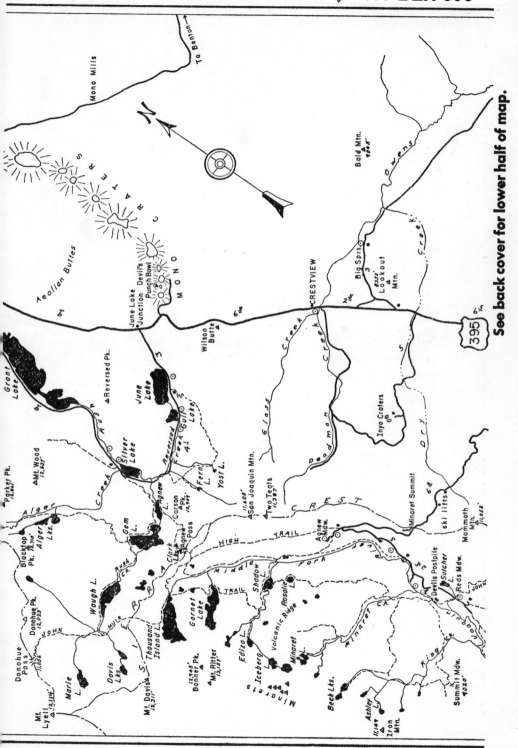

See back cover for lower half of map.

MAMMOTH LAKES SIERRA

A handbook for roadside and trail

Edited by
Genny Smith

By
Dean Rinehart
Elden Vestal
Bettie E. Willard

Illustrated by
Susan Rinehart

Fourth edition

Mammal drawings by
Jean McEachern

Maps by
Dean Rinehart

Historic photographs from
**The collections of Adele Reed, Genny Smith,
Laws Railroad Museum, Eastern California Museum**

Trail scouting by
Larry Eastman

Photographs by
**Ed Cooper, David J. Dunaway, LaMoine R. Fantozzi,
Philip W. Faulconer, Robert C. Frampton, Don Gibbon,
Philip Hyde, T J Johnston, J. W. MacBride,
H. W. Mendenhall, Edwin C. Rockwell, Tom Ross,
Gerhard Schumacher, John S. Shelton, Julius Shulman,
Bev Steveson, Stephen H. Willard, Billy Young**

Copyright © 1976 by Genny Smith
Genny Smith Books, Palo Alto, California

ISBN 0-931378-00-1
Library of Congress Catalog Card Number: 76-7970

First printing, May 1959
Second printing, October 1959
Third printing, August 1961
Second edition, July 1964
Third edition, June 1969
Second printing, August 1971
Fourth edition, June 1976
Second printing, May 1980

Design of cover and photo section by Stephanie Furniss
Front cover photo, Lake George and Crystal Crag, by Stephen H. Willard
Back cover photo, Winter, Mammoth Mountain, by T J Johnston

Distributed by:
WILLIAM KAUFMANN, INC.
One First Street, Los Altos, California 94022

The Fourth Edition, 1976

The most significant changes in this edition come from geological studies published in 1975 and 1976. Since this edition is the first popular book to incorporate this new material, don't be surprised if our text differs markedly from trail and highway signs and most books, including our own previous editions. The major work we draw on is that of Roy Bailey, U.S. Geological Survey, who mapped the geology basic to evaluating Long Valley's potential for geothermal energy. He has pieced together the geologic history of the Long Valley caldera, where violent explosions 700,000 years ago emplaced much of the volcanic rock that forms the land surface today. From other geologists we have gleaned exciting details: King Huber, who helped unscramble the volcanic events of the Devils Postpile area; Glen Izett, Ray Wilcox, and others, who have identified volcanic ash from the Long Valley explosions as far east as Nebraska; Spencer Wood, who worked out dates for the two most recent pumice eruptions and located probable sources; and Howard W. Oliver, whose calculations indicate that the Sierra Nevada continues to rise today. A wealth of geologic material on this area has been published; but most of it is available only from scientific libraries, is technical, and requires some acquaintance with geologic jargon. Two basic publications containing valuable bibliographies are: *Geology and Mineral Deposits of the Mount Morrison Quadrangle* by C. Dean Rinehart and Donald C. Ross, U.S. Geological Survey Professional Paper 385, 1964; and "Volcanism, Structure, and Geochronology of Long Valley Caldera" by Roy A. Bailey, G. B. Dalrymple, and M. A. Lanphere in *Journal of Geophysical Research* 81:725–44, 1976.

Another change comes from the graduate studies of Diana F. Tomback, U.C. Santa Barbara. She has given us a whole new understanding of the interdependence between the Clark's nutcracker and the whitebark pine. Bird collects seed and caches it in the ground; some seed sprouts and grows into trees; tree depends on bird to plant seed; bird depends on tree for seed, and so on *ad infinitum*.

The Contributors

This is a very personal guidebook. At some time most of us have lived east of the Sierra. While each one of us has tried to present facts objectively, our deep affection for the eastern Sierra can't help but shine through. We wouldn't want it otherwise, for we care about this land and its wild flowers and wild creatures.

Each author is an acknowledged authority in his field. Dean Rinehart, with other members of the U.S. Geological Survey, mapped the geology of the Mount Morrison, Casa Diablo, and Devils Postpile quadrangles during seven summers. Elden Vestal, first Regional Fisheries Biologist for Inyo-Mono with the California Department of Fish and Game, lived and worked in the area for thirteen years. Bettie Willard, plant ecologist, lived summers with her parents at the Willard Studio from 1925 to 1957; she was appointed by President Nixon in 1972 to the Council on Environmental Quality. Genny Schumacher Smith, free-lance writer and editor of the companion book *Deepest Valley: Guide to Owens Valley,* has been a summer resident of Mammoth Lakes since 1955. We welcome corrections, additions, and suggestions. Send them to the editor c/o the Southern Mono Hospital Auxiliary.

We are privileged to publish prints from the life work of the late Stephen Willard, landscape photographer from 1913 to 1966. He and his wife Beatrice established the Willard Studio at Mammoth Lakes in 1924; she has kept the studio open since his death. Prints were made by Rick Warner of Whittier. Photographers who live east of the Sierra include Edwin C. Rockwell, staff member of the U.S. Forest Service since 1951; first at Mammoth Lakes, now in Bishop. T J Johnston is photographer for Mammoth Mountain Ski Area. Tom Ross, well-known mountain climber, lives at Independence. Bev Steveson has lived summers at Mammoth since 1974. Some of the historic photographs are by the late Harry Mendenhall, who operated a photo studio in Big Pine from about 1910 until 1952. He may have taken his first photographs of Old Mammoth in the early 1900s; his signature is in the Wildasinn Hotel register in the summer of 1908. Other historic photos come from the collection of Adele Reed, author of *Mammoth Lakes Memories* and other books on local history. She and her husband Bill lived at Mammoth from 1927 to 1948. Billy Young worked for the power company out of Bishop from 1910 to 1953.

Susan Rinehart, who drew most of the illustrations, lived summers in Mammoth with husband Dean and their two small children. Larry Eastman, trail scout part-time and cook full-time, has lived at Mammoth during the summer since 1964 and year-round since 1972.

To the dozens of people who over the years have contributed ideas and information to our new editions, we are sincerely grateful. Thanks to Stephanie Furniss Murphy, this is the most handsome of our four editions by far. She made the final photo selection and designed the photo layout and cover. For help with this fourth edition I thank especially Edwin C. Rockwell, U.S. Forest Service, and Larry Mangan, biologist, BLM, both of Bishop; also John Derby and Larry Wade, Mammoth Lakes, and Tom Whear, Lee Vining, USFS; Jim Wickser, Independence, DWP, City of Los Angeles; Florence McAllister, who proof-read this edition; and most of all, Ward Smith, the editor's editor.

Genny Schumacher Smith

Palo Alto and Mammoth Lakes
June 1976

Contents

		Page
Roadsides	*Genny Schumacher, Bettie Willard*	1
Trails	*Genny Schumacher, Bettie Willard*	34
Geologic Story	*Dean Rinehart*	73
Climates and Life Zones	*Genny Schumacher, Elden Vestal*	85
Trees	*Genny Schumacher*	88
Wildflowers and Shrubs	*Bettie Willard*	93
Mammals	*Elden Vestal*	107
Fish	*Elden Vestal*	116
Birds	*Genny Schumacher*	121
Background	*Genny Schumacher*	128
Notes		143
Index		145

Writing in his journal from a hill near San Francisco Bay, Pedro Font, a Franciscan missionary, described what he saw: "Looking to the northeast we saw an immense treeless plain into which the water spreads widely, forming several low islets; at the opposite end of this extensive plain, about forty leagues off, we saw a great snow-covered range [una gran sierra nevada] which seemed to me to run south-southeast to north-northwest."

The Eastern Sierra

Over the crest of that great snowy range, directly east of San Francisco Bay where Font stood in 1776, lies a superbly beautiful portion of the 400-mile-long Sierra Nevada, the Mammoth Lakes Sierra. Six hours north of Los Angeles and three hours south of Reno, this 50-mile portion of the eastern Sierra slope extends from Rock Creek to Lundy Canyon. It is bordered by Long Valley and the Mono Lake Basin, both around 6500 feet in altitude. Magnificent mountains rise abruptly more than six thousand feet above these high desert valleys. A long snow season supports famous ski centers on two of them—Mammoth Mountain and June Mountain.

In a broad opening in the steep mountain front, below a mile-wide lakes basin, is the resort village of Mammoth Lakes. Although Mammoth Mountain is lower than neighboring peaks, its great hulk dominates the landscape for miles around. Into the mountain front north and south of Mammoth, water and ice have cut the deep-gashed canyons of Hilton, McGee, Convict, Parker, Walker, Lee Vining, and Mill creeks. Rock Creek drains a much longer canyon; at its head, Little Lakes Valley cradles more than a dozen small lakes. Rush Creek drains a broad basin below the Sierra crest and empties into June Lake Basin lying below the dramatic vertical face of Carson Peak. June Lake's resorts cluster around its large lakes.

The Sierra Nevada's short, steep eastern slope has distinctive qualities that make it seem a world apart from all of western California. In contrast to the Sierra's western slope that spans forty to seventy miles in its gradual upward rise from the fertile Great Valley near sea-level to its snowy crest, the eastern slope abruptly drops off thousands of feet to arid valleys far below. In contrast to west slope rivers and dense forests, east slope streams are small, its forests few and without underbrush. The land is spacious and open to the sky, the views immense. Akin to the arid lands eastward, the eastern slope receives little moisture from Pacific rain clouds, for the high Sierra crest blocks them.

In the Mammoth Lakes region, however, at the center of the generally arid eastern Sierra, two low passes let Pacific storms spill over the crest, bringing heavy snows and a long ski season. Blowing across Mammoth Pass and Minaret Summit, on either side of Mammoth Mountain, these storms provide late-lying snowbanks that account for pockets of wildflowers and unexpected meadows. They also water the Jeffrey pine forest that extends miles to the east. (If you are surprised that we consider 9,000-foot passes *low,* you may be even more astonished to know that you can't find a lower pass for a hundred miles south and seventy-five miles north. South of Lake Tahoe for two hundred miles, few gaps breach the Sierra crest. Most of its passes stand ten, eleven, and twelve thousand feet high, little lower than its peaks.) In addition to having more water, the Mammoth Lakes Sierra has far more color in its rocks. Instead of only gray Sierra granite, here more ancient rocks show a hundred shades of maroon, red-gold, dark brown, blue-gray, pink-tinged purple, and bright rust. Younger volcanic eruptions have splattered the region with red cinder cones, pinkish-tan flows, whitish pumice, and black obsidian.

The abrupt changes in altitude, from thirteen-thousand-foot peaks to seven-thousand-foot valleys, make possible an unusual diversity of plant and animal life within short distances. Alpine willow covered by nine-month snowbanks flourish only a few miles west of desert sagebrush; the white-tailed jackrabbit only a few miles from his black-tailed low-country cousin.

As if all this were not enough, a few miles west rise two more grand ridges, the Silver Divide and the Ritter Range. Crowning the Ritter Range, the tantalizing glacier-spangled peaks of the Minarets, Mount Ritter, and Banner Peak tower a thousand feet above the Sierra crest. With all these variables, each canyon, each camp, each trail is a unique combination of views, of colors, of flowers and forest, and of birds and furry creatures that live therein.

Unlike most high mountain ranges, the eastern Sierra welcomes campers and mountaineers with long summers that are relatively warm and dry. It is also readily accessible—by scheduled airline, by bus, and by roads. Eleven highways cross the Sierra, though some are closed in winter. From any of them you can link up with Highway 395, surely one of the most scenic highways in all the west, which follows the eastern Sierra for almost its entire length from Susanville south to Reno and Inyokern. From 395, dozens of roads wind far up the canyons, others head east into the desert—all lead to countless surprises and magnificent viewpoints. From the road ends, good trails lead farther into the mountains and on over the passes. Then, once you have learned the landmarks, this open, friendly country invites you to wander cross-country and to explore. Miles of joy and endless days of wonder are yours for discovering.

The Inyo National Forest: Sources of Mountain and Trail Information

Most of the roads and trails described in this guidebook lie within the Inyo National Forest. Adjoining the Inyo Forest along its western boundary are the Sierra National Forest and Yosemite National Park. Adjoining the Inyo Forest on the north is the Toiyabe National Forest. It's all glorious mountain country regardless of which agency administers it, although there are some important differences between park and forest regulations. Firearms, dogs (even on leash), and other pets are prohibited on all park trails; they are allowed on forest trails. For maps, wilderness permits, and information on just about everything—campgrounds, trail conditions, weather, bird check-lists— stop in at the ranger stations in Bishop, Mammoth Lakes, Lee Vining, and Bridgeport. Or write, or telephone:

Inyo National Forest, Supervisor's Office, Bishop 93514
Toiyabe National Forest, Bridgeport Ranger Station, Bridgeport 93517.

Maps

Forest Visitors Map, Inyo National Forest, 1972, 30 x 40 inches, 4-color. Scale: ½ inch = 1 mile. This is by far the best single map of the area. Road and trail information, which is sadly out of date on topo and other older maps, is accurate as of 1972. This map covers the entire Inyo Forest, from its boundary south of Owens Lake north to Mono Lake. It includes the Sierra Nevada crest and most of the Inyo and White Mountains. Available at ranger stations.

USGS Topographic Maps, 15-minute series. U.S. Geological Survey. Scale: 1 inch = 1 mile. The following quadrangles cover the area described in this guidebook: Mount Abbot, Mount Tom, Casa Diablo Mountain, Mount Morrison, Devils Postpile, Tuolumne Meadows, Mono Craters, Cowtrack Mountain, Bodie, and Matterhorn Peak. Inquire locally where they are for sale. Purchase by mail from Topographic Division, USGS, Federal Center, Denver, Colorado 80225. Write also for the free Descriptive Folder, Map Symbol Sheet, and Index to Topographic Mapping in California. If you don't know how, find someone to show you how to read topo maps. Even though some road and trail information is out of date, they are invaluable. Eighty-foot contours accurately depict altitude and relief.

Sources of Other Information

California Department of Fish and Game. Maps and information at the office in Bishop. See also page 120.

Chambers of Commerce. For accommodations and services, winter and summer, write: June Lake Loop Chamber, June Lake 93529; Mammoth Lakes Chamber, P.O. Box 123, Mammoth Lakes 93546; Mono County Chamber, P.O. Box 514, Bridgeport 93517.

City of Los Angeles, Department of Recreation and Parks. For information on Camp High Sierra and boating at Crowley Lake write: 200 N. Main St., Los Angeles 90012.

Eastern High Sierra Packers Association. Guided trips, horses, mules, burros. Write: P.O. Box 147, Bishop 93514.

Mono County Department of Parks. For a list of county parks and campgrounds write the department: Courthouse, Bridgeport 93517.

Mono County Museum, Bridgeport. Extensive historical collections. Located in the 1880 Bridgeport Elementary School building. Adjacent picnic area.

Wild places, wild things

This is mainly a book about the wild places in the Mammoth Lakes Sierra and the things you may discover there. We can't guarantee that you will find them, though, for the essence of wild things is that they live in their world in their way. They appear and disappear for their own reasons, not because we whistle a call. This is part of the thrill of a wild place—the brief encounter, the unexpected moment you remember a lifetime. You may go for weeks without ever seeing an alpine columbine or a mountain quail or a pika. Then one day in a rock pile that looks no different than a hundred others you have passed, you will see a pika carrying wildflowers in its mouth and spreading them out to dry like hay. Then, if you care, you can learn about him and his rock pile, how he manages to survive nine-month winters, who his neighbors are, what he feeds on and who feeds on him. The next time you hear a pika's nasal call, the experience may then be a deeper one and you may feel more at one with the pika. For you realize that he sees you as a creature at a rock pile, briefly in his wild place.

And what's happening in the Sierra's wild places? Something of a miracle did happen to keep them wild at all. Few there would be if all the sheepmen, lumbermen, road-builders, and miners had had their way. If no one had objected to their doings, the Sierra would probably resemble the Alps—beautiful but tamed, far from wild. Fortunately for us, John Muir and his friends did object, and we have them to thank for Yosemite Park. Others continued the fight—wild lands for everyone versus dollars for someone—so that today there is a glorious strip of wild land along the Sierra crest where one can hike for more than two hundred and fifty miles without ever seeing a road and hearing all the noise that roads bring. With one noticeable exception, this wild land is firmly protected by law and will be preserved forever wild within national parks and national forest wilderness areas. That exception is the four-mile-wide "corridor" that extends west of Reds Meadow between the John Muir and Minarets wilderness areas. Since the 1930s a trans-Sierra road through the corridor has been repeatedly proposed and repeatedly rejected. The Forest Service now has the corridor under study as the proposed San Joaquin Wilderness. Wilderness status for this land is essential.

By a strange twist, the greatest threat to the High Sierra today comes from the very people who love it the most—the hikers and fishermen and back-packers. Around some popular lakes there have been just too many of them. In the wilderness areas reached by this book's trails—the John Muir, Minarets, and Hoover—the use in 1975 was one and a half million visitor days. That's double the use in 1969. As back-country use multiplied during the 1960s, a few botanists and ecologists noticed subtle scars at some of the heavily used lakes—Bullfrog, Rae, Shadow, and the Desolation lakes—but no one paid much attention to their warnings. It wasn't until around 1970 that the danger signals became so glaringly evident that few people could *not* notice—plants trampled to death, water polluted, down wood scarce. Shadow Lake—in one of the most beautiful settings of all the Sierra, and a natural stopping place on the John Muir Trail—is a good example. From years of camping concentrated around its upper end, the lake shore was hard-packed, denuded of grass and flowers, and covered with charcoal and blackened stones.

There is no question that we must bow to the physical capacity of the land, limiting people to numbers within the soil's capacity to absorb and filter human waste, to numbers that will not trample lake shores and meadows to destruction. But there is still another dimension to consider. How close to-gether can people hike the same trail and camp around the same lake before their very closeness destroys the quiet and wildness they came for?

If all this sounds grim, don't be discouraged. If you hear the Sierra is crowded, don't be fooled. There is solitude for the finding even in the Sierra, especially on weekdays and in the off-season. There's lots of it a quarter-mile off any trail, and more of it up those canyons with no trails that I hope no one ever writes a guidebook about. Even more promising, we are learning how to tread more gently in the winderness, to think of each meadow, each lake shore as a high mountain garden we would no more trample than we would our garden at home. And so remarkable is the ability of plants and soil to recover from abuse that a few years of rest are already working their wonders. Within the short time back-country rangers have been diverting campers from damaged areas, grass and flowers have started to return to the shore of Shadow Lake.

Too, there's an awarenes—more keenly felt than ever before—that the world is a small planet, created not for man to dominate for his benefit alone, but a marvelous place inhabited by many creatures. Since we alone have the power to annihilate our brother creatures—and have—the more reason we have to assume responsibility for their welfare. In this perspective the preser-vation of wild creatures and their living space is a legitimate aim that needs no other justification. Wild things should be preserved because they are on this earth along with us. Because they happened. That is reason enough.
G. S. S.

Roadsides

THE DRIVE FROM SHERWIN Summit to Conway Summit, the section of U. S. Highway 395 described in this guidebook, can be made in less than two hours. Yet between these two summits —both fittingly named after pioneer settlers—are so many scenic and interesting roads and trails, that a two-weeks vacation allows only a beginning acquaintance with all there is to see and do.

In the following pages are descriptions of points of interest along Highway 395, as well as along most of the sideroads branching east and west from it. The material is arranged from south to north, beginning at Sherwin Summit about twenty miles north of Bishop, and ending at Conway Summit twelve miles south of Bridgeport. Sideroads and their attractions are described at their junctions with U. S. 395. An original map, with the most accurate and up-to-date trail and road information possible at the time of publication, has been prepared for this guidebook. It is on the end papers. Refer to it while reading the guidebook, for the text will then be considerably more meaningful. For more details on points of interest mentioned in the auto trips, turn to the appropriate sections following: trails, geology, trees, flowers, shrubs, mammals, fish, birds, and history.

Highway 395 was first known as "El Camino Sierra," a romantic name probably inspired by El Camino Reál (The Royal Highway), the old trail connecting the California missions. East of the Sierra, from earliest times trails had connected the Indian settlements and had also led west across several Sierra passes. These trails were followed by the first prospectors, who came about a hundred years ago when their feverish search for gold led them from the played-out placers of the Mother Lode to the land east of the Sierra. The cattlemen, farmers, traders and soldiers who came next followed the old paths, as well as trampling new ones to the mining camps. With heavy use, the trails widened into "roads" which were fairly adequate for slow, large-wheeled wagons, but not for the speedy, thirty-mile-per-hour automobiles which began traveling them in the early 1900s.

The first bond issue to acquire and construct a State Highway System was approved by California's voters in 1910. With pressure from the Inyo Good Road Club, El Camino Sierra (220 miles between Mojave and Bridgeport) was included in the state's first highway plan, and work was begun on the worst part of the old wagon road, Sherwin Hill. The completion of ten miles of graded, oiled road was celebrated in 1916 with a barbecue in Rock Creek Canyon attended by almost a thousand people. Something to celebrate, indeed—the long trip from Bishop to Mammoth Lakes could now be made in two and a half hours! Bit by bit the entire route, two ruts through sand and sagebrush, was paved or oiled. Since cars often sank to their axles in the loose pumice of Deadman Summit and in the sand near Division Creek, these two projects were next; then bridges across some of the creeks; then a road over Conway Summit; and

1

finally in 1931 a hard-surface road was completed all the way from Bishop to Los Angeles. The new four-lane highway connecting Round Valley with Tom's Place was completed in 1956.

In its ascent from Round Valley, the new road cuts through sparkling pink and pale gray volcanic rock called Bishop tuff, one of many indications of volcanic eruptions that can be seen along the highway between Bishop and Mono Lake. This tuff—120 cubic miles of it—exploded long ago from vents now buried beneath the floor of Long Valley. Its surface has weathered to a rosy tan color. Since the tuff is relatively soft and easily quarried, it was used as a building stone by some of the early settlers.

HIGHWAY 395 SHERWIN SUMMIT TO MAMMOTH

Just north of Sherwin Summit (7000 feet) watch for the first glimpse (northwest) of the Ritter Range's thirteen-thousand-foot crest. As the road drops from the summit to Rock Creek, to the left the old Sherwin Grade road branches off, leading to lower Rock Creek and joining 395 in Round Valley. This paved road follows the general route of the historic Sherwin Tollroad, built during the 1870s by James L. C. Sherwin. In 1859 Sherwin and his bride from Kentucky had come west to Virginia City, lured by tales of the fabulous Comstock Lode. Eventually Sherwin homesteaded in Round Valley, at the foot of the grade bearing his name, and in 1874 built a wagon road up Rock Creek for a sawmill he established there. Several years later when the rush to the Mammoth mines began, Sherwin extended his road and operated it as a tollroad. It is hard today to imagine the dangers of the old road. Wagons occasionally got out of control going down the steep road and crashed down the slope, killing the mules or horses. Several boilers being freighted to the Mammoth mill broke loose and rolled all the way to the bottom of the grade.

Sideroad to Rock Creek Canyon and Little Lakes Valley.—A good paved road branches left from the highway to the many campgrounds along Rock Creek and to the resort, store, and pack station near Rock Creek Lake, up the canyon. A short walk beyond the road end there is a fine view of the valley. Weeks could be spent exploring this one canyon for it is one of the longer ones and has over fifty lakes within half a day's hike. The gray-green

Figure 1. Little Lakes Valley.

trees dotting the brush slopes are pinyon pine; a few large reddish-barked Jeffrey pine tower above them. Along the creek grow birch, cottonwood, willow, and the quaking aspen which turn brilliant colors in late September, making this road in fall a glorious drive through a golden forest. Trails lead from this canyon to Tamarack Lakes, Morgan Pass, Mono Pass and Hilton Lakes.

Sideroads to Tom's Place and Owens Gorge Road.—The turnoff to Rock Creek also connects with the old highway, which leads to several resorts off the freeway. The first of them is Tom's Place, named for Tom Yerby who had a store and cabins for many years. The Owens Gorge Road crosses Long Valley Dam, leads to the southeast tip of Crowley Lake, and joins a network of back roads leading east toward Casa Diablo Mountain and north toward the Benton Crossing road. The Owens Gorge is a 700-foot deep gash cut by the Owens River into the Bishop tuff. Part of the gorge is inaccessible; part of it is busy with hydro plants. However, it's possible to hike a similar gorge cut by Rock Creek. (See page 143, 7, for this unusual trail.)

395 [resumed].—The highway skirts the lower edge of Little Round Valley, whose meadows have long provided summer pasture for sheep or for Owens Valley cattle. On the upper side of the road, among the squat, symmetrical pinyon pine, grow numerous mountain mahogany—large angular shrubs that in late summer have a silky, silvery appearance caused by the fuzzy, spirally-twisted "tails" on its seeds. Mountain mahogany is a favorite food of deer.

Sideroads to Crowley Lake and Hilton Creek.—This large reservoir is well known for its "big ones" which thrive on the lake's plentiful, rich food supply. The lake is fished heavily; an opening weekend generally attracts more than 10,000 anglers. The lake has a short season, sometimes closing July 31, partly because during the warm summer months the fish acquire a musty taste, and partly because such heavy use over a longer season would make it impossible to maintain the fish population. Hilton Creek, in the opposite direction, has some of the largest, loveliest aspen trees anywhere along the highway. At the base of the hill near the creek, Richard Hilton operated a milk ranch and supplied butter to mining camps from the 1870s to the turn of the century.

Scenic viewpoint.—A full-circle panorama from this point includes Boundary Peak in Nevada. Pastoral Long Valley to the east gives only a few hints today of its violent birth 700,000 years ago when an underground reservoir of molten rock began to erupt showers of pumice and smaller fragments, "ash." Pumice piled up as much as twenty feet deep; volcanic ash drifted as far as Nebraska, 1100 miles away. Then a series of shattering explosions hurled out glowing, gas-propelled clouds that shot out in all directions and blanketed 450 square miles between Bishop and Mono Lake with layers of incandescent fragments, hundreds of feet thick. The fragments welded together and cooled to form the volcanic rock, Bishop tuff. These prodigious explosions, which ejected a total of two hundred cubic miles of tuff and pumice together, culminated in the collapse of the roof of the reservoir. The elliptical basin twenty miles long formed by that collapse is called a caldera. Long Valley lies in the eastern half of the caldera; Laurel and McGee mountains behind you form its south wall; Bald and Glass mountains its north wall; and San Joaquin Mountain its west wall.

Filling the lowest portion of Long Valley is Crowley Lake, the largest reservoir on the Los Angeles Aqueduct. In 1941 the Department of Water and Power completed the Long Valley dam across the Owens River, inundating lush meadows that had long been grazed by cattle. Crowley gathers the waters of the upper Owens River as well as most of the streams flowing into Mono Lake and sends it down the river's natural channel to the aqueduct intake south of Big Pine. The lake was named for Father J. J. Crowley, the Desert Padre, beloved by men of all faiths. Promoting Inyo-Mono as a summer vacation land, he was a major force in helping people establish a new faith in the future—a faith that had dwindled to hopelessness as they watched Owens River water flow away from the ranches and into the aqueduct. A monument to Father Crowley stands on the old highway north of Hilton Creek. He was killed in an auto accident in 1940.

Far east of Crowley Lake the White Mountains shape the skyline. (White Mountain Peak, 14,246 feet, see page 143, 8.) How much better if the mapmakers had retained the Paiute name for the entire range—Inyo, dwelling place of a great spirit. Atop the White Mountains grow the oldest of living things, the bristlecone pine, some more than 4,000 years old.

To the west, below flat-topped McGee Mountain, a 700-foot high pile of gravel and rock curves out of McGee Canyon. This boulder-strewn ridge—a glacial moraine—consists of rock debris that was carried down-canyon by a glacier and then melted out from the edges of the ice. Farther left, up on the Sierra slope, a high, stubby moraine blocks the mouth of Hilton Creek Canyon. This "dump moraine" marks the snout of the Hilton Creek glacier. At the lip of its hanging valley it just dumped its load of debris onto the steep mountain slope. Well-preserved moraines, some of them over a mile long, stand hundreds of feet high at the mouth of almost every canyon between Sherwin Summit and Sonora Pass.

395.—Continuing north, the highway passes close to the Sierra's sheer east face. Its colorful, striped rocks—red, rust, purple-brown, blue-gray, white—

Figure 2. Sierra peaks west of Highway 395.

Mount Ritter and Banner Peak   J.W. MacBride

Discovery!
This book is mainly about wild places and the wild things

you may discover there. That is, if you are lucky you will discover them, for the essence of wild things is that they appear and disappear for reasons of their own, not because we whistle a call. They live in **their** world in **their** way. They may give us a glimpse now and then of that world, and the thrill of those unexpected moments, those brief encounters, may linger always.

So in this guide there is no attempt to tell you "all about" the wild places of the eastern Sierra. Their secrets will become yours only as you wander about and discover them yourself. We want to help you form a comfortable acquaintance with the landmarks, the plants, the rocks, and the animals, but we can only open doors. You are on your own — to choose, or not, to walk through some of those doors, to explore, to discover.

Thousand Island Lake   Stephen H. Willard

T.J. Lake   Stephen H. Willard

Old Mammoth   Stephen H. Willard

Stephen Willard discovered the Sierra a lifetime ago.

Wintering in the desert and summering here, Willard devoted most of his life to photographing scenic landscapes. He and his wife Beatrice opened a studio in Mammoth in 1924 and operated it until his death in 1966. We are privileged to publish a selection of photographs from his life's work. You will find them scattered throughout the photo sections. Contact prints from his eight-by-ten negatives were made especially for this edition.

Lake George, Crystal Crag   Bev Steveson

were formed hundreds of millions of years ago (during Paleozoic time) from sediments deposited in a shallow sea then extending across California and several other western states. The walls of deep-slashed McGee Canyon expose the colors and folds of this ancient layered rock in elegant fashion. Along McGee Creek, among the cottonwood and willow, flourishes a tree that is rare in this region—the copper birch, named for its shining, copper-colored bark. Landmarks are named for the McGee brothers—Alney, John, and Bart— pioneer cattlemen who had their headquarters near McGee Creek. Alney later worked as foreman for T. B. Rickey, a prominent land baron in the 1890s who owned most of Long Valley and grazed several thousand head of cattle.

Sideroad to McGee Canyon.—This road winds steeply up the canyon's large moraine, then levels off and follows the creek to a pack station. Trails lead to the lakes and streams of upper McGee Canyon and over McGee Pass to the headwaters of Fish Creek. On the north side of the canyon, at an altitude of over 11,000 feet, a small tungsten mine operated intermittently from 1942 to 1954. If you begin watching about a mile and a half up the road and if you have afternoon shadows to help, you may locate an extraordinary fault scarp that cuts across the moraine. (See photo section, "Fire!") Movements along the fault zone at the base of the mountains formed this striking 50-foot break.

395.—Left of the highway is the old McGee Mountain ski area where in the late 1930s the Eastern Sierra Ski Club of Bishop built a rope tow, the first tow of any size. The highway swings left, abruptly revealing one of the most spectacular views along 395—hulking Mammoth Mountain and behind it the jagged peaks of the Ritter Range.

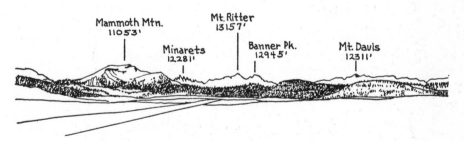

Figure 3. Mammoth Mountain and peaks of the Ritter Range.

Sideroad to Whitmore Hot Springs, Owens River, Benton Crossing, Benton.—This is the first of several roads leading east from the base of the Sierra, which take you into a desert world that is totally unlike the mountain world to the west—a world of plants and animals and colors that is fascinating and beautiful in its own very different, special way. (See page 143, 9.) This road passes Whitmore Hot Springs, several natural pools that were a favorite bathing place for as long as anyone can remember. Later enclosed, at times it has been operated as a public plunge. The water averages over 80°F; nearby springs vary in temperature from barely warm to very hot. In a region such as this, where there have been abundant and recent volcanic eruptions, hot springs are to be expected. Generally they represent the last activity of subsiding volcanic forces. Part of the water may have its source in the subterranean reservoir of molten lava from which earlier eruptions came. Much of the water discharged, however, probably originates as rain which percolates to depths where it subsequently becomes heated. Pressure, caused by the heat, forces the water through fissures to the surface.

About three miles from the highway junction, the road passes near the shallow Alkali Lakes, part of the network of resting ponds on the Pacific Flyway, the north-south route flown by migrating ducks and geese. It is another three miles to Benton Crossing on the Owens River. The original crossing of the old Benton-Mammoth City wagon road is several miles south of the present one and is now covered by Crowley Lake. The river, called "Wakopee" by the Paiutes, was named by Captain John Frémont for Richard (Dick) Owens, one of the leaders of Frémont's 1845-46 expedition. Owens River drains the Sierra Nevada's eastern watershed all the way from Deadman Summit near Mono Lake to Owens Lake near Olancha. Rainfall on the western Sierra slope being much greater, the comparable portion of the west slope is drained by *four* major rivers.

From Benton Crossing, the view west to the vast Sierra—all the way from the canyon of Hilton Creek north to Mount Dana—is superb, with Mount Morrison particularly impressive. Directly behind the Crossing is a high ridge of volcanic rocks, Glass Mountain Ridge. Beyond Benton Crossing, a graded dirt road leads south, following the shore of Crowley Lake. The road then winds through the sagebrush and pinyon pines of Watterson and Wildrose Canyons, retracing the general route of the wagon road built in 1878 from the supply center of Benton to Mammoth City. About thirty miles after leaving Highway

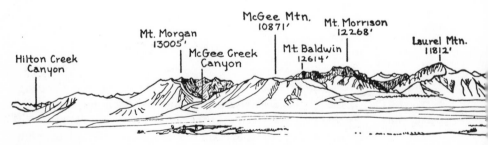

Figure 4. Sierra peaks, seen from Benton Crossing.

395, the road joins State Highway 120 coming from Mono Lake. For an interesting loop trip, turn left and return by this paved road—passing Adobe Meadows, Mono Mills, the Mono Craters and re-joining 395 a little south of Lee Vining (see below, Highway 120 East).

If you turn right, it is but a short detour to Benton, known at one time as a wide-open, shooting mining town. It also vied with the other early settlements of Aurora, Bridgeport, Bodie, and Monoville for the honor of being selected the county seat. For almost twenty years the town throve on the production of the famous Blind Springs Mining District, located on the hill of the same name just east of Benton. From 1864, when it was organized, until 1881, the district's mines produced almost four million dollars' worth of silver. In 1883 the narrow-gauge Carson and Colorado Railroad was completed from Mound House, Nevada, south to Keeler at Owens Lake, and Benton Station, a few miles to the east, served as a train stop and shipping point. Several buildings dating from Benton's early days still stand—the slaughter house, Madam J. Lynch's Benton "Hotel," and the thick-walled metal-shuttered Wells Fargo office. Inquire at the general store for the location of these buildings as well as of the old cemetery. Ask also to see the fine, large collection of Indian arrowheads—ranging from the very small ones used for killing birds to the large ones used for deer, and including some made from the rare brown obsidian. Tools, books, drugs, dishes, and other antiques are also on exhibit. Occasionally an Indian basket made by a local Paiute is for sale. Benton may have been named for Frémont's wife (Frémont was a national hero of his time) or for Senator T. H. Benton of Missouri, who favored metallic currency and who was also Frémont's father-in-law.

395.—Northward along 395 there are fine views westward of Mammoth Mountain and of the sheer cliffs of Convict Canyon. The highest, light-colored peak directly left is Mount Morrison. In the dark ridges in front of it, a very important geological find was made in 1953 (see Fig. 5) when small fossils called graptolites were discovered. They proved to be nearly 500 million years old, making these dark rocks the oldest known anywhere in the Sierra.

Sideroad to Convict Lake. On either side of this road, as it leaves the

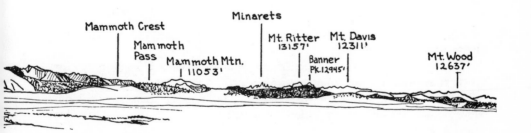

highway, may be seen areas recently burned by brush fires, probably caused by careless smokers. The area on the left was burned in 1956, the one on the right in 1947. The latter was reseeded in the fall of 1947 and a portion of it fenced in order to study the reëstablishment of range plants. The shrubs here are part of the winter range of eastern Sierra deer herds. Bitterbrush, the deer's preferred food, may take as long as fifteen years to reëstablish itself after a fire.

After a gentle ascent of one mile, the road climbs steeply up the moraine. A true wild-west story is behind the naming of these landmarks. In September, 1871, twenty-nine desperadoes broke out of the state penitentiary in Carson

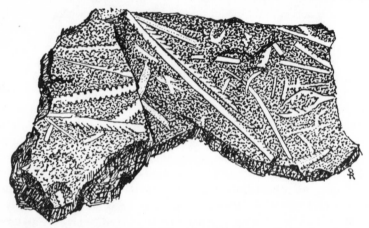

Figure 5. Graptolites from Mt. Morrison, oldest Sierra fossils. Actual size.

City, Nevada. One group of six—murderers, train-robbers, horse thieves—headed south. On the way, they brutally murdered a young mail rider of Aurora, mistaking him for a former prison guard they intended to kill in revenge for shooting two former convicts. Posses from Aurora and Benton took up the chase, sighting them near what was then called Monte Diablo Creek, now known as Convict. The posses stayed all night at the McGee place, and next morning cornered the criminals in Convict canyon. A fierce fight ensued during which Robert Morrison, a Benton merchant was killed, and the convicts escaped. Three of them were captured several days later, near Round Valley. Enroute to the Carson penitentiary, two were lynched north of Bishop, contrary to a popular myth that places the lynching at the "hangman's tree," a large snag near the outlet of Convict Lake.

The lake's setting is majestic. Mount Morrison, named for Robert Morrison, rises precipitously from the canyon's south side and Laurel Mountain, with its red, brown, white, and rust-colored cliffs, from the opposite side. Numerous flowers, including many-colored penstemon and the brilliant yellow blazing star, grow in the rich soil along the shores of the lake. A trail follows Convict Creek upstream.

Sideroad to Hot Creek.—A graded gravel road branches right, crossing sagebrush flats and meadows and then following the bank of Hot Creek. Several parking places on the left indicate trails leading to the creek. About three miles from Highway 395, a large parking area and sign mark a popular swimming area. Hot Creek rises in the complex of warm springs issuing from beneath the basalt lava table bordering the fish hatchery, which is not far to the west. Mammoth Creek is tributary to Hot Creek. Along a two-mile segment of Hot Creek here are many hot springs, warm springs and fumaroles (gas vents), which heat the water sufficiently to allow pleasant bathing even in winter. Hot springs come and go unpredictably along Hot Creek. In late August 1973 two new geysers erupted, tearing holes ten feet in diameter in the bank downstream from the bathing pool and gushing scalding water, mud, and pebbles three to six feet high for months. Two years later they had dwindled to small hot pools. In mid-December small hot springs and geysers erupted from some other new vents upstream. Similar hot-water activity in the past, which chemically altered the rocks, is responsible for the creek's colorful banks.

Sideroad to Hot Creek State Fish Hatchery.—This is an interesting sidetrip of only one mile. Visitors are welcome daily and employees are happy to answer questions. Trout of various sizes are segregated into separate pools, including fingerlings 3–5 inches long, "catchables" 7–9 inches long, and large breeding stock. Over five million fish from this hatchery are planted annually in eastern Sierra waters. In addition, millions more are hatched from the excellent breeding stock and transported to other hatcheries for rearing. The successful operation at Hot Creek is due largely to the warm springs which supply 56°-58° water the year round, an ideal temperature for fish rearing. The fish grow continually, about one inch per month, without a dormant period in winter.

A large hot spring that maintains the high temperature of 186° F. may be visited by driving through the hatchery and walking across the bridge over Hot Creek toward the clay plant. Follow the northern branch of the creek upstream about ½ mile and look for a deep pool at the meadow edge.

Sideroad to Laurel Creek and Sherwin Creek.—This road turns left from the highway, winding through the meadows and sagebrush flats of Laurel Creek. The sagebrush-covered, thousand-foot high mass at the mouth of the first canyon—Laurel Canyon—is a very large, well-preserved glacial moraine, loose material deposited along the margin of an advancing glacier thousands of years ago. Its arc-shaped form stands out clearly, since this moraine is free of trees and since Laurel Creek has washed away relatively little of it. From behind the moraine it is also possible to see the many small concentric ridges, nestled one inside the other, which mark the glacier's fluctuating retreats and advances. In autumn, the curving green band of aspen following Laurel Creek down the moraine turns yellow, making a brilliant streak of color through the dull gray sagebrush. Climbing the moraine is a rough jeep road, built by tungsten interests in 1955 to their claim high on the slope of Bloody Mountain, at an altitude of 11,200 feet. Many people wonder why this mining road was permitted, for when it was built Laurel Canyon was included within the High Sierra Wilderness Area; supposedly, motorized vehicles are prohibited in wilderness. The prominent road scar on the canyon's slope is visible miles away; the road itself has destroyed all wilderness quality the canyon once had. The explanation of this paradox lies in the law governing mining on National Forest land (explained in trail section, see "Agnew Meadow to Shadow Lake").

In the aspen near Laurel Creek still stand some old ranch buildings of the Summers family, early cattlemen who settled here around 1900, grazing their cattle in these mountain meadows during spring and summer and driving them to Owens Valley for the fall and winter. Continuing on, signs to the left indicate several boys' camps. The road crosses several lava ridges, passes the Sherwin Creek Campground, then joins the Old Mammoth Road (see below).

395.—The highway continues across rolling brushland. Scattered in the brush are hummocks of chunky black lava, basalt, which is common throughout the area. It erupted from different sources at many different times. The meadows bordering Mammoth Creek in June usually are covered with western blue flag, or mountain iris. Just beyond the creek crossing, on the hill to the right, is a whitish clay deposit. Prospect pits have been dug in this kaolinite, a mineral used as a paint filler and in making fine china.

MAMMOTH LAKES ROADS

Highway 203 to Mammoth Lakes, Devil's Postpile National Monument, Reds Meadow.—This state highway leads over low hills of lava to the community of Mammoth Lakes (7800 feet) and its all-year resorts. The first large building on the right is the Mammoth Visitor Center and Ranger Station. The Inyo National Forest has a varied year-round program including guided tours, evening programs, and self-guiding nature trails. Stop in for information on these events, on the weather, on campgrounds, and on road and trail condi-

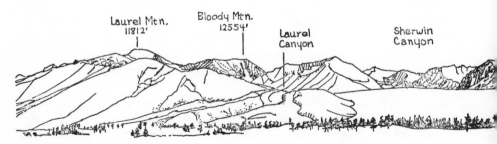

Figure 6. Approach to the Mammoth Lakes basin.

tions; also for maps, fire and wilderness permits, trail guides, and nature books. Handsome exhibits explain this region's unusual features. Beyond the Visitor Center the main road leads to the lakes basin and Reds Meadow. The old Mammoth Road leading to the site of Mammoth City turns left.

The name Mammoth came from Mammoth City, the largest camp in this area during 1878-79, which in turn was named for the principal mining company. It has been known as Mammoth ever since, but when the post office was established "Lakes" was added to the name, to avoid confusion with another Mammoth in northern California.

Highway 203, continued, to the Ski Area, Minaret Summit, Agnew Meadow, Devil's Postpile, Reds Meadow.—A mile and a half beyond the Visitor Center, turn right, north. (The road to the lakes continues straight ahead, see p. 15.) This continuation of Hwy. 203 offers one of the most spectacular auto trips in the region. A full day can be spent exploring all its possibilities.

The road winds through a magnificent Jeffrey pine forest, passing hills which are some of the volcanic domes described in the geology section. A side road leads to the locally famous rift known as the Earthquake Fault. Near the parking area exhibits explain the origin of the crack, and a self-guiding nature trail takes one down into the bottom of the crack. This long crack though the best-known, is only one of many fractures in the glassy volcanic rock covering the area north of Mammoth Mountain. It is really not a "fault" at all, for a fault—as the term is used by geologists—is generally defined as a crack along which the rock on one side *moved,* in a different direction from the rock on the other side. The Earthquake Fault shows no such movement; it simply opened. Examine the crack carefully. Would not the sides fit together perfectly if the crack could be closed again? The crack, however, is aligned with faults to the north along which movement did occur, suggesting that the cracks opened in response to the same stress that caused movement there. Probably an earthquake took place, but there is no record that it was felt by man. Since large red fir grow from its sides, this crack must be at least hundreds of years old, and possibly thousands. In the days before refrigerators were common, Mammoth residents used to come to the Earthquake Fault

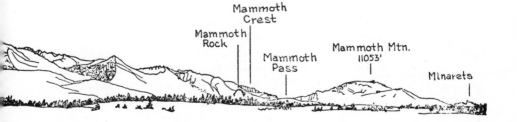

in summer for down in its shaded depths was always snow, which they dug to make ice cream or to cool their food.

The paved road continues through red fir-lodgepole pine forest to Mammoth Mountain's north slope, one of the finest skiing areas in California, developed since 1945. Early snows drift over the mountain into the shade on its north side, often providing enough snow to ski on in early November. The high elevation and the lack of exposure to winter sun keep ice formation at a minimum, the snow remaining packed and each new storm adding a few inches of

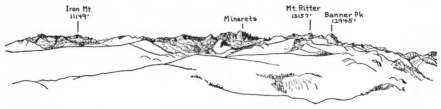

Figure 7. The Ritter Range.

powder to the surface. Skiing usually continues to Memorial Day weekend, some years into July. During the summer one of the lifts runs every day, providing a novel sightseeing trip and fine views west to the Ritter Range.

Beyond the ski lift, the road winds among mountain hemlock and then tops Minaret Summit, the ridge dividing the streams flowing east into Owens River from those flowing west into the San Joaquin Valley. At the summit, turn right to reach the observation point and self-guiding Nature Trail at Minaret Vista—one of the grandest views—magnificent Sierra peaks stretching for more than thirty-five miles, from Mount Lyell in Yosemite Park south to Kaiser Crest above Huntington Lake. In the deep canyon below winds the Middle Fork of the San Joaquin River, its headwaters at Thousand Island Lake, which lies below Banner Peak. Above the river, notice the canyon's smooth, almost bare walls. Their rounded form resulted from the pressure and scouring of the huge glaciers that once flowed down these canyons. Small glaciers of a more recent "Little Ice Age" remain on the cool northern slopes of most of the Ritter Range peaks. The entire Ritter Range is an exceptionally rugged divide partly because glaciers from both the east and west sides carved great steepsided amphitheater-shaped basins (cirques) into it, leaving a narrow saw-like crest. The range is jagged because its peaks and pinnacles were never sculptured into round, smooth ridges by overriding glaciers. Instead, these peaks stood well above the surface of the ice, where the rock-shattering effects of freezing and thawing were most intense. Rainwater seeps into the cracks and expands as it freezes, wedging the cracks a little farther open with each new freeze, until finally the loosened rock tumbles onto the glacier below. Thus these rugged frost-riven spires stand in marked contrast to the rounded ridges below them.

Much of the high country viewed from the observation point is National Forest wilderness, accessible to the rider, hiker, and fisherman by a network of good trails, its primitive beauty protected against roads and commercial development.

Beyond Minaret Summit, the road down to the Devil's Postpile and Reds Meadow is rough and dusty, though graded and wide enough for passing. Photographers who wish to catch the rainbow of Rainbow Falls should arrange to be there by noon, when the rainbow is at its best, then see other points of interest on the return trip. The road from Minaret Summit on was built in the late 1920s by the Minaret Mines Company. The mine operated through two winters, completely dependent on dog teams for supplies and mail from Mammoth. Half a mile down from the summit, on the left, is a widened area for parking—a favorite place for pictures and viewing the Middle Fork canyon.

Descending through a forest of towering red fir trees, the road skirts the edge of Agnew Meadow, named for Theodore (Tom) Agnew, a miner who in 1877 settled here in the North Fork District, as the area was then known. Agnew worked part time as a guide for the U. S. Army troops administering Yosemite Park (there was no National Park Service until 1916), which at one time included much of the Ritter Range and the Devil's Postpile. Remains of what may have been Agnew's cabin have been found recently near one of the meadows. To reach Agnew Meadow campgrounds and pack station, take the road that forks to the right; from its end, trails lead to the high country of Shadow, Garnet, and Thousand Island lakes.

The road's left fork continues on down the canyon, passing Starkweather Lake, named for a prospector called by some "the human gopher," who had claims on the slopes above during the 1920s. The road then crosses a grassy expanse known as Pumice Flat, named for the layer of light-weight pumice blanketing much of this region. Try floating a piece of this frothy volcanic rock on water. On the flat, best seen in the early morning, are many Belding ground squirrels, also known as "picket-pins" for their characteristic stance. Here the road nears the meandering San Joaquin River, named about 1805 for Saint Joaquim by Gabriel Moraga, a Spaniard exploring what we now call the San Joaquin Valley, far to the west. A spur road branches to the right half a mile to Minaret Creek campground, just opposite Minaret Falls, which slithers and cascades down over massive glacier-polished granite. Be sure not to miss this sight, especially in early summer.

Continue on the main road a short way to the spur road on the right leading to Devil's Postpile National Monument and ending at a large parking area, where there is also a Park Ranger Station and campground. To reach the main feature of the monument, a ten-minute walk, take the wide trail leading across the meadow.

Devil's Postpile is an unusual formation of tall columns of basalt, other

well-known examples of columnar basalt being the Palisades of the Hudson
and the Giant's Causeway in Ireland. The molten basalt flowed southward
from a vent near Upper Soda Springs Campground, pouring into the Middle
Fork valley and filling it from one side to the other to a minimum depth of
400 feet, from Pumice Flat south to Rainbow Falls. As the lava cooled and
solidified it shrank, developing cracks which radiated out from centers spaced
1-2½ feet apart. The cracks grew until they joined one another, and also grew
downward—the result being the four-, five-, six-, and seven-sided columns of the
Postpile. The enormous glacier which later formed and moved down the Middle Fork valley quarried away most of the columns, leaving on both sides of
the valley small remnants which can be seen at several places along the river.
The Devil's Postpile is the largest of these remnants. The mosaic-like top of the
Postpile, easily reached by a short trail, still shows some of the scratches and
the high polish made by the slow-moving, tremendously heavy ice mass—
though during the thousands of years since the glaciers melted, much of the
polished surface has weathered away. Frost action, the prying effect of freezing
water which has collected in the cracks, continues today—as it has for many
years—to destroy the Postpile columns slowly, pushing them outward until
they fall and shatter into the huge blocks of broken "posts" lying all about the
bottom. The Postpile is the starting point for numerous trails into the scenic
Ritter Range; trails also go downstream to Rainbow Falls (see trail section).

Near the Postpile the John Muir Trail—coming down from the passes and
high lakes of the Ritter Range—crosses the bridge over the Middle Fork and
then immediately swings back up to the timberline country, near Purple and
Virginia lakes. This famous trail, named for the man who did so much to protect the Sierra's wild beauty, is a true wilderness trail, the only one in America
where one can hike over 200 miles in the same direction without crossing a road
or passing a settlement of any kind. It travels the grand country of the High
Sierra, shunning the easy passes and the canyon bottoms in favor of the sweeping views and rugged spaciousness of the timberline country.

Back on the road to Reds Meadow, after one-half mile there is a short spur
on the left leading to Sotcher Lake, known also as Pond Lily Lake. This small
lake is famous for the mass of yellow pond lilies, usually in full bloom in late
July, that cover the surface of the water near its outlet. Beyond the lake the
road passes the first of the meadows known as Reds Meadow, named after
Red Sotcher (or Satcher)—a large red-bearded man who came here in 1879
herding sheep. It is said that Sotcher began raising vegetables when he found
that they grew well in the meadows and that there was a great demand for fresh
produce in the bustling camps near the Mammoth Mines. Turnip plants, possibly originally planted by Sotcher, were found in the meadows in the 1920s by
Mrs. Emma McLeod, a ranger's wife. True or not, the story also goes that
Sotcher was a cattle and horse thief, stealing animals on one side of the Sierra
and selling them on the other.

The mining boom at Mammoth also led to the construction of a trans-Sierra toll trail, which passed through Reds Meadow and was known as the Mammoth Trail or the French Trail, after J. S. French who built it. It led for fifty-four miles from Fresno Flats on the Sierra's west slope over Mammoth Pass to Mammoth City, the trip taking two days or more. Stock being driven to the Mammoth markets and pack trains carrying all kinds of supplies made this a busy trail during the few years that Mammoth flourished.

A left turn leads to Reds Meadow campground and public bath house providing water from a natural hot spring. Above the campground is a large meadow famous for its profusion of wildflowers from early July through August; most conspicuous are the tall blue larkspur or delphinium, Queen Anne's lace, evening primrose, old man's beard, and tiger lilies. The floral display is due to the exclusion of grazing. Mountain meadows are fragile areas; their beauty can be destroyed quickly by trampling. Enjoy the flowers from the edge of the meadow, and at the same time preserve them for others to enjoy the rest of the summer. Reds Meadow is fed by numerous springs, some of them warm, flowing from the hill behind and also from the meadow itself. East of the bath house is a log cabin which is unusual in that the logs are set vertical rather than horizontal as in most log buildings. It was constructed by Malcolm McLeod, District Ranger here from 1921 to 1929, and his assistant, from lodgepole pine cut nearby. It is for him that McLeod Lake on Mammoth Pass is named.

The main road ends about a half mile farther at the pack station, store and resort. Before you reach the pack station, a very bumpy but passable road turns off to the right and goes down about 100 yards to the beginning of the Rainbow Falls trail, a gentle hike of little more than a mile. The famous mountaineer, Walter Starr Jr., considered Rainbow Falls to be "the most beautiful in the Sierra outside of Yosemite." Here the water of the San Joaquin's Middle Fork pours over a resistant ledge of lava. The rainbow is particularly colorful at noon, across the mist that sometimes rises two-thirds the height of the falls. Use caution nearing the edge of the cliff, for loose pumice makes footing precarious. A steep path descends to the base of the falls.

Mammoth Lakes Road.—Where Highway 203 turns north toward the ski area, another paved road continues east, to the lake basin south of Mammoth Mountain. Near the post office, the forest was mostly Jeffrey pine—large reddish-barked trees with long needles—but as the road gains altitude, mixed Jeffrey pine and white fir are encountered. Still higher, at the observation point, the forest is predominantly red fir. Such changes indicate the colder climate and the longer snow season of the higher elevations. A large parking area left of the road provides the first good view of Mammoth Crest with its year-round snowfields. Behind brush-covered Panorama Dome, is Red (or Gold) Mountain—focus of an exciting, though brief, mining boom, 1878-80. To the right are the rough lava cliffs of Mammoth Mountain's east slope; below, Mammoth

Falls plunges over a ledge of lava. Eastward, in the distant valley, lies Crowley Lake; beyond it, on the horizon, the White Mountains stretch out of sight. Above the observation point, the road is cut along a glacial moraine, a mass of debris ranging in size from particles of fine clay to large angular boulders, then levels off to cross the outlet of Twin Lakes. Twin is the first of the Mammoth Lakes—a group of thirteen lakes, none of which is named "Mammoth Lake." At the far end of the lakes, Twin Falls tumbles down three hundred feet into the upper lake. The Forest Chapel, where outdoor Sunday services are held in summer, is at the base of the lava cliffs. Above the bridge a paved road forks right, leading to Twin Lakes store, resort, and campgrounds.

Old Mammoth Road, secondary road to Old Mammoth, the Mammoth Mines and Mammoth City.—About ½ mile above the Twin Lakes bridge a dirt road, known as the Old Mammoth Road, branches left and leads to the site of Mammoth City. In this gulch during 1878–79 sprouted a mining camp of perhaps a thousand people, who had come from everywhere to seek wealth and fame at the Mammoth mines, supposedly "the largest bonanza outside of Virginia City." Mammoth City—the center for the nearby, smaller camps of Pine City, Mill City, and Mineral Park—is reported to have had twenty-two saloons, thirteen stores, two breweries, two livery stables, five restaurants, and two newspapers. (Lest the number of business houses give the impression of a permanent "city," let it be remembered that a ten-foot square tent or shack plus a barrel of whiskey and a few glasses were all that was needed to make a "saloon.") As in most boom camps, supplies were scarce and brought big prices. Jim Sherwin carried in eighty pounds of potatoes on his back, and was paid a dollar a pound for them.

The major cause for the sudden excitement was the organization of the Mammoth Mining Company, which incorporated in 1878. To the right of the road is the steep slope of Mineral Hill (now known as Gold or Red Mountain) into which the company drove four tunnels. Their dumps are still clearly visible. The lowest tunnel is easily reached by crossing the creek. Though its opening has collapsed, there is much to explore—the large dump, big timbers, bits of machinery, rusted tram cars. A row of neatly piled rocks, above and just left of the opening, marks the foundation for the tracks which carried the ore cars down from the next highest tunnel on the slope. Above that is No. 3 tunnel, supposed to have provided the richest ore. To process the ore a 20-stamp mill was erected half a mile down the slope, and to provide water-power dams were constructed on Lake Mary and Twin Lakes and a flume was built from Twin Lakes' outlet. An elevated tramway carried the ore cars to the mill. According to Chalfant, one day when the tracks were icy, the train got out of control and the brakeman was badly injured. After that, a mule was used to control the cars. One stormy day, a wind roaring down the canyon blew the poor beast off the track. Thereafter whenever a fierce wind threatened, the wise mule lay down on the tracks until the blast subsided.

Cabins of the miners were dug into the hillside to the left of the road; stone foundations may still be found in the brush. Only two buildings are recognizable—the large log building next to the road, near it another log building partly collapsed. Most of them were salvaged for their wood; one by one the others fell, usually under the weight of winter snow. Among old-timers there is a difference of opinion as to whether these buildings date from the boom days of 1878, or whether they were built about twenty years later when Dr. Doyle of Bishop reopened the mines long enough to lose some money on them. Square nails are often a clue in dating old buildings, for round nails were not widely used until after 1890. Since all of these structures contain square nails or nail-holes, it is likely that they are pre-1890 and the only standing remains of Mammoth Mining Company times. They were no doubt used by later prospectors, trappers, and sheepherders, who added the round nails which are there also.

A year and a half later, during the severe winter of 1879-80, the company mill suddenly shut down, never to run again. A reported disagreement among the stockholders probably meant that they were unwilling to pour more money into the project. The company stock, worth up to $20 a share in 1879, was worthless the next year. In 1881 the property was sold at a sheriff's sale. The Mammoth Company was said to have spent almost $300,000; the only reliable estimate of Mammoth's gold output, as reported in the *Eighth Annual Report of the State Mineralogist*, 1888, is $200,000. Deep snows—it is said that twenty-eight feet fell during December—hastened the departure of people after the mill closed. The *Mammoth City Times* on one occasion reported the exodus whimsically, saying, "Twenty pairs of snowshoes, each with a man on top, left this morning."

Later a Judge Doyle of Chicago invested some money in the Mammoth mines, sight unseen. In the late 1890s he sent his son, a young doctor, to see why the mines were bringing no return. Young Dr. Doyle invested more money, building a 10-stamp mill (the remains of this mill—large timbers and a stone foundation—can be found in the willows along the creek). His crew used the two log buildings for a cookhouse and bunkhouse. Across the road was a sturdy frame building that was the assay office. But the mines did not pay, and the property changed hands. Since then, the Mammoth and the other mines on Red Mountain have been worked now and then on a small scale. Some people, however, still believe there is high-grade ore within Red Mountain. There is no doubt that there *is* gold, but the ore discovered so far is a mixture of minerals that is difficult and expensive to mill. Blasting and prospecting go on almost every summer. And who knows—perhaps "the largest bonanza outside of Virginia City" *is* there, waiting to be discovered.

Down the Old Mammoth Road, from the edge of the first sharp curve, a wide ditch can be seen in the gully below. This is believed to be the site of a roofed tramway that was built partly underground, that the ore trains could supply the mill despite deep snow. Above juts a prominent white crag, Mammoth Rock, known in the old days as Monumental Rock. It is composed of marble (metamorphosed limestone) and fine-grained sandstone, being an erosional form and not a volcano as is popularly believed. Near the base is a blue-gray limestone containing small white disks ⅛"-¼" in diameter. These are fossil crinoids, ancient relatives of the sea urchin (see figure 12, trail section). Hot springs, once active here, have decomposed the surrounding rocks into the white clay which is abundant below Mammoth Rock. A faint sulfur smell can still be detected, and a careful search will reveal a little native sulfur that was deposited near the old vents. Farther down the road, in the trees to the right, is the grave of Mrs. J. E. Townsend, who died in November 1881, thirty-four years old. Since the ground was covered with deep snow when she died, her hand-made coffin was packed in snow until she could be buried the next March. An old picket fence around the grave has been replaced by a more sturdy one. The story goes that this young mother of three dreamed of someday having a house with a picket fence. Her grieving husband then gave her the only picket fence he could—around her grave.

To see the big flywheel, which is about all that is left of the Mammoth Company's old mill, drive a little farther, park along the road, and then walk up the dirt road past the Mill City Tract cabins, turning right beyond the last cabin. Stone foundations mark the outline of the mill buildings. A large water-wheel, turned by water from the Twin Lakes' flume, drove the twenty stamps which crushed the ore. The next year, twenty more stamps were added and a steam engine, but it is believed that the mill closed before the engine was ever used. Over the years the machinery has been taken, much of it for scrap. The water-wheel and the mill buildings were burned purposely in 1929 because they were considered a fire hazard. A cluster of miners' cabins on the hill above was known as Mill City. A large white house near the creek was built by C. F. Wildasinn, who in the early 1900s owned most of the land near Old Mammoth, grazing cattle and operating a sawmill and small hotel during the summer. (Valentine Eastern Sierra Reserve, see page 143, 11.)

The road continues down to the low hills and meadows known in the early days as Mineral Park. A sawmill on Mammoth Creek supplied lumber to Bishop for many years. The corrals to the right of the road indicate the approximate site of the original Mammoth Lakes. Nearby was the Summer's hotel, built in 1918, a garage, dairy, bakery and store—complete with barber chair, butcher shop, post office, and pot-belly stove which served as the community center. Only an occasional trapper or a lone caretaker stayed through the winter, until in 1928 freight and passenger service by dog sled was inaugurated. Until they were disbanded during the war years, the dog teams—mostly Greenland malamutes weighing up to one hundred and forty pounds—supplied color as well as winter communication and transportation for this snow-bound country. A few hardy souls began living at Mammoth year-round, and a few skiers (mostly

Europeans, since at that time few Americans had ever seen a ski), came to enjoy the snow. Besides carrying passengers at twenty dollars a head and freight at ten cents a pound from Sherwin Hill to Mammoth, the dog teams carried mail, snow surveyors, workmen to repair power breaks, hauled ice, and made a number of emergency runs such as rescuing people from stalled cars and racing the sick to a doctor. In 1937, when the present Mammoth highway was completed, business moved to better locations on the new road, and this meadow area has since been known as Old Mammoth. The Old Mammoth Road continues on to rejoin Highway 203.

Mammoth Lakes Road (resumed).—

At the Old Mammoth Road turnoff, there is a good view of the bald, pumice-covered summit of Mammoth Mountain and of its lava cliffs. Mammoth is a volcano that, according to geologic studies published in 1976, is much younger than was thought. Born about 180,000 years ago, it spewed out lava and fragments during ten or more major eruptions, the last one 40,000 years ago. Although at a distance its profile is that of a typical, symmetrical volcanic dome, at closer range its surface seems markedly irregular. This is due partly to glacial sculpturing and partly to the eruption of lava flows that, too small and viscous to spread out, cooled as stubby, steep-sided blobs on the volcano's flanks.

A paved sideroad turns left to the inlet of Lake Mary, where there is a store, resort, and a narrow road leading to the extensive Coldwater Campground. Near the junction are the remains of an arrastra, a crude mill for crushing ore, built in the late 1890s. In contrast to stamp mills, which were expensive, arrastras could be built by one man with practically no capital and were often powered by burros that walked around and around, pulling heavy stones over pieces of ore and pulverizing them. At one time a waterwheel ran this arrastra; its ditch can still be traced through the trees. Among the lodgepole here were scattered the cabins of Pine City, a mining camp contemporary with Mammoth City.*

The highway then tops a rise near Lake Mary, the largest of the Mammoth lakes, nearly a mile long. It was named after Mary Calvert of Pine City.** Lake George was named for her husband. The thumb of gray rock towering above Lake Mary is Crystal Crag, a "cleaver" or "island" of resistant granitic rock around which flowed the two arms of a glacier. It is a remnant of a once high ridge separating the drainages of Crystal and T. J. lakes. Glacial quarrying steepened the sides of the ridge, finally cutting through and destroying it, except for Crystal Crag itself, which apparently was more resistant. Close to its base is a small pond jokingly called "Mammoth Lake." Since visitors long have queried, "Where is Mammoth Lake?" this tiny pond was christened in answer to their question.

---

* *See page 143, 1.*
** *See page 143, 2.*

A paved road branching left from the highway crosses the outlet of **Lake Mary**, a favorite place for enjoying sunsets and the view of Duck Pass. The road then winds up the hill to Lake George, where there are more campgrounds, a resort and the beginning of the Mammoth Crest trail. Lake George (9008 feet), is the highest of the Mammoth group accessible by car. On the far side of the lake, where several small streams enter, there are small meadows lush with a large variety of flowers. Above them rises Crystal Crag; from Crystal Lake at its base tumbles Crystal Falls. A striking variation in vegetation may be discovered around Lake George. On the warmer, drier south-facing brush

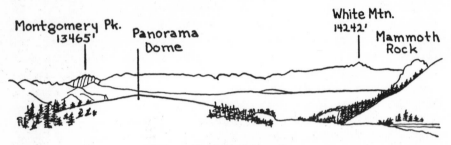

Figure 8. The White Mountains.

slope below the resort grow several stocky Jeffrey pine, while on the cool shaded slope across the lake, mountain hemlock grow down to the water's edge.

The highway continues along the Rim, a bench of volcanic rock in which glaciers carved the basins of Mary, Mamie, and Horseshoe lakes. Lake Mamie (8898 feet), sometimes incorrectly spelled "Mayme," is believed to be named for Mamie Clarke, at one time the superintendent of schools in Bishop. Beyond, to the right, is a large parking area with excellent views eastward, particularly enjoyable at sunset. The road ends at Horseshoe Lake, ten miles from Highway 395. Horseshoe is the only lake in the Mammoth group with wide sandy shores; since it also has no outlet, it is ideally suited to swimming. (Swimming is prohibited in all the other lakes, for they supply drinking water). Much of the "sand" is pumice, typical of this region. Horseshoe's water level varies considerably with the season and the year. Undoubtedly the lake loses its water through underground drainage into the porous volcanic rock in which it lies. Camping on Horseshoe Lake is for organizations only; permission must be obtained from the Ranger Station.

HIGHWAY 395—MAMMOTH TO CONWAY SUMMIT

From the Mammoth Lakes junction, a short spur leads north to Casa Diablo, a hot spring long enjoyed by whites and Paiutes alike. The *Mammoth City Times* in 1879 described its wonders in a lyrical article. Steaming pools, a small lake fringed with tules, and a stream created an unusual oasis for birds and animals and gave rise to a small resort. Drilling for geothermal steam in the 1960s dried

Mammoth Mountain   Bev Steveson

Fire!
Known in Paiute legend as "the burnt land," the eastern

Sierra between Bishop and Mono Lake has been a center of intense, often explosive volcanic activity the last three million years. The marks of that violence are everywhere — craters, volcanoes, red cinder cones, black glassy obsidian cliffs, acres of pumice, and miles of lava.

Mammoth Mountain is one of the volcanoes. Born about 180,000 years ago, ten or more major eruptions built the mountain up to about the size it is today. Its last eruption occurred around 40,000 years ago.

Boiling springs, Hot Creek   LaMoine R. Fantozzi

Casa Diablo geyser,1959   Gerhard Schumacher

Obsidian flow   Bev Steveson
(detail, 17 inches wide)

Explosion pit,   Edwin C. Rockwell
Inyo Craters

Rhyolite domes and stubby flows of the Mono Craters   Robert C. Frampton

Another rhyolite dome, Wilson Butte   Robert C. Frampton

Large as it is, Mammoth Mountain is insignificant compared to the enormous eruptions centered at Long Valley 700,000 years ago. Pumice and fine-grained glassy fragments called "ash" exploded in such quantities that the skies must have been darkened for months at a time. Shattering explosions hurled out glowing gas-propelled clouds that shot out in all directions and blanketed four hundred and fifty square miles with layers of incandescent fragments hundreds of feet thick. Two hundred cubic **miles** of volcanic material was ejected, and ash from these eruptions has been identified as far away as Nebraska.

Steam vents and hot springs tell us that the volcanic fires are not yet spent. The most recent explosions we know of, those that ripped out the Inyo Craters, have been dated at about 1400 A.D. A hundred and fifty years earlier, the pumice that mantles the Mammoth area exploded from a vent south of Deadman Creek.

The Mono Craters are a chain of rhyolite domes and stubby flows. Their flat-topped shapes were determined by the viscous nature of the lava that formed them. When pressures below pushed it upward, instead of flowing, it solidified, piling up on itself in a jumble of blocks that spread sluggishly outward. Wilson Butte was formed in the same way.

Devils Postpile, remnant of a basalt flow   Bev Steveson

Basalt column   Ed Cooper

Glacier-polished columns   Bev Steveson

Rainbow Falls dropping over lava cliff

Ed Cooper

Devils Postpile is a spectacular remnant of a basalt flow

that erupted close to a million years ago in the valley of the Middle Fork of the San Joaquin River. Unlike the almost-solid rhyolite that formed the stubby domes of the Mono Craters, basalt flows freely. It flowed at least three miles, filling the valley to a depth of several hundred feet. As the basalt cooled and shrank, an intersecting network of cracks produced the five- and six-sided columns or "posts." The glaciers that later flowed down the Middle Fork valley quarried away much of the flow. They also planed off and polished the top of the rock columns, producing an extraordinary parquet-floor effect.

Downstream from the Postpile, Rainbow Falls drops a hundred and forty feet over a cliff of lava. The height of the falls is maintained by an upper layer of massive, resistant lava. Underlying it is a softer layer of platy lava that is easily undercut by the plunging water at the base of the falls.

Abrupt eastern Sierra front formed by repeated faulting,
Sawtooth Ridge above Bridgeport Valley

Bev Steveson

Fifty-foot fault scarp in moraine, McGee Creek

John S. Shelton

During this period of volcanic fury, large-scale faulting

occurred along the 400-mile length of the eastern Sierra. Breaking along faults at the base of its eastern slope, the entire Sierra block tilted downward to the west. Its eastern portion lurched upward, while many of the adjacent blocks to the east dropped downwards. This faulting occurred not as one great cataclysm, but probably as hundreds of repeated jerks, of about the same intensity we experience during earthquakes today.

Perhaps the fifty-foot break in the McGee Creek moraine, pictured above, can help us understand the large-scale faulting of the entire eastern slope. Recognizing this break for what it is — a recent, very fresh fault scarp — is a key to understanding much about the eastern Sierra, its origin, its rocks, even its weather. It was formed by movement along a fault; one side moved up relative to the other. Repeated movement, similar to this, along the fault zone that extends the length of the Sierra accounts for the abrupt mountain front characteristic of the eastern Sierra. The steep mountain front above Bridgeport Valley (opposite) and the sheer face of Carson Peak (following page) are colossal examples of ancient, eroded fault scarps.

Sheer face of Carson Peak, an ancient fault scarp

Stephen H. Willard

Probably the Sierra crest is rising today,

and probably at about the same rate as in the past. Geophysicists haven't been measuring the Sierra long enough for their data to be conclusive. But measurements made in 1940 and again in 1957 indicate that at least part of the Sierra may now be tilting farther westward. A comparison of precise measurements at Tioga Pass and at White Wolf to the west show that Tioga Pass has risen relative to White Wolf. They indicate a differential rate of uplift of twenty-eight inches per century.

up the spring and left Casa Diablo as it is today—a mess of concrete and pipes. (See page 143, 3.) The old log cabin still standing here in the 1960s was probably the original way station on the Bodie-Mammoth City stage line. One old-timer says that inside there was little more than a couple of barrels of whiskey and a single glass, which was passed from hand to hand. Colorful deposits of travertine and kaolinite across the highway indicate intense hot water activity in times past. Both of these materials form around volcanic vents and hot springs, as acid-charged hot water slowly disintegrates the surrounding rock.

Beyond Casa Diablo, the highway enters an extensive forest of Jeffrey pine covering some two hundred square miles, the largest Jeffrey pine forest in the world. At present, most of the forest is being managed for sustained-yield logging. Because of its unique character and its scenic beauty, a few local citizens attempted, several years ago, to have a portion of it preserved in its natural state and protected from the network of roads and the disturbance by bulldozers that logging always brings. They were not successful.

Many of the gaps along the Sierra Crest are protected from the brunt of winter storms by other high peaks to the west. Here, however, storm clouds blown inland from the Pacific Ocean can come straight up the Middle Fork of the San Joaquin and over the relatively low saddles of Minaret Summit and Mammoth Pass, dumping their load of moisture as rain and snow east of the Sierra Crest. North and south of here the high crest causes the clouds to drop more of their moisture on the west slope. The additional water is one of the factors that enable this forest of Jeffrey pine to grow on what otherwise would be dry sagebrush-covered hills.

Sideroad to the Inyo Craters and their lakes.—A well-signed, graded road branches left to the Inyo Craters picnic and parking area. An easy fifteen-minute walk takes you to the craters themselves and to an unusual self-guiding nature trail. These two explosion craters represent possibly the last volcanic activity in the area, and indicate a relatively mild form of volcanism, which might be thought of as the dying volcanic forces' "last gasp." Gases burst through weak spots, hurling out whatever was above and leaving these funnel-shaped craters. Craters are not uncommon in this area, but craters with lakes are rare. One contains opaque jade-green water; the other is a deep clear green. These lakes are fishless, though every year a few anglers hopefully looking for a new spot visit them. From radiocarbon age determinations on fragments of buried wood and from tree-ring counts, the date of the explosion that formed the craters is about 1400 A.D.

Sideroad to an Outstanding Viewpont.—See page 143, 4.

Sideroad to Owens River resorts and Big Springs Campground.—A paved road to the right leads to two ranches that were homesteaded years ago, which now have resort facilities, and also to Big Springs Campground on the Owens River. Here springs gush into Deadman Creek, coming from San Joaquin

Mountain, increasing the flow of water to such an extent that Big Springs is commonly considered the headwaters of the Owens River.

Sideroad to Deadman Recreation Area.—A graded road branches left and goes to a campground on Deadman Creek, which received its name from the story of a man named Farnsworth, who in 1861 in Monoville claimed he had discovered rich ore while searching for the Lost Cement Mine. Eventually Farnsworth made a deal with a Robert Hume, who was to put up money for a small mill. Hume, with $700 on him, went with Farnsworth to his Owens River camp to see the ore. Some weeks or months later, Farnsworth returned to Monoville—hatless, knife cuts in his clothing, and a bullet hole in the calf of his leg. He told a harrowing story of being attacked by Indians, and of Hume's being killed. A party was organized to punish the Indians, the group by coincidence staying overnight at Farnsworth's camp. One of the men, collecting firewood in the dark, lifted a heavy log from the creek only to discover it was the body of a man. Other details led the men to believe that Farnsworth had killed his own partner and hidden his body in the creek. Farnsworth escaped from the jail he was placed in, and was never heard of again. Treasure hunters of today should refer to chapter three in Chalfant's book, *Gold, Guns, and Ghost Towns*, for details about the Lost Cement Mine. Many believe it to be on Deadman Creek; others believe it to be a dozen different places, including the east slope of Gold Mountain at Mammoth, above Windy Flat.

395.—The highway passes Crestview, which commands an exceptional view of the Sierra crest to the south. The view is even better just north of

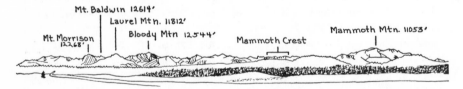

Figure 9. The Sierra crest south of Crestview.

Crestview, where there is a turnout left around a rock promontory. In front of the resort are two huge wheels used for lumbering in the early days. Heavy logs were slung *under* the axle, somewhat as lumber today is carried under high straddle-trucks, the driver sitting on top. Around a large Jeffrey tree nearby a fence has been built, in memory of a courageous mail carrier who in the fierce winter of 1879 set out from Mammoth to get the mail at Bodie. Just half a mile from Deadman Station, near here, he and his mule were overwhelmed by snowdrifts. He was found after several days half frozen, and died later at Mammoth. To see the tree follow the power line about one-quarter mile north, up the wash from the resort. The highway swings up over Deadman Summit.

Sideroad to Bald Mountain Lookout.—See page 143, 5.

Sideroad to an obsidian dome.—Just beyond the summit, a dirt road branches left through the snow fence to an obsidian (volcanic glass) dome. The road forks left about one-half mile from the highway and goes directly to the base of the large, three-hundred-foot-high dome. This is one of the best places to see a hill of solid obsidian. Obsidian is often pure black, or it may be sprinkled with tiny white crystals as it is here, suggesting the name "snowflake obsidian." The streaks of bubbly gray material—obsidian also, but more frothy—show well the contorted flow lines of the molten material as it welled up. Obsidian forms when thick viscous lava reaches the earth's surface and then cools rapidly, giving the various minerals in the lava no time to crystallize.

395.—As the highway crosses a pumice flat beyond Deadman Summit, Wilson Butte is straight ahead. It is another obsidian dome but quite different in rock texture from the one described just above. Examine some of the broken blocks at its base. Their texture reminds one of a fine-grained sponge—not as dense as obsidian nor as frothy as pumice. This dome, one of the most recent, erupted probably less than five thousand years ago. Much of the forest north and south of Wilson Butte was blown down in the early 1920s, when heavy rains were followed by violent winds. The trees, rooted in the rain-soaked loose pumice soil, were easily felled by the wind. Remnants of the phenomenon remain today, large weathered tree trunks all lying in the same direction. Past Wilson Butte a road turns left into the forest leading to Hartley Springs. To the right of the highway may be seen a circular, steep-sided explosion pit similar to the Inyo Craters. On its far side is a large V-shaped gully that formed in a few hours in the loose pumice, when a pipeline broke during construction of the Los Angeles aqueduct.

Sideroad to the Devil's Punchbowl.—A narrow road turns off to the right to this large explosion pit. Stay in the road tracks, for it is easy to get stuck in the loose pumice. Several signs indicate the road leading up to the lip of the Punchbowl. This crater may be considered to have reached a slightly more advanced stage than the one just seen from the highway, for the formation of explosion craters follows a definite sequence: first, explosions that produce cone-shaped pits—like the ones holding the Inyo Crater lakes; second, the rise of a stiff, more-or-less solid obsidian dome from the floor of the pit, as at Wilson Butte and at Panum Crater near Mono Lake; third, the continued rise of the dome until it may spill over the side in a short, chunky flow. To see a baby dome that rose only about forty feet above the crater's floor, look down into the Punchbowl.

Everyone familiar with the country between Mammoth Lakes and Mono Lake eventually comes to realize how many square miles are covered with pumice, and then begins to wonder where so much pumice could have come from. Yet the amount of pumice is relatively small, compared to the outpourings of lava that lie hundreds of feet thick under the pumice, and that built mountains thousands of feet high—the Mono Craters, Glass Mountain Ridge, San Joaquin Mountain, Mammoth Mountain, and dozens of smaller ridges and hills. All came from the depths of the earth. Pumice is just lava in another form —a gas-charged, once-molten froth. The pumice here was hurled out explosively from a series of vents aligned northward from Mammoth Mountain to the Mono Craters. The youngest pumice, that which blankets the Mammoth area, probably exploded from a vent now buried by the dome south of Deadman Creek, about 1240 A.D. Fragments from this explosion have been identified in Sierra meadows as far away as the valley of the Little Kern, 120 miles south.

June Lake Loop Road.—A paved road branches left to the June Lake basin—where there are campgrounds, resorts, stores, boat landings, and a pack station—and rejoins Highway 395 north of Grant Lake. The wide, sandy beach at the east end of June Lake offers some of the best swimming in the area. To the right of the lake is Reversed Peak, named for the creek that rises in June Lake and flows *toward* the mountains—an unusual situation, for streams usually flow *away* from mountains. Following the shore of June Lake (7616 feet), the road cuts through a rocky outcrop on which is balanced a huge granitic boulder, over thirty feet in diameter and estimated to weigh ninety tons, which was left on this perch by a melting glacier. The road then leads through the community of June Lake and past Gull Lake, named for the many gulls that fly over from their nesting area on Mono Lake to fish. On the left are the lifts and tows of the June Mountain Ski area. The five-month ski season usually begins at Thanksgiving. As the road winds through the small valley of Fern Creek with its many large aspen trees, in May and June there are splendid views of Rush Creek Falls cascading down twelve hundred feet over glacier-smoothed rock. Left of the falls are the sheer cliffs of Carson Peak, named for the first owner of the Silver Lake resort.

At the base of **Rush Creek Falls** (which no longer flow in summer, their water going instead through penstocks) is a powerhouse now belonging to the Southern California Edison Company and built in 1916. The original company that built most of the eastern Sierra powerhouses was established in the early 1900's. It delivered its first power in 1905 to the then prosperous Nevada mining towns of Goldfield and Tonopah, from a plant on Bishop Creek and over a

Figure 10. Sierra peaks near June Lake Junction.

113-mile-long transmission line (then the longest in the world) across the White Mountains. The water for the Rush Creek Powerhouse comes from three lakes in the basin of upper Rush Creek, where dams were constructed at Agnew and Gem lakes and at Rush Meadows.

Silver Lake takes its name from the silver-gray color of its water on overcast days. The stretch of Rush Creek connecting Silver Lake to Grant Lake is a lovely bit of stream-meadow landscape. From the aspen- and willow-lined banks of the creek, there are fine views back toward Carson Peak. From early June, when the wild roses and iris bloom, to late autumn when the aspen turn yellow to reddish orange and burnished pink, there is something of interest and of beauty. Grant Lake was once a small marshy basin at the foot of Reversed Peak. In connection with its work on the Mono Craters tunnel, the Los Angeles Department of Water and Power built a dam at Grant Lake. The lake now collects the diverted water of Lee Vining, Walker, and Parker creeks in addition to Rush Creek water; and it acts as the control point for shunting this Mono Basin water through the Craters tunnel and into Owens River, Crowley Lake, and on through the aqueduct. The present lake has inundated formerly extensive meadows and Jeffrey pine and aspen groves, and now reaches up into the canyon of Rush Creek.

395.—Just beyond June Lake junction there is a glimpse of some Ritter Range peaks to the southwest. The landscape in the foreground combines two quite different geological features—glacial moraines and volcanic cinders. Most of the red cinder used locally on driveways comes from this area. Left of the highway there is a fine example of a long moraine—the low brush-covered ridge, sprinkled with boulders and a few trees, extending from left of Reversed Peak toward Mono Lake for over a mile. The highway winds down a canyon cut through Bishop tuff, the same pinkish rock you first encountered on Sherwin Grade. Here the winds have sand-blasted some tuff into grotesque sculptures. A short walk east takes you to them, the Aeolian Buttes.

Left of the highway on the skyline are the summits of Mounts Gibbs and Dana, the latter named by the Whitney Survey after Professor Dana of Yale, the foremost American geologist of his time. The Whitney Survey was organized in 1860, when the legislature appointed Josiah Whitney, of Harvard, state

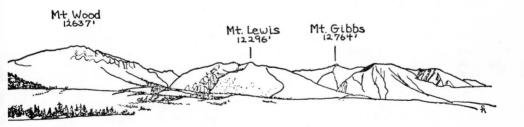

Mt. Wood
12637'

Mt. Lewis
12296'

Mt. Gibbs
12764'

geologist and directed him to make a geological survey of the state. Since much of California had never been mapped, members of the Survey were privileged to name many Sierra Peaks—such as the Minarets (for their resemblance to the slender spires of a mosque) and Red Slate Mountain. Several peaks were named after members of the Survey—Whitney, Brewer, Gabb, Gardiner, Hoffmann, and Clarence King. Other peaks were named for prominent men of the time, both Americans and Europeans—California Senator John Conness (who helped set aside Yosemite), the eminent English geologist Sir Charles Lyell, and the famous German geographer Karl Ritter.

Figure 11. Mono Pass, Mt. Gibbs, and Mt. Dana.

The broad saddle left of Mount Gibbs is historic Mono Pass; below it is Bloody Canyon, whose perils were described graphically by William H. Brewer, leader of the Whitney Survey party that travelled it in 1863. In a letter to his family, Brewer wrote: ". . . a terrible trail. You would all pronounce it utterly inaccessible to horses, yet pack trains come down, but the bones of several horses or mules and the stench of another told that all had not passed safely. . . . The horses were so cut by sharp rocks that they named it 'Bloody Canyon' . . . and it is appropriate—part of the way the rocks in the trail are literally sprinkled with blood from the animals." Over Mono Pass there had long been an Indian trail, used by the Paiutes of Mono Lake and the Miwoks of Yosemite when they crossed the Sierra to trade with each other. Probably the first white men to cross Mono Pass were soldiers under Lt. Tredwell Moore, who in June 1852 were sent from Fort Miller in Mariposa County to Yosemite Valley to punish Indians for killing two prospectors. Five Indians were captured in the Valley and shot; the rest fled east to hide among their friends, the Paiutes of Mono Lake. The Indians were never caught, but in chasing them over the Sierra crest Moore's men picked up pieces of gold ore. Displayed back in Mariposa, the ore came to the attention of a prospector named Leroy Vining, who set out to find its source. Vining and a few companions, coming via Mono Pass and Bloody Canyon with one of Moore's men as guide, were probably the first to prospect the Mono Basin. Later prospectors and pack trains, swarming to the gold strikes at Mono Diggings and later Aurora, followed the general route of the ancient Indian trail which came to be known as the Mono Trail.

To the right of the highway, the steep-sided Mono Craters cut the sky-line with their odd flat-topped forms. This unusual chain of obsidian domes and stubby obsidian flows rises about 2400 feet above Pumice Valley, approaching in height the famed volcanoes Stromboli and Vesuvius. Yet they probably excite much less comment than is due them, dwarfed as they are by neighboring Sierra peaks which tower three and four thousand feet above them. Unlike the lava of the well-known Hawaiian volcanoes, which flows down-slope in large fiery streams, the lava that built the Mono Craters was very thick, almost solid, when it reached the surface. Some of it rose as gigantic columns of solid obsidian, building dome-shaped mountains such as the three high domes at the center of the Mono Craters chain. Some of it rose as not-quite-solid obsidian and spilled over in stubby steep-faced flows, as can be seen both north and south of the central domes. Much of the pumice in the area came from explosions connected with the rise of the domes. On the leeward (east) side of the Craters, pumice is known to be twenty feet thick; and wind-blown pumice drifted east as far as the Nevada boundary, thirty miles away. On the windward (west) side, pumice is seldom more than five feet thick. Probably the Mono Craters were built during thousands of years, though most of them are recent, having formed since the Ice Age—that is, less than 10,500 years ago. The volcanic fires in the eastern Sierra have been quiet for many years, with hot springs and steam vents the only surviving traces of activity. However, it takes little imagination to picture the Craters again hidden by clouds of steam, hurling ash and pumice as far as the eye can see. It may happen again.

Highway 120 East, Sideroad to Mono Mills and Benton.—This road, paved all the way to Benton, turns right from Highway 395. On hot summer days, plan this trip so most of it can be enjoyed during the cool hours of early morning or late afternoon. About three miles from the junction a graded road branches left to Panum Crater (called North Crater on the new topographic map). Panum, an Indian word meaning "lake," is the name given it by I. C. Russell, an early geologist who in 1889 published his classic report on the Mono Basin. Panum is an excellent example of an explosion crater which passed through two stages: first, violent explosions hurled out bits of frothy lava which fell as pumice around the vent in a crater-shaped mound; second, a mass of stiff, quickly cooling obsidian rose and effectively plugged its own vent. The contrast between the gently sloping, pale gray circular rim and the dark jagged plug (or dome) in its center is striking.

As the road nears the base of the Mono Craters, there are many opportunities to observe their rough, blocky obsidian flows and their smooth steep-sided pumice slopes. A safe but unimproved road turning off left leads to the south shore of Mono Lake. On any of these pumice roads, always stay in the road tracks. Farther on, as Highway 120 enters a forest of Jeffrey pine and lodgepole, notice that most of the trees are small—few exceeding 8–12 inches in diameter, though there are many stumps of 3–4 foot diameter. In the early days, parts of this forest were clear-cut to supply the tremendous demand of nearby mining camps for wood. It is hard today to appreciate the mining camps' complete dependence on wood for fuel as well as for building purposes. Besides quantities used for cooking and domestic heating, the mills and hoisting works needed enormous amounts to run their steam engines. It is said that Bodie used as much as 45,000 cords in a year. Millions of feet of lumber were needed to construct mills, flumes and houses, to shore up tunnels and shafts. Dozens of sawmills employing hundreds of men kept busy the year around—among them several large sawmills west of Big Meadows (as Bridgeport was then called) which supplied Bodie and Aurora, and a wood ranch in Lee Vining Canyon.

A large sign by the highway indicates the site of Mono Mills, an important sawmill operating over thirty-five years. Behind the sign is the depression of the large millpond, and portions of the flume bringing water to it. At first wood was sent to Bodie via barge across the lake and then via team. Then during Bodie's flush days, the Bodie Railway and Lumber Co. was incorporated to build a 31-mile narrow gauge track around the east end of the lake to Mono Mills. The Bodie and Benton Railroad (which never went on to Benton) was completed in 1881. Especially powerful locomotives—named the Inyo, Mono, Tybo, and Bodie—were built to haul the lumber trains up the steep grade to Bodie, a 1900-foot rise in ten miles. Though the tracks were taken for scrap years ago, parts of the route still can be traced.

After the highway crosses Sand Flat, there are impressive views east of Montgomery Peak. In the foreground are scattered juniper trees and pinyon pine. Quantities of pinyon were cut for the mining camps, as they make excellent fuel. For lumber, however, the Jeffrey pine were prized most highly. Just beyond Black Lake at the lower end of Adobe Valley, thirty-nine miles after leaving Highway 395, a graded road turns right and loops back to 395, joining it near Convict Lake. (For a description of this road and of Benton, see above "Sideroad to Whitmore Hot Springs, Benton Crossing. . . .")

395.—After the highway crosses Rush Creek, there is a road sign indicating the Mount Diablo Base Line. This is a line running east and west from Mount Diablo, a prominent peak east of Oakland and the starting point for all the surveys in California. Before California became a state, property boundaries—particularly of the old Mexican land grants—were described in vague terms (so many paces toward the large oak tree, etc.). A fixed point on top of Mount Diablo was chosen in 1851 and a meridian line and a base line surveyed from it. After that, all property was described in relation to these lines.

Sideroad to Grant Lake.—This is the northern end of the June Lake Loop Road, described in detail above.

395.—For some distance the highway crosses large meadows, formerly lush and flooded during summer with ample mountain water now diverted into Grant Lake and the Aqueduct. Indians live in the small houses to the left of the road just south of Lee Vining, many of them descendants of the Paiutes who have long made their homes along the shores of Mono Lake. Before the white man changed their lives, one of their important trading items was obsidian, so plentiful here yet scarce on the other side of the Sierra, which they exchanged with Yosemite Indians for acorns, berries, and bead money. The Paiutes were excellent basket weavers; fine collections of their baskets may be seen at the Bodie Museum, and the Inyo Museum in Independence. Before the road turns left into Lee Vining Canyon, there are good views of Panum Crater, the low crater at the end of the Mono Craters chain that is closest to Mono Lake (see above, Highway 120 East).

Highway 120 West, sideroad to Tioga Pass and Yosemite National Park.—Twelve miles from this junction, Highway 120 enters Yosemite Park at Tioga Pass (9945 feet), the highest highway pass in the state. It is a spectacular road and a safe one, though frightening to some people not accustomed to mountain driving. The road follows Lee Vining Creek and then passes the Lee Vining Ranger Station.* There is no record of Vining's having made any important gold discoveries, though it is known that in 1863 he was operating a sawmill on this creek and delivering lumber to Aurora, where he was later accidentally killed by his own revolver. Vining's Gulch, a name on early maps, may have been a humorous name for the immense chasm of Lee Vining Canyon, or it may have referred to Vining's "rancho" which was on the same creek nearer Mono Lake.

In the vertical walls of upper Lee Vining Canyon, there are striking contacts of gray and multi-colored rocks. The tremendous heat and pressure accompanying the intrusion of the gray granitic material twisted and baked some of the old sedimentary rocks beyond recognition. At the top of the grade are Ellery and Tioga lakes, both dammed for use in the power plant below. A road branches off right to Saddlebag Lake, a large reservoir in this system. On the colorful slopes to the right (north) of Tioga Lake are a few well-preserved buildings dating from the time of the Tioga Mine and the camp of Bennettville. To develop this mine, eastern investors organized the Great Sierra Consolidated Silver Mining Company in 1881. The camp was set up, a road constructed to Crockers on the west side of the Sierra, and a tunnel driven eight hundred feet. The camp also had a sawmill and prepared quantities of charcoal for the furnace that was to be built to handle the ore that never was mined. Three years later, before any ore was worked, the mine closed, never to reopen, and was later sold by the sheriff for taxes. (See also history section, "The Lundy and Tioga Mines.") Tioga is an Iroquois Indian name, meaning "where it forks," applied to certain towns and rivers in Pennsylvania and New York. Probably the eastern owners of this mine transferred a name that was familiar to them to their new mine in California, which in turn gave the name to the pass and the lake. Near the pass is the Tioga Tarns (self-guiding) Nature Trail.

---

* *Exhibits, maps, fire permits, information. See also page 143, 6.*

Yosemite Park is one of the scenic wonders of the world. Information on all aspects of the Park may be obtained from rangers at Tioga Pass or at Tuolumne Meadows, six miles west.

395.—Near Mono Lake there had been a small settlement called Lakeview for many years. When a post office was to be established there, "Lakeview" was already the name of another post office, so the name Lee Vining was chosen.

Near Lee Vining, the highway borders Mono Lake, an alkaline body of water ten miles wide and fifteen miles long. It has no outlet, and evaporation has concentrated the water's mineral content, making it bitter and about twice as salty as the ocean. When Ice Age glaciers fed it, Mono Lake was three or four times larger and its water level was over six hundred feet higher. Shorelines of the Ice Age lake show clearly on the mountain front hundreds of feet above the present level. You can see them best in late afternoon light, looking west from the pole-line road.

Mono Lake's two islands are unusual in that they are both volcanic. Negit Island, the black one, is a volcanic cone and lava flow, part of the flow forming tiny islands to the north of Negit. Negit is an Indian word for "blue-winged goose." Possibly this was an Indian interpretation for "gull," for there are no records of concentrations of geese, while gulls nest on Negit Island by the thousands. Paoha, the white island, is an Indian name to encompass "diminutive spirits, having long, wavy hair, that are sometimes seen in the vapor wreathes ascending from hot springs." Paoha is formed of old lake sediments and younger lava flows; it has some hot springs and small craters, one of them containing a jade-green lake. The story is told that Paoha served as a haven for Chinese laborers who were building the Bodie and Benton Railroad, during an anti-Chinese agitation in Bodie. Learning of plans to run the coolies out, the railroad contractors sent messengers on swift horses to the construction camp east of Mono Lake. The Chinese were loaded on barges and ferried to the white island, and returned only after the trouble-makers' enthusiasm (and liquor) had given out.

The knobby white *tufa towers* scattered about the shore are deposits of calcium carbonate. These limy deposits, usually clustered where fresh-water springs rise from the lake bottom, formed under water and are exposed only because the water level has dropped. Tiny plants, calcareous algae, are responsible for the deposition. A chemical reaction between the fresh spring water and the mineral-rich lake water causes some calcium carbonate to precipitate upon a framework of algae. The algae also deposit much of the tufa themselves, a process that may be likened to the formation of coral—a limy deposit secreted by tiny animals—in the ocean.

To a casual observer, Mono Lake seems barren—no trees, little grass, no fish. Yet it supports great numbers of birds throughout the year, for its waters teem with a brine shrimp *(Artemia)* and with the larvae and pupae of a brine fly *(Ephydra)*. Migrating twice yearly along the Pacific flyway, millions of grebes, phalaropes, and shovellers, mallards, teal, and other ducks stop to feed. More than 500,000 eared grebes at one time rest on the lake in fall. Common in summer are the "Mono Lake pigeons"—phalaropes, dainty birds smaller than ducks that whirl around and around, stirring up insects with their slender bills. Conspicuous also in summer are the gulls that fly inland to nest by the thousands on Negit Island. More than a dozen other bird species nest on the islands and in the fresh-water marshes around the lake.

Mono Lake's rapidly declining level and the increasing alkalinity of its waters are a potential catastrophe to this complex of life—shrimps, flies, and birds. Its shoreline indicates how far the water has receded since its historic high in 1919. This white band is widening rapidly. Between 1919 and 1940, owing to natural causes, the lake dropped ten feet. Between 1940 and 1970, with its inflow partly diverted into the Los Angeles Aqueduct, the lake's level dropped twenty-eight feet. Since 1970—with the Second Aqueduct completed and the total flow of the four major streams feeding Mono Lake diverted—the lake level has been dropping nearly two feet a year. According to one DWP estimate, the lake will stabilize fifty or sixty feet below the 1974 level, and the lake surface will be smaller by half. The exposed white shore will be from one-half to over two miles wide, and a land bridge will make both Paoha and Negit islands part of a peninsula.

Possibly by the time you read this, we will already know the effect on the nesting gulls—whether they can defend their rookery from land predators, or whether they will abandon it. The larger questions are whether a shrunken Mono Lake will continue to be a haven and a source of rich and abundant food on the Pacific flyway; and if not, what the effect will be on migrating birds if another of their major resting places is removed. The answers to these questions ultimately depend on the ability of two small creatures—shrimp and fly—to survive in increasingly concentrated alkaline water, and to survive in sufficient quantities.

This same brine fly has given us the Indian names *Mono* and *Monache*—names the Paiutes never used, but names applied to them by their western neighbors, the Yokuts. They come from a Yokut word meaning *flies*. In Yokut eyes, the people at Owens and Mono lakes were the *fly people,* after the pupae that were a food staple and an important trade good. The Paiutes at Mono Lake called them *"koo-cha-vee"* or *"cu-za-vi."* They scooped them from shallow water and also gathered quantities from the heaps that drifted to shore. Brewer, mentioned before, described the dried pupae as "oily, very nutritious, and not unpleasant to the taste," and as resembling yellow grains of rice that would make a fine soup. Brewer also told of a man who capitalized on the gulls' eggs on Negit Island. With hens' eggs selling in Aurora during 1863 for up to $1.50 a dozen, he had a ready market.

Three miles north of Lee Vining, on the left, are two historic buildings moved around 1900 from two of the old mining camps—a store from nearby

Lundy and a saloon from Bodie. The saloon was used for the same purpose here until 1914 when Mono County went dry. Notice a small stream gushing out from under it; this is no accident. Water was diverted to run under the saloon's north side, where the bar was, in order that the beer could be let down through a trap-door and kept cool.

Just north of the old saloon, to the right of the highway, is a creek flowing through a fan-shaped mass of mud and debris, now somewhat disguised by vegetation. Part of this debris came roaring down the creek's steep gully in the summer of 1955, when a cloudburst started the movement of mud and rock particles from the slopes high above. As the mudflow acquired more and more load and more water, it gathered momentum and rushed down the canyon, stripping everything in its path, including boulders the size of a car. When the mass reached the mouth of the canyon, it burst out onto the fan already built by previous outbreaks, sweeping houses and cars into the lake within minutes. At the mouths of many steep canyons there are similar masses of debris, called alluvial fans. These can be easily identified in desert areas such as the eastern Sierra or the White Mountains, where the fans are not covered by trees.

Sideroad to Lundy Lake.—This is a scenic drive any time of year, but in late September or October when the aspen turn brilliant gold, it is unequaled. Above the road is the flume (the wood-stave line built in 1910 has been replaced with pipe) that carries water from Lundy Lake to the Mill Creek power plant. About three miles from the junction the road forks—the left fork going down to the dam at the outlet of Lundy Lake and leading to the May Lundy Mine road, the right fork going to a resort at the west end of the lake and to the beginning of the Lundy Falls trail.

William O. Lundy started a sawmill in this canyon in 1878 or earlier, selling lumber to Bodie. In '79 gold was discovered by a William Wasson, and the same summer Lundy and two partners located claims also, among them the May Lundy Mine named after Lundy's daughter. The May Lundy was high on a steep slope in Lake Canyon (south of Lundy Lake), its lower tunnel over 11,000 feet. It was worked continuously from 1879 to 1898. The town of Lundy was near the resort at the end of the lake, where foundations can still be seen in the brush. A toll road led from Lundy Lake up Lake Canyon to the small mining settlement of Wasson, near Crystal Lake below the mine. Toll rates, as published in 1881, were: a wagon and two animals, $1.50; saddle animals, 50¢; loose stock, 10¢. A trail was built from Lake Canyon on to Bennettville and the Tioga Mine, so that high camp could get supplies from Lundy. It was impossible, however, to transport heavy machinery such as boilers and pipe by pack-train. (Tons of equipment were carried from Lundy to Bennettville, see history section, "The Lundy and Tioga Mines.")

Sideroad to Hawthorne and Bodie, the "pole-line" road.—This road goes east fifty-five miles to Hawthorne, Nevada, and is an important auxiliary road for Mono Basin residents when winter snows temporarily block Highway

395 to the north. Seven miles from the junction, a graded dirt road climbs Cottonwood Canyon to Bodie, one of the best preserved ghost towns in California. If you look west from the pole-line road the shorelines of ancient Lake Russell, the large lake that occupied this basin during glacial times, show clearly in the late afternoon light on the steep Sierra slopes, hundreds of feet above the present lake. Though the trip to Bodie is dusty, and may be hot and tiring, there are few old mining camps where there is so much to see. Since loop trips are always more interesting and since parts of this road are steep, it is suggested that visitors to Bodie continue on 395, and about six miles north of Conway Summit take the turnoff to the right leading to Bodie; then return by this Cottonwood Canyon road. Bodie is now a State Historic Park.

Bodie was Mono County's largest mineral producer by far (see history section). It also claimed the wildest street, the wickedest men, the worst climate, and the best water. No superlatives were too great for Bodie's boom years. No attempt will be made here to condense Bodie's colorful history into a few paragraphs. Interested persons are urged to visit Bodie, particularly the museum, and to read the books suggested at the end of the history section. From Bodie a road leads northeast, down a canyon to the ghost town of Aurora, Nevada, another famous boom town. Inquire at Bodie whether this road is open, for flash floods and washouts frequently make it impassable.

395.—Past the Hawthorne junction, Highway 395 skirts the edge of an extensive meadow belonging to the family of John Andrew Conway, who settled here in 1880 and for whom Conway Summit is named. Construction of a new route over the summit was completed in 1962. Nearing Conway Summit (8138), stop at the parking area on the highway shoulder to appreciate the panoramic view south over much of the country that has been described in this chapter— Mono Lake and Mono Craters in the foreground, the White Mountains, and the Sierra Nevada as far south as Bloody Mountain.

RECOMMENDED READING

Bowen, Ezra. *The High Sierra.* New York: Time-Life, 1972. A personal narrative. Exceptional photographs, good reproduction.

Kauffman, Richard. *Gentle Wilderness: The Sierra Nevada.* San Francisco: Sierra Club, 1964. Text from John Muir, 76 exquisite color photographs, superb reproduction. A book of shimmering beauty and loving craftsmanship.

Roth, Hal. *Pathway in the Sky: The Story of the John Muir Trail.* Berkeley: Howell-North Books, 1965. Not a trail guide, but a collection of essays on many aspects of the high country. Fine references. Good photographs.

Storer, Tracy I. and Robert Usinger. *Sierra Nevada Natural History.* Berkeley: University of California Press, 1963. Cloth and paper. Excellent illustrations and an incredible amount of information crammed into this outstanding small handbook.

Teale, Edwin Way. *The Wilderness World of John Muir.* Boston: Houghton Mifflin, 1954. Cloth and paper. My first choice of John Muir books. Brief biography of Muir plus the best of his writings.

Trails

RUGGED AND MAJESTIC, THE SIERRA Nevada is also friendly, welcoming, and lavish with her beauty. Long summers of little rain provide a hiker's paradise the length of the narrow strip that straddles her crest. Fondly known as the High Sierra, this strip of blue lakes and shining rock begins at an elevation somewhere around 9,000 feet—wherever it is that the trees thin and the views begin.

THE JOHN MUIR TRAIL, THE PACIFIC CREST TRAIL

Wild and rugged though it is, this magnificent mountain wilderness abounds with good trails. Shunning the valleys and the easy routes, the famous John Muir Trail winds among the loftiest peaks and passes of the High Sierra. It is the longest mountain wilderness trail in the country, touching no towns nor paved roads along its two hundred miles between Tuolumne Meadows and Mount Whitney. Yet for all its wildness the Muir Trail is readily accessible by trails intersecting it from dozens of roadends—including those at Reds Meadow, McGee Creek, Mammoth Lakes, and June Lake.

The Pacific Crest Trail when completed will reach 2400 miles from the Mexican to the Canadian border, generally following the mountain ranges of the Pacific states. With two exceptions, the Pacific Crest Trail follows the Muir Trail through the central Sierra. One of those exceptions is north and south of Reds Meadow, between Thousand Island Lake and Crater Meadows. Here the Pacific Crest Trail will follow a new route, to be constructed during the late 1970s. New construction is also scheduled for the Muir Trail, to re-route it around the congested area at the Devils Postpile; a new bridge will cross the Middle Fork downstream from the Postpile. These changes may affect many of the trails in the Middle Fork Canyon; inquire at the Mammoth and Postpile ranger stations.

WILDERNESS PERMITS

A wilderness permit is required to hike most mountain trails in the High Sierra, for a one-day hike as well as a backpack trip. Permits are free and are available at the ranger stations listed in the front of the book and at the seasonal entrance stations. Inquire about reservations and limitations as far in advance as possible, lest you arrive at the roadend packed and ready to take off, only to find the day's quota is full. Within the broad policy of accommodating as many people as possible without destroying the very wilderness qualities they come for, back country rules vary from place to place. That policy may include: a reservation system; limits on size of groups and length of stay; daily quotas; where wood is scarce, prohibitions on wood fires (stoves required); where forage is scarce, limits on grazing; where meadows and lakeshores are hard packed from trampling, closure to all camping and grazing until plants return.

ALTITUDE FITNESS

The higher the mountain, the less oxygen in the air. In that simple fact lies the cause for many a misery—nosebleed, headache, nausea, shortness of breath, rapid pulse, irritability, insomnia, lack of appetite. Lack of oxygen—particularly insufficient oxygen to the brain, which is especially sensitive to lack of oxygen—causes many of these symptoms of *altitude sickness*. Some people feel the altitude at 5,000 feet. Almost everyone feels it at eastern Sierra roadends that are 8,000 and 9,000 feet high. Age and strength have little to do with it. Athletic teen-agers are sometimes hit the hardest. There is no way to prevent altitude sickness—no pills, no pre-conditioning. Your body needs *time*. It will adjust.

Dr. Andrew J. Smatko, editor of the 1972 *Mountaineer's Guide to the High Sierra,* who has climbed over five hundred Sierra peaks, offers these suggestions to ease your adjustment to high altitude. Camping one night at a half-way altitude can help immensely. Then camp no higher than 8,000 feet for another night or two. Take it easy; walk slowly; take short hikes; eat small amounts of carbohydrate-rich foods frequently, especially quick-energy sugars; and drink as often as you are thirsty, for the dry air of the eastern Sierra increases the body's need for water. Do all these things for as many days as necessary; your body will tell you when it's ready for longer hikes and higher altitudes. Pushing yourself and your children is the worst you can do, for above 10,000 feet reactions usually become only more severe.

DEFENSES AGAINST CHILLING

Generally hospitable and good-natured, the Sierra Nevada can be unexpectedly harsh and brutal. If you approach her with humility, she will reward you with safe journeys and days of happiness. But if you fail to accord her the respect due one of the world's great mountain ranges—if you fail to prepare for her black moods, her bitter weather, her high altitudes—she is unforgiving. You may pay with your life, as did four of the five climbers on Mount Ritter, Memorial Day weekend 1971. And the two boys, in separate parties, who died one Labor Day weekend less than ten miles from roadends, when an unexpected storm soaked their clothes and their sleeping bags.

Hypothermia is the medical term for the body's losing heat faster than it can produce heat. We used to call it "freezing to death," but death can occur in temperatures well above freezing. If your clothing is wet and a high wind begins to blow, you are in deadly peril. A drop in body temperature of just a few degrees causes physical collapse. The defenses against chilling are proven: ample down or wool clothing and water*proof*, not water repellent, jacket or poncho. There are certain things to remember: that wool is the only fabric that stays warm when wet; that a chilled person must be warmed immediately; that if you are caught unprepared, there is no time to lose in getting down and out of the mountains.

MOUNTAIN-WISE

Happiness in the mountains is keeping warm, dry, and safe. The wise mountaineer—

Doesn't succumb to the myth that "it never rains in the Sierra in summer." He is prepared for rain, hail, and snow. Yes! Even in August.

Carries these essentials in his knapsack: flashlight, matches, whistle, extra food, map and compass, dark glasses.

Always tells someone where he is going and when he expects to return.

Avoids risky stream crossings and steep snow slopes if possible, making detours instead. If fording a stream is necessary, he wades across with boots *on* (socks in pack to keep dry); boots dry after a few minutes of walking.

A special happiness lies in being aware of all the other creatures—plant, animal, and human—that share the mountains. The thoughtful mountaineer—

Gives stock the right of way, moving several yards off the trail, standing still and talking quietly so that the animals will see and hear him. Realizing the precarious balance of heavy-laden, short-tied mules, he guards against spooking them by *not* waving his arms and not letting his poncho flap in the wind. He parks his gear well off stock trails, lest a mule take the notion to kick it to pieces—why? Well, although mules are among the most patient and faithful of animals, they are also sometimes quite beyond understanding.

Refrains from cutting across switchbacks lest he start gullies.

Goes as far as practical—at least 100 yards—from water to dispose of human waste; digs and covers; burns or carries out toilet paper.

Leaves the least possible evidence that he has passed. He carries out all that he carries in. He walks *around* meadows instead of trampling the grass and flowers. He steps *over* small plants lest he break off stems that have taken several years to reach stubby lengths, so brief are alpine summers. Most important, he does all these things without being odiously virtuous about it. He is almost a paragon, but there are more and more like him. This is a good thing, because there are lots of people camping in the wilderness. His kind take up less room.

ROCK CREEK

The road up Rock Creek Canyon goes higher than any other in the area, ending at 10,250 feet above sea-level. From its end it is possible to reach the high timberline country with less climbing than from any other starting point. This is one of the longer canyons, containing more than forty lakes; a few miles over Morgan and Mono Passes, many other lakes are accessible.

Topographic maps needed: Mount Abbot and Mount Tom quadrangles.

Rock Creek Lake (9682 feet) to Kenneth, Francis and Tamarack Lakes.

Kenneth Lake (10,350 feet), intermediate hike, 3 miles.

Francis Lake (10,870 feet), intermediate hike, 4 miles.

Tamarack Lakes (11,580 feet), strenuous hike, 6 miles.

Starting Point: From Highway 395 follow the Rock Creek road about 9 miles up the canyon. Turn left at the sign pointing to Rock Creek Lake, park on the east side of the lake, and look for the sign which marks the beginning of the trail.

The trail goes up a brushy slope for half a mile, then follows an old logging road into the wide basin of the East Fork of Rock Creek. The basin is bounded on the east by Wheeler Crest, a massive granite ridge whose sheer east face is so impressive from the highway north of Bishop. The trail turns right (S) from the logging road (where it is joined by the route coming from Rock Creek Lodge) and winds through a forest of whitebark pine to the large meadow surrounding Kenneth Lake. Gentian are abundant in late August and September.

Just before reaching Kenneth Lake, the trail branches into three. The left branch goes to the lake's inlet. The right branch follows a small stream to Francis Lake, which lies in a small canyon on the north slope of Mount Morgan (13,748 feet). The middle branch crosses the meadow above Kenneth Lake and ascends a low ridge where the trail forks again. The left fork leads to Dorothy Lake. (The lake always known as Dorothy is a mile SE of Kenneth Lake. See back cover map. On the 1949 Mount Tom topo sheet Dorothy is shown incorrectly one-half mile NE of Kenneth.) The right fork leads to the stream coming from Tamarack Lakes and follows its gentle little valley for about a mile and a half, until it is blocked by abrupt cliffs. The trail swings to the right (W) and switchbacks up to the high basin of Tamarack Lakes 800 feet above.

At the outlet of Tamarack Lakes, there is a distinct change in the color of the cliffs—light gray to the left (N), dark brown to the right (S). Both are igneous rocks, that is, they once were molten and welled up from the earth's interior. But they differ in mineral composition and in age, the dark being older. This is an excellent example of a geologic "contact"—the place where two different rocks touch each other. Easterners may wonder about the name of these lakes, for their "tamarack" is the eastern larch tree which is not native to California. In parts of the west, the name "tamarack" somehow became attached to the lodgepole pine. Tamarack Lakes are poorly named, however, for there are no trees of any kind in their high basin.

Rock Creek Lodge to Kenneth, Francis and Tamarack Lakes.

Starting Point: Rock Creek Lodge. Follow the Rock Creek road about 8 miles up the canyon from Highway 395. Then turn left (E) to the lodge.

Distances to the lakes are about the same as on the preceding trail. But a bit more climbing is involved, since the lodge (9360 feet) is 300 feet lower in altitude than Rock Creek Lake. The trail from the lodge crosses a meadow, climbs steadily, levels off, and then meets the trail coming from Rock Creek Lake. Proceed as described above.

★Road End (10,250 feet) to Long Lake, Morgan Pass and Morgan Lakes.

Long Lake (10,543 feet), easy hike, 2 miles.

Morgan Lakes (10,708 feet), intermediate hike, 4 miles.

Starting Point: Drive to the very end of the Rock Creek Canyon road, 1 mile beyond the pack station.

This route follows the old road of the Pine Creek Tungsten Mine, abandoned after a more direct road was built to the mine from Round Valley via Pine Creek. Beyond the parking area the road is blocked to vehicles, for this is a boundary of the John Muir Wilderness Area. Wilderness Areas are established by Congress under the Wilderness Act on some portions of national forest land which have outstanding wilderness character and scenic value. The beauty of such areas can be kept natural only by prohibiting roads and commercial development within them. Access is provided by a network of good trails.

The road winds past lake after lake—Mack, Marsh, Heart, Box, Long, Chickenfoot—close under the high peak of Mount Morgan (13,748 feet) to the left (E), and past several rugged unnamed peaks all nearly 13,000 feet. East of this string of lakes, there are at least a dozen more lakes and ponds. All are less than half a mile of easy walking from the trail, though there is no trail to them. To reach Eastern Brook Lakes, from the parking area head directly east, or from the outlet of Mack Lake strike out to the northeast. Hidden Lakes are directly east of Heart Lake, not more than $\frac{1}{4}$ mile away. Between Box and Chickenfoot Lakes are several more small lakes and ponds, reached easily by following up the stream draining into Box Lake or following down the stream from Chickenfoot's outlet. Gem Lakes, to the south, cluster under Pyramid Peak and are reached by going up the stream draining into Chickenfoot Lake— the stream that the trail crosses just before beginning its climb up Morgan Pass. This entire basin, known as Little Lakes Valley, is a very special place— gentle walks, wildflowers throughout the summer, many small streams, and dozens of lakes, all encircled by ridges towering two and three thousand feet above and dominated by snowy Bear Creek Spire (see figure 1, Roadsides).

The road is almost level until the short, gradual climb over Morgan Pass (11,104 feet). From Lower Morgan Lake, in the 1950's, trucks could be seen carrying ore from the famous Pine Creek Mine, the largest known tungsten deposit in this region and one of the most productive in the country. The mine is now operating on many levels, the highest close to 11,000 feet.

Road End (10,250 feet) to Mono Pass*, Summit and Trail Lakes.

Mono Pass (12,000 feet), strenuous hike, 3 miles.

Summit Lake (11,900 feet), strenuous hike, 3½ miles.

Trail Lakes (11,240 feet), strenuous hike, 5 miles.

Starting Point: Drive to the very end of the Rock Creek Canyon road, one mile beyond the Pack Station.

---

*There are two Mono Passes. The one referred to in historical writings, famous as an old Indian trail, is forty miles to the northeast, just south of Tioga Pass.

Start early up these steep zigzags, to avoid being sun-broiled on the shadeless slopes. There are fine views back into Little Lakes Valley and across the canyon to Mount Morgan. West of the pass is the Mono Creek drainage and its Recesses, wonderful country for a wilderness vacation. For an even better view into the Mono Creek country, scramble up another 900 feet to the top of Mount Starr, just east of the pass. From there, at least seven stately peaks each more than 13,000 feet in altitude can be seen—Mount Mills, Abbot, Dade, Gabb, Bear Creek Spire, Hilgard, Red Slate—and a dozen others only slightly lower. Just over the pass are the still waters of Summit Lake and farther down, the Trail Lakes.

Rock Creek Road (9840 feet) to Hilton Lake 2 (9900 feet).

Intermediate hike, 3½ miles.

Starting Point: Follow the Rock Creek road up the canyon to a point about ½ mile beyond the Rock Creek Store. Look to the right (W) for the start of the trail.

This is the easiest route into the Hilton Lakes Basin for it starts high, rises only 500 feet to cross the Hilton Creek–Rock Creek divide, and then drops down to meet the Hilton Creek trail. At this junction, a trail goes left to the upper lakes, 3–10. The other trail goes right to Lake 2 and Davis Lake. See below for a description of the Hilton Lakes Basin.

HILTON CREEK

Ten lakes and five streams tributary to Hilton Creek lie close together in a high granite basin. Both Hilton and neighboring McGee canyons have outstanding displays of golden aspen in fall.

Topographic maps needed: Mount Abbot and Mount Morrison quadrangles.

Hilton Lakes Pack Station (7200 feet) to Davis Lake and Lakes 2–10.

Davis Lake (9801 feet), strenuous hike, 5 miles.

Lake 2 (9900 feet), strenuous hike, 6 miles.

Lake 4 (10,400 feet), strenuous hike, 7½ miles.

Starting Point: Hilton Lakes Pack Station, ½ mile west of Highway 395.

In early summer or in fall, this can be a pleasant hike; but in mid-summer take a horse or hike the cooler, less dusty route from Rock Creek (see preceding trail). The hot, dusty trail gains 1600 feet in altitude as it climbs to the top of a sagebrush- and pinyon-covered moraine. There it joins a mining road and follows it toward the Hilton Creek Tungsten Mines, which produced small tonnages in the 1940s and '50s. The trail leaves the road, crosses the creek, and then enters more scenic country with large meadows and many aspen. To the right (W) of this broad canyon is a high varicolored ridge with 13,005-foot Mount Morgan* at its summit. As the trail climbs, it enters a forest of lodgepole

---

*This Mount Morgan is 700 feet lower than another Mount Morgan 9 miles south, near Rock Creek.

pine. The Jeffrey forest, which normally occurs between the forests of pinyon and lodgepole is "missing" on this slope, a phenomenon often encountered on the Sierra's steep eastern slope.

The trail passes Davis Lake and Lake 2, the two largest of the Hilton Lakes, and is joined by the trail connecting with Rock Creek. From this junction, a good trail continues to Lakes 3 and 4. To reach Lake 5, from 4 boulder-hop up the ridge to the SE. Beyond, there isn't much of a trail; to reach the smaller, higher lakes follow the streams. Lake 10, quiet and remote at the end of the canyon, lies just below Mount Huntington.

McGEE AND CONVICT CREEKS

Don't be fooled by the uninviting sagebrush entrances to these two canyons. Red, rich brown, blue-gray and white rock-layers—tilted, folded and contorted —are exposed in these spectacular canyons to provide some of the most colorful of all displays of east-side Sierra sculpture.

Topographic maps needed: Mount Abbot and Mount Morrison quadrangles.

★ McGee Creek (8100 feet) to the Beaver Dam, Round Lake, Big McGee Lake.

Beaver Dam (9000 feet), intermediate hike, 2½ miles.
Round Lake (9950 feet), strenuous hike, 4½ miles.
Big McGee Lake (10,480 feet), strenuous hike, 6½ miles.
Starting Point: Take the McGee Canyon road to its end, a mile above the pack station. Park in the cleared space below the locked gate, which bars all vehicles except those of the Scheelore Tungsten Mine. The road is kept closed to assure that the region will revert as nearly as possible to wilderness when the claim is abandoned.

On hot August days, start this trip at least by 8 o'clock, for there is little shade until the road enters the lodgepole forest above the beaver dam. Besides, the canyon walls are especially colorful in the early-morning light. By the gate watch for the rare copper birch, named for its copper-colored bark. About a mile above the gate is another uncommon tree, the limber pine, with silver bark on its upper trunk, long branches curving upward, and a 3–10-inch cone. In the eastern Sierra, this tree usually grows well above 9000 feet; but here in the canyon bottom a few trees have found a suitable climate. During high water it is very dangerous to ford McGee Creek on foot. Instead, between the two fords used by horses, follow the foot trail on the west side of the creek.

In the shallow lakes by the road watch for signs of beaver planted here in 1955, in hopes that they would dam the creek and eventually make this swampy area into a fine large fishing lake. (For a discussion of beaver problems, see the section on mammals.) Continue on the road until a trail branches off to the left. Follow it up the main canyon to Round Lake and then Big McGee Lake, which is walled in by Mount Crocker (SE) and Red and White Mountain (SW). From the lake, the trail ascends steeply to 11,900 feet at McGee Pass, then down to the high, wild back-country of Upper Fish Creek.

McGee Creek (8100 feet) to Grass and Steelhead Lakes.

Grass Lake (9800 feet), strenuous hike, 4½ miles.

Steelhead Lake (10,400 feet), strenuous hike, 6 miles.

Starting Point: Same as above.

Proceed as described above for about 1½ miles beyond the beaver dam. A trail branches to the left (E) and climbs steeply up the canyon's east wall to Grass Lake, which is surrounded by a fine high-mountain meadow. It is a steep climb to Steelhead Lake above, which lies in a large cirque almost at timberline. Its setting affords a spectacular view of the red and gray rocks of Mount Baldwin ridge to the west. The color difference results from complicated folding of iron-stained quartz-rich rocks and gray marble. The Scheelore Tungsten Mine lies just below Mount Baldwin at an altitude of about 11,000 feet, where the marble is in contact with granitic rocks.

McGee Creek (8100 feet) to Meadow, Golden and Crocker Lakes.

Meadow Lake (10,160 feet), strenuous hike, 5 miles.

Golden Lake (10,400 feet), strenuous hike, 6 miles.

Crocker Lake (10,900 feet), strenuous hike, 6½ miles.

Starting Point: Same as above.

Follow the road and then the trail as described above, past the beaver dam to the turnoff to Grass and Steelhead lakes. Another mile up the main trail is the turnoff left (E) to Meadow, Golden, and Crocker lakes. Cross McGee Creek, then follow the meadow downstream about a hundred yards, past a mass of granite boulders to the mid-point of the meadow. From there the trail proceeds up a forested slope. Just beyond its junction with a connecting trail to Grass Lake, the trail may seem lost in a small meadow. Go along the upper side of the meadow toward the sound of a noisy stream. Cross it, and follow its right bank to clear, shallow Meadow Lake. For a discussion of Mount Baldwin across the canyon, see the preceding trail.

Beyond Meadow Lake, the trail is less distinct, though fairly well marked by rock cairns. Follow the meadow around to its upper end, cross the stream coming from a small waterfall visible above, and follow its right bank to the waterfall, at the head of which lies Golden Lake. Crocker Lake can be reached by scrambling up the boulder slope at the inlet of Golden Lake (no trail) and following the stream to its source, just below the peak of Mount Crocker to the left (SE). Mount Crocker and the three peaks near it (but not visible from this basin) were each named for one of the "Big Four" of Central Pacific Railroad fame: Charles Crocker, Mark Hopkins, Collis Huntington, and Leland Stanford.

★ Convict Lake (7580 feet) to Lakes Mildred and Dorothy.

Lake Mildred (9760 feet), strenuous hike, 5 miles.

Lake Dorothy (10,250 feet), strenuous hike, 6 miles.

Starting Point: Parking lot at Convict Lake boat landing. If Convict Creek is high, postpone this trip until mid-July. Inquire locally.

The trail to Lake Mildred is steep all the way, but rewarding for those who appreciate rugged mountain scenery enhanced by extraordinary exposures of highly-colored and folded rock formations. The trail proceeds along the north shore of Convict Lake, then follows Convict Creek upstream. Three miles up the canyon, the trail crosses the creek. In early summer this can be a dangerous crossing, for the stream is very swift and there is no bridge. In the stream bed and along the trail just below Lake Mildred, look for black platy rocks within which are circular light-gray or white structures about the size of an 8-penny nailhead. These are fossil stems of crinoids (sea lilies), animals which lived in the shallow ocean covering this region 300,000,000 years ago. The stem was made up of a stack of small hard disks held together by soft tissue.

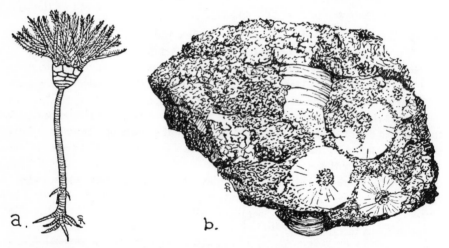

Figure 12. *a*. A living crinoid, less than life size. *b*. Fossil crinoid stems, actual size.

The U-shaped valley behind Lake Mildred is a fine example of a glacial canyon, a broad trough gouged out of bedrock by a moving glacier. After the glacier melted, the bottom of the trough filled with water and became a long lake. Over thousands of years, gravel and dirt have been carried in by streams, and now most of the trough has become meadow and marsh and Lake Mildred is slowly being filled with sediments. Straight ahead (S) is Red Slate Mountain (13,163 feet). From Lake Mildred, the trail climbs over a 500-foot ridge to Lake Dorothy, a large lake about the length of Convict Lake. From Lake Dorothy it is possible to reach Constance Lake (no trail) at the very base of Red Slate Mountain, or to follow a good trail about a mile north to Lake Genevieve.

Road End (7620 feet) to the Inlet of Convict Lake (7580 feet).

Easy hike, 1 mile.

Starting Point: At Convict Lake, take the paved road which forks left, and follows around the left (S) shore of the lake for half a mile. The trail begins at the road end.

This is a rough fisherman's trail following close to the shore of Convict Lake and occasionally dipping down to the water's edge and passing through willow, aspen, cottonwood, copper birch, and a few limber pine. In July watch for a brilliant yellow flower several inches across with five broad petals. This is the beautiful blazing star, which opens in the evening and closes the following afternoon. Near the end of the Lake to the left (S) of the trail, are cliffs of dark gray and reddish rocks, some of which contain fossil graptolites (see figure 5, Roadsides), tiny marine animals that lived in the ocean covering this region 500,000,000 years ago. At the inlet, where Convict Creek cascades into the lake, is a small gravel beach which makes a nice picnic spot.

MAMMOTH TRAILS

Mammoth Lakes basin is the most popular of the east-side canyons, with many campgrounds, summer homes, and resorts. It has many lakes, streams, and quiet meadows, nestled below Mammoth Crest and Mammoth Mountain. There are a number of trails leading to the lakes within the basin itself, besides trails leading out of the basin over Duck Pass, Mammoth Crest, and Mammoth Pass. From many high points there are fine views across to the Minarets, Mount Ritter, and Banner Peak.

Topographic maps needed: Devils Postpile and Mount Morrison quadrangles.

Laurel Canyon (9770 feet) to Lake Genevieve (10,150 feet).

Strenuous hike, about 3 miles.

Starting Point: Take the Old Mammoth Road to the Mammoth Creek bridge. Drive down the road branching left (S and E) to Laurel and Sherwin creeks about four miles. Climb the rough jeep road up the Laurel Canyon moraine and continue up the canyon to the point where the trail starts, just east of the lakes. If you don't have 4-wheel drive and start hiking at the bottom of the moraine, add four miles and 2,000 feet of climbing to the figures above.

Magnificent views, precipitous canyons, and wildly colored rocks make this hike spectacular every step of the way. In fall glittering yellow aspen in the meadows behind the moraine add even more color. The trail switchbacks up to the saddle between Laurel and Bloody mountains, passes through a strange bowl-shaped basin, and climbs the ridge to its east. Shrub-like whitebark pine manage to cling to the exposed ridges, but few manage to grow more than a few feet high. Wind-driven ice particles shear them off as neatly as any hedge-trimmer. Once you have reached the top of the ridge (10,800), find a high point and take time to immerse yourself in the glorious views. (See sketches pp. 10,

20, 75.) Eastward a broad view encompasses Long Valley and all the highest peaks of the White Mountains. Most dramatic of all are the airplane-like views straight down to Convict Lake more than 3,000 feet below. From this viewpoint, if you squint your eyes, it is not difficult to imagine a great white tongue of ice lying where Convict Lake is now. The curving arc-shape of the canyon's huge moraine clearly outlines the size and shape of the vanished glacier's snout. From another great viewpoint, on the small ridge SE of Lake Genevieve, looking up-canyon you can easily picture the upper glacier—heading in the broad cirque below Red Slate Mountain and filling the U-shaped canyon behind Lake Mildred with ice more than a thousand feet thick.

The precipitous walls of the scooped-out canyon also expose the long, tortured history of the ancient rock layers—a history of tilting, folding, and squeezing. The striking rusty red and gray colors near Mount Baldwin come from layers of gray marble and iron-stained quartz-rich rock. Lake Genevieve is encircled by the dark red slopes of Bloody and Laurel mountains. On the far side of Genevieve, the Convict Creek trail comes in from Lake Dorothy. It is twice as far to hike out by this trail and you'll have to arrange a car shuttle at Convict Lake, but the loop makes a superb day. See above, "Convict Lake to Lake Dorothy."

★Sherwin Creek (7800 feet) to Valentine Lake (9650 feet).

Strenuous hike, about 5 miles.

Recommended starting point: 1¼ miles down the Laurel-Sherwin creeks road from Mammoth Creek bridge (see preceding Laurel Canyon trail), turn right (S) and drive ¼ mile to a parking area. Follow the trail to Sherwin Lakes described below. From the upper lakes a connecting trail now swings east to pick up the Valentine Lake trail. This route is more gradual than the old Valentine trail and starts higher.

The following paragraph describes the old Valentine Lake trail that begins two miles farther down the Laurel-Sherwin creeks road. It is shorter, much steeper, and the parking less convenient, but we leave it in for variety.

A dusty trail zigzags up the 800-foot moraine of Sherwin Canyon, gradually levels off and then winds through the most beautiful juniper forest in the area. Sheltered from the fierce winds which distort so many junipers, the trees grow tall, straight and symmetrical here. To the right of the trail, shortly after leaving the juniper grove, is an unusual spring with clear cold water bubbling up from a sandy-bottomed pool. The trail follows the canyon, climbs steeply by a waterfall (watch for water ouzels), and comes suddenly to the brink of rock-bound Valentine Lake, named after Los Angeles businessman W. L. Valentine—one of the owners of Valentine Camp, an exclusive club camp built at Mammoth in 1920. High, almost perpendicular granite cliffs wall in this narrow, deep lake on three sides.

Sherwin Creek (7800 feet) to Sherwin Lakes (8620 feet).

Intermediate hike, 2½ miles.

Starting Point: Same as above.

The five Sherwin Lakes lie close together in a basin just behind the steep-fronted glacial moraine that blocks the mouth of Sherwin Creek Canyon. To reach them, follow the trail as it leads through the manzanita-covered lower slopes and then in long, easy zigzags climbs the moraine's upper slopes. The trail leads to the two upper lakes; the three smaller lakes are downstream.

Twin Lakes (8540 feet) to Mammoth Falls and the Old Mammoth Road.

Mammoth Falls (8400 feet), easy hike, ¼ mile.

Starting Point: Left (E) side of the highway about 50 yards above the bridge at Twin Lakes outlet.

In the placid Lakes Basin, Mammoth Creek tumbles suddenly out of Lake Mamie to fall 250 feet into Twin Lakes. Racing from the outlet of Twin, it leaps over lava cliffs to form a second fall, before cascading on down its gorge into the forest below. This walk—through a streamside woods of aspen and pine to a viewpoint of this lower fall—is particularly dramatic in early summer when the creek is high and also in October when the aspen are golden.

This trail follows along Mammoth Creek for a short distance, is joined by the Valley View Point trail coming in from the right, and then crosses a wood-lined flume—the ditch that carried water from Twin Lakes to turn the water wheel of the Mammoth Mining Company's mill during the 1870s. It is believed that the flume was built as an open ditch but that it became necessary later to cover it (partly with felled trees which can still be found) to prevent its being choked with snow. From the flume the trail winds down through the forest, a spur path turning left to Mammoth Falls.

Twin Lakes (8540 feet) to Panorama Dome and Valley View Point.

Panorama Dome (8892 feet), easy hike, ½ mile.

Valley View Point (8700 feet), easy hike, 1 mile.

Twin Lakes outlet (8540 feet), loop trip, easy hike, 1½ miles.

Starting Point: About 250 yards above the bridge at Twin Lakes outlet, on the left (E) side of the highway.

The dome and the point both provide excellent views east across the meadows of Mammoth Creek to the White Mountains, especially lovely at sunset. Leaving the highway, the trail plunges into dense red fir forest. Notice many old 2- to 4-foot stumps throughout this forest—some rotted and toppled over, but many still standing, weathered to a silver gray and half decayed at their base. These probably date from Mammoth's mining days of 1878–80, having been cut for lumber and fuel. The trail forks, its right branch going to the top of Panorama Dome, whose sheltered north-facing slope has a snowbank lasting most of the summer. A few whitebark pines border the trail near the top, another indication that this side is colder than the west side of the dome where Jeffrey pines grow. The dome itself is composed of resistant volcanic rock, but is almost completely covered with glacial moraine, debris left by a melting glacier—much of it probably carried from Mammoth Crest and Coldwater Canyon. Among the brush bloom dry-hillside flowers from June to August. The top of the dome is one of the best places to view Mammoth Crest, Crystal Crag, and Mammoth Mountain, as well as the old Mammoth mines across on the steep slope of Gold Mountain. (For details of the mines and Mammoth City, see section on Roadsides.)

The trail to Valley View Point meanders downhill to the left, from the fork mentioned above. This trail may be indistinct because of broken fir branches. If so, go generally downhill to the old flume where the trail can be picked up again, turning off to the right and heading east across a wide forested bench. At its edge is Valley View Point. On the volcanic outcrops, patches of shining glacial polish remain, scoured by a glacier as it pushed its way down the canyon. To make the loop trip ending at Twin Lakes outlet, return to the flume and turn right onto the trail that follows it almost all the way to Twin Lakes.

Twin Lakes (8540 feet) to Twin Falls and Lake Mamie (8898 feet).

Easy hike, ½ mile.

Starting Point: Cross the auto bridge to the campground on the far side of upper Twin Lakes. Follow the one-way road leading to the mountain in a gradual left hand curve. Do not turn off sharp right or sharp left onto branching campsite roads. About 200 yards from the bridge turn sharp left, walk toward the base of a steep slope, and there intersect the trails leading to Twin Falls (left, S) and Mammoth Mountain (right, N).

This short walk is particularly pleasant in the early evening, when the sunset colors over Long Valley can be enjoyed. For a one-way trip, plan to be met at Lake Mamie by car. Or for a really easy hike, start at the bridge across Lake Mamie's outlet and be met at Twin Lakes. In early summer, be prepared with mosquito repellent.

The trail passes to the left of a cool mountain spring and wanders through wet meadows lush with a variety of tall flowers, before climbing through a shady hemlock forest that covers the lower slopes of the Rim. Glacial polish and grooves can be seen on some of the outcrops on top of the Rim. The trail's first switchback borders the edge of Horseshoe Falls, a mass of boulders marking a former outlet of Horseshoe Lake. The trail nears Twin Falls several times, finally reaching the top of the Rim at Lake Mamie. In August there are many pink monkey flowers on this trail. Stay on the trail, for short-cutting across switchbacks deepens gullies, destroys flowers, and eventually results in trail washouts.

★ Twin Lakes (8540 feet) to the Bottomless Pit, Seven Lakes Point, and Mammoth Mountain.

Bottomless Pit (Lava Cliffs) (9300 feet), intermediate hike, ¾ mile.

Seven Lakes Point (9800 feet), intermediate hike, 1¼ miles.

Mammoth Mountain (11,053 feet), strenuous hike, about 3½ miles.

Starting Point: See trail above.

For panoramic views of Mammoth basin, Long Valley, the White Mountains, and parts of the Sierra Crest, this is the finest trail in the region. After leaving Twin Lakes campground, the trail winds upward gradually through a forest of tall red firs and "creeping" aspen, bent from the weight of winter snows, then switchbacks across the sunny, rocky base of Mammoth Mountain to the top of the lava cliffs, where the trail levels out. Use caution in approaching the edge, for loose pumice makes it unstable. At the end of this bench is the Bottomless Pit, and at its bottom a natural lava arch—both probably formed by erosion and weathering. The trail down into the arch has been closed for the safety of visitors, several people having had trouble getting out of the pit.

Where the well-worn horse trail swings away from the Pit and leads up a forested slope, keep a sharp lookout to the right for the beginning of the foot trail. Both trails lead to Seven Lakes Point, but hikers will enjoy the foot path more. It is less dusty and offers a continuous succession of fine views of Mammoth basin and Long Valley. As the trail crosses a sheer slope to the Dragon's Back—a long, dark-colored lava ridge jutting from the mountain's east flank—be careful not to dislodge loose rocks, for they could seriously injure people at the lakeshore below. Several sturdy limber pines cling to this steep slope. Rare in this region, they are named for their flexible branches which can bend in any direction with the wind. From Seven Lakes Point, Twin Lakes, Mary, T.J., George, Mamie, and Horseshoe Lakes can be seen. Crowley Lake, created since the point was named, is visible in Long Valley, making eight lakes in all.

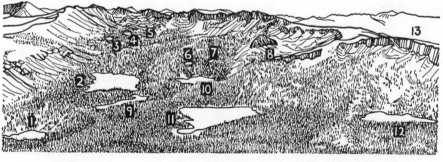

1—Twin Lakes	5—Barney Lake	10—Lake George
2—Lake Mary	6—Barrett Lake	11—Horseshoe Lake
3—Arrowhead Lake	7—T. J. Lake	12—McLeod Lake
4—Skelton Lake	8—Crystal Lake	13—Mammoth Crest
	9—Lake Mamie	

Figure 13. The Mammoth Lakes Basin.

The trail to Mammoth Mountain continues up the Dragon's Back. This is a steep, dry, and arduous hike, but the sweep of the view from the top cannot be duplicated elsewhere. Besides the lakes and peaks of the Mammoth area, these others can be seen: the Mono Craters and Mono Lake to the north; the White Mountains (just inside the California state line) to the east; the Silver Divide, and on the horizon Kaiser Crest above Huntington Lake, to the south; the entire Ritter Range to the west; Donohue, Koip, and Parker peaks, Mount Dana and Mount Warren to the northwest. (See figures 7 and 8, Roadsides, for sketches that will help identify some of these peaks.)

Since there is now a bulldozer road and a gondola from the ski area to the summit, you may prefer to hike elsewhere for your views, such as to Mammoth Crest or San Joaquin Mountain. Be sure to take a windbreaker and a canteen of water.

Coldwater Canyon (9050 feet) to Heart Lake (9590 feet).

Easy hike, about 1 mile.

Starting Point: From the upper end of Lake Mary, turn left (S) up the Coldwater Creek Camps road, go to the end of the road and park. Just below the parking area is a dirt road going across a bridge marked "Mammoth Mines No Trespassing." Cars are prohibited, but the mining company does not object to hikers using their bridge.

No short hike within Mammoth basin offers a better view of Mammoth Pass and the Ritter Range beyond it. Stay on the road; do not wander among the buildings on the left. This is private property and trespassers are not welcome. After the road passes the buildings on the left, take the left fork that goes up the hill and then switchbacks up a brush-covered slope. Many hillside flowers may be found along the way. From the upper part of the road are impressive views back over Mammoth basin. To the left is the entire expanse of Mammoth Crest, in the foreground is Lake Mary. In the distance, over Mammoth Pass, are Mount Ritter and Banner Peak; to the right, Mammoth Mountain. The road dwindles to a trail that contours along the mountainside to Heart Lake, pocketed on the steep slope of Gold Mountain and named for its perfect heart shape. The lake has also been called "Dart Lake" for the prospector whose claims were nearby.

★Coldwater Canyon (9050 feet) to Arrowhead, Skelton, and Barney Lakes, Duck Pass, Duck Lake and Purple Lake.

Arrowhead Lake (9660 feet), easy hike, 1¼ miles.
Barney Lake (10,200 feet), intermediate hike, 2½ miles.
Duck Lake (10,427 feet), strenuous hike, 5 miles.
Purple Lake (9900 feet), strenuous hike, 8 miles.

Starting Point: See above. Go to the end of the road and park. A large sign marks the beginning of the trail.

The Duck Pass trail, one of the most heavily used in the Mammoth area, climbs steadily and is very dusty for the first mile. The network of gullies and old routes visible from the trail was caused by short-cutting prior to construction of the present route. It is slowly healing. After the trail levels off, Arrowhead Lake can be seen to the left through the trees. A side trail drops down to its shore. To make a loop trip back to the parking area, descend the steep footpath which follows Mammoth Creek downstream from the lake's outlet. Proceed cautiously on this path, for it goes along the brink of several rushing falls. The trail continues another half-mile to Skelton Lake, named for the "Skelton boys," early prospectors who had a 3-stamp mill below the lake. From Skelton the trail climbs over several low ridges, worn round and smooth by glacier movement, and through lush mountain meadows to Barney Lake, which rests in a glacier-scoured basin as do all the lakes in this canyon. Barney Lake is noted for its unusual jade-green color, possibly caused by algae growing in its waters.

From Barney Lake the trail climbs very steeply to Duck Pass (10,790 feet). In July clumps of alpine columbine—creamy white with tints of pink, blue, or yellow—make outstanding displays among the rocks. Alpine buttercups bloom at the edges of melting snowbanks lying late in the gulches. As the trail passes over Duck Pass, a lake is glimpsed which may be mistaken for Duck Lake. This is Pika Lake, however, named for the pika (cony or haymaker), a small rabbit-like animal that lives in abundance among the rocks in the narrow ridge separating the two lakes. Rounding a bend, the full expanse of Duck Lake comes in view, stubby whitebark pine in the foreground, the Silver Divide and Sharkstooth Peak in the distance across Cascade Valley. Duck Lake is unusual among Sierra lakes for its intense deep-blue color, appropriately compared to that of Crater Lake. So deep and clear are its waters that the light from the sun is absorbed, except for the deep blue portion of the spectrum which is reflected back. The setting of Duck Lake is typical of timberline country— barren, rough, lonely, but having a beauty all its own. There are two stories about the lake's name, one claiming that at certain times the letters DUK are spelled in snow on the dark rocks of the Duck Lake-Purple Lake divide across the lake. The other relates that one fall a group of ducks landing on the lake to rest for the night were found next morning frozen in the newly formed ice.

From the outlet of Duck Lake the trail drops down to join the John Muir Trail, then rounds a granite slope to Purple Lake. Many-hued rocks reflect into its water, giving it a purple tint at certain times of day. These are some of the ancient metamorphic rocks discussed in the geology section.

★**Coldwater Canyon (9050 feet) to Emerald Lake and Sky Meadow.**

Emerald Lake (9440 feet), easy hike, ¾ mile.
Sky Meadow (9700 feet), intermediate hike, 2 miles.
Starting Point: At the upper end of Lake Mary, turn left (S) up the Cold-

water Creek Camps road, drive to its end, and park on the west side of the parking area near Coldwater Creek.

To enjoy high-mountain flowers, icy streams, and a tranquil forest of hemlock—all in a timberline setting at the base of the Blue Crag and Mammoth Crest—hike to Sky Meadow. From the end of the road, the main trail climbs upward through a red fir forest. To its right is a much more scenic route, a footpath following Coldwater Creek upstream almost all the way to the lake. Occasionally a dark gray bird, the dipper, or water ouzel, will be seen bobbing up and down on the rocks in the cascades.

Emerald is a deep green lake nestled in trees, the sheer cliffs of Mammoth Crest looming behind it. (It is incorrectly named Way Lake on the topographic map.) Many rare and lovely mountain flowers bloom during late July and August in the meadows at the lake's inlet. Near the inlet the trail forks, the left fork climbing the hill and a dim trail eventually leading to Skelton Lake. The right fork crosses one small creek, and then follows the bank of a larger creek upstream a short distance to Gentian Meadows. In late summer, after the snows that lie late in this north-facing glen have melted, Gentian Meadows is a choice spot to see alpine flowers—alpine shooting stars just after the snow is gone, red heather and bog laurel in late July, and in late August thousands of blue gentian.

From the meadows, the trail veers right up over a low ridge. Though it is less distinct from here on, a watchful hiker can trace the trail and follow the cairns marking its way. It crosses a wooded slope, then crosses a second low ridge, descends to a small creek, and climbs steeply up a slope of mountain hemlock. The trail continues upward past the cascades of Coldwater Creek to Sky Meadow, which lies at the base of the great Blue Crag at the east end of Mammoth Crest. The meadow and the surrounding rocky slopes are one of the few truly alpine areas in the Mammoth basin. Long snow duration, ample water all summer, fertile stable soil, and protection from winds all make this protected hollow an ideal habitat for many plants rarely found elsewhere. (In early summer carry insect repellent; mosquitoes as well as flowers thrive in dampness.) From early August until the snow flies, this is a flower garden in miniature, for—typically alpine—the flowers are tiny. In mid-July alpine shooting star covers the ground, in August elephant heads and purplish-red paintbrush, in September blue and white gentian. On the rocky slopes above, the first to bloom are the Sierra primrose, followed shortly by white columbine and stonecrop.

★ **Lake George (9008 feet) to Barrett Lake and T. J. Lake.**

Barrett Lake (9210 feet), easy hike, ¼ mile.

T. J. Lake (9260 feet), easy hike, ½ mile.

Starting Point: At Lake George turn left and follow the road to its end at a parking area.

The trail crosses the creek at the outlet of Lake George, then forks above the first meadow. The left fork is the horse trail and is the better path to follow going up. A loop trip for hikers will be described that returns by the right fork, a footpath only. Along the left fork, the trail passes under an old western white pine of exceptionally large size, then enters a small meadow. After crossing a small creek, the trail again forks—the right fork bypassing Barrett Lake and going directly to T. J. Lake, the left fork (the main trail) ascending a hill through a fine stand of mountain hemlock to Barrett Lake, named for early forester Lou Barrett, and then continuing to T. J. Lake. T. J. are the initials of Tom Jones, one of the first supervisors of the Inyo National Forest; the spelling Tee Jay is incorrect. Through red heather and Labrador tea, two high-mountain plants, a footpath follows the left (E) shore of T. J. Lake to its upper end, where wildflowers are abundant during the summer. Riders must return by the same route, but hikers may follow the footpath along the creek's cascades from the outlet of T. J. Lake to Lake George. Along the shore of Lake George there are a number of springs which are ringed with spectacular displays of flowers in mid-summer.

★ Lake George (9008 feet) to Crystal Lake, Mammoth Crest, Deer Lakes.

Crystal Lake (9640 feet), intermediate hike, 1¼ miles.

Mammoth Crest (10,640 feet), strenuous hike, 3 miles.

Deer Lakes (10,660 feet), strenuous hike, 5½ miles.

Starting Point: Park at Lake George. The trail begins on the right (N) side of the paved road.

From the ridge separating Lake George and Horseshoe Lake, the trail zigzags up through stands of mountain hemlock, some of the finest in the area. At several points where the trail nears the precipitous dropoff above Lake George, there are striking views into its blue depths, Lake Mary and Gold Mountain forming the background to the east. The trail to Crystal Lake, which lies in a glacial cirque at the base of Crystal Crag, branches off to the left.

To reach Mammoth Crest continue on the main trail, each switchback bringing wider views of the surrounding country. The rock underfoot suddenly changes from cream-white granite to deep red cinder. Long ago the cinder, as well as the gray lava nearby, broke through the older granite and covered part of it. Lava of the same type occurs on top of Gold Mountain to the east, suggesting that perhaps the surface of the land between Gold Mountain and Mammoth Crest was once gently sloping, and that the lava patches now found atop each are remnants of a once continuous flow. Since the eruption Mammoth and Coldwater Creeks, aided by the ancient glaciers, have excavated the canyon now separating Gold Mountain from Mammoth Crest.

The trail forks, the left fork crossing a shallow basin which is possibly a crater, the right fork climbing a ridge of red cinder, from which there is a stirring view of the Sierra, from the Silver Divide north to the Ritter Range.

(See figure 7, Roadsides, for identification of peaks.) From the ridge, circle left (toward the south) around the rim of the basin mentioned above and join the left fork. Do not take the trail that turns off right for it is no longer maintained. After the two forks rejoin, the trail follows the gently sloping top of Mammoth Crest. Viewed from the crest itself, the contrast between the vertical east-facing cliffs and the gentle west-sloping surface is particularly striking. Such contrasts are not uncommon in the high country. Since the leeward, shady side of a ridge favors the accumulation of snow, glaciers grew largest there during the Ice Age and did their most extensive cutting on the slopes most protected from sun and winds, often the east and north slopes.

Small clumps of wind-torn, dwarfed whitebark pine and occasional lodgepole grow on the Crest. Severe weather and exposure account for their low, spreading growth forms. Wind is the most effective agent in the environment here. Nearly always blowing, it nips the growing tips of the branches on the windward side, producing these lopsided forms. Branches closest to the ground grow most successfully because they are most protected from the winds' blasts, especially in winter when drifting snow covers them. Many cushion-type alpine plants grow along the Crest, among which are tiny lupines and sulphur flowers. Watch along the trail for granite slabs having shallow, circular cavities worn in them. These are neither potholes such as are often worn in stream beds by rotating gravels, nor Indian grinding holes. They are formed by water collecting in small depressions in the rock and dissolving some of the minerals, thus enlarging the depression and allowing more water to collect. The shallow basin resulting is known as a weather pit, and may be one to three feet in diameter though only a few inches deep. They are found in the Sierra in areas of granitic rock, such as Yosemite Park.

From the main trail several short side trails branch to the east, leading to the edge of the Crest where there are fine views down to the Mammoth Lakes basin. See figure 13 for identification of landmarks. The trail continues along the Crest, then descends to Deer Lakes, the headwaters of Deer Creek. The lower lake is bordered by alpine meadows in which there are dwarf willows only three or four inches high.

Horseshoe Lake (8950 feet) to McLeod Lake, Crater Meadows, the Red Cones, Deer Creek.

McLeod Lake (9250 feet), easy hike, ½ mile.

Crater Meadows (8800 feet), intermediate hike, 3½ miles.

Starting Point: At the end of the highway at Horseshoe Lake, go straight ahead from the pavement toward the base of a hill. Do not turn left to the bathhouses or follow the jeep trails used for maintaining the water system.

The first part of this trail is steep, apt to be sunny, and in deep pumice, but there is shade here and there from the lodgepole pine and mountain hemlock. McLeod Lake is named for an early forest ranger of Reds Meadow, Malcolm

Mount Morrison

Ed Cooper

Ice!
A land
born of fire and
sculptured by ice.

For several million years, fire and ice have played their antagonistic roles, shaping the landscape we see today — the one building and adding, the other quarrying, scouring, tearing down.

During summer when only a few snow patches spangle Sierra peaks, it takes considerable imagination to picture the Ice Age landscape. It was a time of fluctuating climates that began about two million years ago. During the cooler and moister times, ice built up and glaciers advanced down the canyons as they do in the Arctic today. When the climate warmed, the glaciers melted back. Cold, moist times alternated with warmer, dryer times at least four and possibly six times.

Glacier, Ritter Range   Tom Ross

Broad, theatre-shaped basins — cirques —
form the head of most Sierra canyons.
There, snow accumulated and compacted
into the ice masses that eventually sent
rivers of ice flowing down-canyon, planing,
grooving, and rounding all the rock they
overrode. Small glaciers linger in some
High Sierra cirques today. Shading some of
the higher cirques are ridges that never
were rounded by overriding ice. Their
rock, standing above the ice, and subject
to the effects of alternate freezing and
thawing today as in the past, has shattered
into spires and pinnacles. Thus the
Minarets and other jagged peaks of the
Ritter Range stand in marked contrast to
the lower, rounded glaciated Sierra crest a
few miles east.

T J Johnston

Unglaciated peaks of the Minarets   Ed Cooper

Glacier-planed bedrock   Philip Hyde
below Minarets

Rock grooved and polished   Philip Hyde
by glacier

Flat-bottomed glacial valley—upper Rock Creek Canyon   Ed Cooper

Mountains sculptured by glaciers are both more forbidding and

more hospitable than unglaciated mountains — forbidding because of steep canyon walls and jagged pinnacles, hospitable because of broad valley bottoms holding chains of lakes and flower-filled meadows. Although the deep canyons of the Sierra have been cut primarily by streams, it is the glaciers that have given the canyons their distinctive U-shaped forms by widening the valley floors and steepening the canyon walls.

On their way down-canyon, the glaciers scooped out many basins in the bedrock. In some of these basins lie alpine lakes. Other basins contain marshes, slowly filling with mud and gravel washed in by streams. As the marshes fill, they dry and grass growing along the margins will steadily advance until the marsh has disappeared. A meadow of grass and flowers will take its place.

U-shaped canyon, Convict Lake

Stephen H. Willard

Mountain iris

Philip W. Faulconer

Willow catkins

Don Gibbon

Glacial moraines, Green Creek

John S. Shelton

Serving as great conveyor belts, glaciers carry rock

down from the high lands, then dump it where they melt in the lower lands. Such dumps, "glacial moraines," are composed of rock debris ranging in size from sand to boulders. Moraines stand hundreds of feet high at the mouth of almost every canyon between Sherwin Summit and Sonora Pass.

Green Creek moraine, a few miles north of Conway Summit, is one of the longer ones (photo above). Its sinuous shape outlines the path of the lower end of the glacier.

The huge arc-shaped piles of debris at the mouth of Laurel and Convict creek canyons (opposite) are moraines also. They outline the location of the glaciers' snouts at the climax of the last glacial advance.

The Ice Age ended about eleven thousand years ago — or did it? Are we perhaps enjoying only a brief, warm interlude before the next glacial advance which could be triggered by only a few degrees drop in average temperature? We may not live long enough to know whether the Sierra's small glaciers will melt away entirely, or whether ice will again build up and begin flowing down Sierra canyons.

Moraines at the mouth of Convict Creek Canyon   John S. Shelton

Moraines at the mouth of Laurel Creek Canyon   John S. Shelton

Mono Lake

Stephen H. Willard

Tufa deposit, Mono Lake

Bev Steveson

Tufa deposit, Mono Lake

Bev Steveson

During the Ice Age Mono Lake was three or four times larger,

its water level over six hundred feet higher than at present. Shorelines of the ancient lake may be seen clearly at several places. Tufa towers that formed under water now stand high above the water line.

The knobby white tufa is the limy deposit of tiny plants, calcareous algae. These algae have helped to precipitate calcium carbonate from the alkaline lake water. Tufa may be likened to coral, a similar deposit secreted by tiny animals.

McLeod; the spelling McCloud and McCleod are both incorrect. Its pumice beach is inviting, but since the lake provides drinking water for resorts and campgrounds, no bathing is permitted. At the lake take the trail which follows along its north shore, Mammoth Crest's granitic cliffs rising almost vertically across the lake. The trail winds through a forest first of lodgepole pine and then of red fir until it joins the John Muir Trail coming from Reds Meadow, four miles away. Just beyond the junction the trail enters upper Crater Meadow, where Crater Creek rises from springs. To the right are two perfectly shaped cinder cones. (For detail about the cones and the trail on to Deer Creek, see trail below, "Reds Meadow to Crater Meadows, Red Cones . . . via the John Muir Trail.")

Horseshoe Lake (8950 feet) to McLeod Lake, Mammoth Pass, Reds Meadow, Devil's Postpile.

McLeod Lake (9250 feet), easy hike, ½ mile.
Mammoth Pass (9290 feet), easy hike, 1 mile.
Reds Meadow (7600 feet), strenuous hike, 4 miles.
Starting Point: See preceding trail.

Go to the outlet of McLeod Lake as described above. Here the Mammoth Pass trail branches to the right, leading through a lodgepole pine forest to the broad saddle between Mammoth Mountain and Mammoth Crest known as Mammoth Pass. This trail is now little used, most people preferring to drive to Reds Meadow and the Postpile. It can be made a relatively easy trip, downhill all the way beyond Mammoth Pass, if you arrange to be met by car at Reds Meadow Pack Station or at the Devil's Postpile parking area. From the pass, the trail winds through red fir forest, joining the Muir Trail two miles down the slope. Continuing downhill on the Muir Trail for two more miles, it enters Reds Meadow near the pack station and store. To reach the Devil's Postpile, continue on the Muir Trail for another mile and a half.

★Minaret Summit Ridge (9240–10,000 feet or higher).

Easy hike, 1–2 miles.
Starting Point: At Minaret Summit, turn right and drive to the lookout point and parking area.

This hike offers one of the grandest views in the entire region; it is also one of the shorter, easier hikes. Begin this trip at the lookout point, where signs identify the mountain peaks. (See also figure 7, auto trips.) Just below the lookout a trail leads off to the right, shortly joining a jeep road which trends generally north along the crest of the ridge. There is a panoramic view west of the Sierra from Mount Lyell south to Kaiser Crest; these other peaks can also be seen: Mammoth, Bloody, and Red Slate Mountains to the southeast; San Joaquin Mountain to the north; interesting volcanic formations to the east.

From mid-July to early August, the pumice covering the ridge is carpeted with small purple lupine and many other dwarf flowers. Several large snowbanks last until late July. Clumps of whitebark pine make fine shelters for picnic lunches; drinking water must be carried in for there are no springs. A windjacket is needed to protect against the cold wind that often sweeps over the ridge.

SAN JOAQUIN RIVER

From the Middle Fork of the San Joaquin River more trails lead in more directions to more places than from almost anywhere. Reds Meadow, the Devil's Postpile, and Agnew Meadow are the starting points. The Middle Fork lies in a deep broad canyon between the Ritter Range and the Sierra Crest. It is the lofty, jagged peaks of the Ritter Range to the west which dominate the area and command attention; not the Sierra Crest and its pumice-covered San Joaquin Mountain, Mammoth Mountain, and Mammoth Crest.
Topographic map needed: Devils Postpile quadrangle.

Reds Meadow (7600 feet) to Crater Meadows, Red Cones, and Deer Creek.

Crater Meadows and Red Cones (8800 feet), intermediate hike, 3 miles.
Deer Creek (9160 feet), strenuous hike, 5 miles.
There are two routes to Crater Meadows, one following the John Muir Trail, the other following Crater Creek. To make an interesting loop trip take the Muir Trail to the Red Cones, and return by the Crater Creek trail.

Via the John Muir Trail.

Starting Point: Reds Meadow Pack Station.
The Muir Trail circles behind the corrals, and then climbs gradually but steadily through virgin fir forest, some of the larger trees more than fifteen feet around. Compared to some forests, this is a "messy" one—many splintered snags still standing and dead limbs littering the ground. Firs are more subject to rot than many trees; hence they break in many pieces, in contrast to the pines which usually fall as a unit, roots and all. This broken wood, along with decaying leaves, needles, cones, and grass, is not wasted; it will become an important part of the new soil now forming and will help provide nourishment for future generations of trees.
Along the trail, Iron Mountain and other peaks of the Ritter Range can be glimpsed through the trees. To the right of the trail is the first of the Red Cones, excellent examples of volcanic cinder cones. They are symmetrical, have small craters at their summits, and are composed of reddish brown porous lava cinders that were blown out of a now inactive vent. A rubbly lava flow extends west down the slope and appears to have been extruded from near the base of the cones. Near the cones the Crater Creek trail leading to the Reds Meadow pack station branches off to the right. The Muir Trail continues on through the

forest, and then ascends the Crater Creek-Deer Creek divide, where there is an extensive view south to the Silver Divide and lower Fish Creek. From the divide, the trail drops down to Deer Creek.

Some editions of the topographic map show the Muir Trail following Deer Creek to Deer Lakes. This is a serious error. The Muir Trail crosses Deer Creek here and heads for Purple Lake. It is possible to reach Deer Lakes by going cross-country and following Deer Creek upstream, but this is a very strenuous trip and there is no trail.

Via Crater Creek.

Starting Point: Follow the Reds Meadow road to its end at the pack station.

From the pack station, this gentle trail winds through a virgin forest of great firs, passing many small streams and dozens of flower gardens with lupine and larkspur growing shoulder high. The slope east of Reds Meadow seems to be a natural underground reservoir for rain and melting snow water; even in late summer, there is abundant water for springs, streams, and meadows. After crossing Crater Creek the trail climbs steeply up a dusty loose pumice slope, and although not much fun to hike, this section of the trail provides good views of the creek's falls nearby. At Crater Meadows, this trail connects with the John Muir Trail. (See above for a description of the Red Cones and the route to Deer Creek.)

Reds Meadow (7600 feet) to Sotcher Lake (7616 feet). Nature Trail.

Easy hike, ½ mile.

Starting Point: From the upper end of Reds Meadow Campground, the trail to Sotcher Lake leads off to the left (N).

This short, interesting trail may be in somewhat poor condition owing to bogs and down trees. It is a popular walk, however, through forest and lush meadow. Many kinds of wildflowers grow abundantly. The trail follows a creek to the southwest side of the lake. To reach the east shore, cross the creek over a large log near the waterfall which comes in from the right (E) and continue on to the lake. Swimming in Sotcher Lake is allowed but not encouraged because there is no beach; steep cliffs slope into deep, very cold water.

Reds Meadow (7600 feet) to Crater Creek, Fish Creek, Island Crossing.

Crater Creek Crossing (6800 feet), intermediate hike, 3 miles.

Island Crossing (6320 feet), strenuous hike, 8 miles.

Starting Point: Follow the main Reds Meadow road and pass the turnoff to the Reds Meadow Campground. About ½ mile beyond that turnoff, turn right onto the road leading to the parking area for the Rainbow Falls Trail.

This is the only trail in the area which is *down* all the way going, and *up* all the way coming back—always a discouraging situation, made even more so by the very dusty pumice trail and the mid-summer heat at these relatively low altitudes. The trail passes the Rainbow Falls turnoff, and meets Crater Creek at the bottom of a cool ravine lush with ferns, alders, and large aspens. The portion of the trail from here to the creek's crossing deserves to be enjoyed leisurely. Left of the trail, Crater Creek slides over clean slabs of granite; from the top of a small ridge just to the right of the trail are good views of the Middle Fork canyon, which here is composed of massive granitic walls and ridges, all rounded and smoothed by the tremendous glaciers which once filled it. This area is unlike any other described in this book; it is more like the Yosemite high country. Little glacial polish remains here however, since the rock's coarse-grained texture has allowed its surface to weather away readily.

Beyond Crater Creek, carry a snake-bite kit or equivalent for rattlesnakes are not uncommon. Watch for them particularly near wet or damp places. Be duly but not *un*duly cautious; they threaten you far less than an oncoming car.

The trail crosses several small streams, then climbs up out of the trees; here, before it swings left (E) into Fish Valley, it passes some outstanding viewpoints a few yards to the right (W) of the trail. The deep gash of Fish Valley comes in from the left, the broad canyon of the Middle Fork from the right; beyond their junction is the impassable gorge through which the Middle Fork of the San Joaquin River flows west. On the western skyline rises the divide separating the watersheds of the San Joaquin and Merced rivers. From the rim of Fish Valley, the trail drops down steeply to Fish Creek, and then follows it upstream into Cascade Valley. Beyond the first crossing is a camp known as "Iva Bell Camp" at Fish Creek Hot Springs. The camp is named after Iva Bell Clark, whose parents had packed in to the springs to relieve Mr. Clark's arthritis. Iva Bell was born unexpectedly in July 1936, greatly surprising both parents. Neither suspected that a child was the cause of Mrs. Clark's "tumor." Ten days later, mother and child were packed out safely to Reds Meadow.

Reds Meadow (7600 feet) to Devil's Postpile (7559 feet).

Easy hike, 1 mile.

Starting Point: Follow the main Reds Meadow road, pass the turnoff to Reds Meadow Campground, and about a hundred yards beyond turn right (W) up a short dead-end road. Look for the trail on the left.

This mile to the Devil's Postpile is part of the old route of the famous John Muir Trail. It leads through shaded forest around the end of the unusual Postpile basalt flow (described in the section on Roadsides). Look for columns to the right of the trail—some straight, some angled, some curved. To reach the Postpile Ranger Station, from the Postpile follow the wide path which stays on the right (E) side of the river.

Devil's Postpile (7559 feet) to Rainbow Falls (7360 feet).

Intermediate hike, 2 miles.

Starting Point: Parking area, Devil's Postpile National Monument.

Two routes lead from the Devil's Postpile to Rainbow Falls. One winds through a shaded forest on a wide, easily followed path. A rougher, but more scenic route follows a fisherman's trail downstream along the San Joaquin River—a particularly exciting route in early summer when the river is at its height. For a one-way trip, arrange to be met by car at the roadhead near Rainbow Falls (see map).

Via the forest trail.

Take the wide path that crosses the meadow and is then joined by the Muir Trail. Keep on the Muir Trail for about ½ mile, then take the signed trail branching right to Rainbow Falls. Near Rainbow Falls there is a network of trails, all leading to viewpoints. To see the Lower Falls, which are really wide cascades rather than a waterfall, continue downstream about ½ mile. A trail continues downstream another 1½ miles to Lost Camp, the last campsite on the river. Beyond the camp the river gorge becomes narrow and very steep and the surrounding country almost impassable.

Via the fisherman's trail.

Take the wide path across the meadow to the Postpile, then take any one of the trails branching right toward the river. A fisherman's trail follows the left (E) bank of the San Joaquin River, a torrent in early summer. Along the riverbank, watch for basalt columns similar to those of the Postpile, though slanted rather than vertical.

Devil's Postpile (7559 feet) to King Creek and Summit Meadow.

King Creek (7607 feet), intermediate hike, 3 miles.
Summit Meadow (9020 feet), strenuous hike, 6 miles.
Starting Point: Parking area, Devil's Postpile National Monument.

We know of a horse that always balked when started on this trail! She knew what was coming—ankle-deep pumice all the way and little shade above King Creek. Be sure to start before sun-up—or roast on the way. Take the wide path crossing the meadow south of the parking area, then turn right and cross the bridge over the San Joaquin River. A quarter-mile beyond, the trail to Summit Meadow branches left; it climbs a granite hump (8,000 feet), then drops down to the wide clear stream of King Creek. Several large logs downstream provide easy crossing for hikers. The many dead and dying red fir along the trail resulted from an epidemic of fir engraver beetles, 1951–54. The epidemic came to an end naturally, as insect infestations often do, perhaps being halted by prolonged cold weather.

The grind to Summit Meadow begins just beyond the creek. This is a part of the old Mammoth Trail, one of the oldest trails crossing the Sierra and much used by prospectors, stockmen, and sheepherders beginning in the late 1870s. The present trail follows much the same route as the old trail, connecting Reds Meadow with Clover Meadow, a roadhead on the Sierra's west slope twenty miles away by trail.

Summit Meadow, a vast expanse of green, at the very top of a broad ridge, comes as a pleasant surprise. Until 1963 the trail west of the meadow was still used as a sheep trail. In early summer, sheep from the western foothills were driven across the North Fork of the San Joaquin River at Sheep Crossing, up to '77 Corral (named for the dry summer of 1877, when this was one of the few places where feed was available), then to Summit Meadow. Formerly, the sheep went on to Reds and Agnew Meadows. However, grazing has been curtailed until now there is no grazing at all this side of the North Fork. Contributing factors included the disturbing of meadows and young trees, and the conflicts between sheep and wildlife and recreation.

Devil's Postpile (7559 feet) to Beck Cabin, Superior Lake, Beck Lakes.

Beck Cabin (9100 feet), strenuous hike, 7 miles.
Superior Lake (9370 feet), strenuous hike, 7½ miles.
Beck Lakes (9780 feet), strenuous hike, 8 miles.
Starting Point: Parking area, Devil's Postpile National Monument.

Five miles of walking through loose pumice is the price of enjoying the rugged high-country near Iron Mountain and the many lakes and streams of the King Creek drainage. Start early, before the sun comes over Mammoth Crest, for the pumice trail can be endured more easily in the cool of the morning than later when the sun beats down through the sparse forest. Follow the wide path through the meadow, then turn right and cross the bridge over the San Joaquin River. Proceed along the Minaret Lake trail. Just before reaching Minaret Creek, the trail to Beck Lakes branches left. The trail climbs steadily to almost 9500 feet, drops down a bit, then rounds a corner where the whole King Creek basin suddenly comes into view. Iron Mountain, dominating the steep ridge circling the basin, was named for a weathered iron-ore outcrop. Subsequent diamond-drilling showed that the quantity of high-grade ore is small and that the deeper ore is of poorer grade.

A half-mile farther stands a log cabin built many years ago by prospector John Beck. The trail to Lake Superior branches off to the right (W) near the cabin and follows a stream all the way to Beck Lakes. Above Superior the trail is less distinct, though it is ducked (marked with cairns) most of the way. Some scrambling is necessary to reach the upper end of the first lake; from there it is an easy walk to the higher lake. From Beck Cabin it is possible to return to the Postpile by an old trail which leads to Summit Meadow, and there connects with a well-defined trail leading back to the Postpile. This is a very strenuous trip, about a twenty-mile loop, and should be attempted only by experienced travelers with a good map. The trail is rocky and has not been maintained for many years. It is further confused by fishermen's trails, some branching off left into Snow Canyon, some right to the high lakes.

Devil's Postpile (7559 feet) to Holcomb Lake and Ashley Lake.

Holcomb Lake (9500 feet), strenuous hike, 9 miles.

Ashley Lake (9600 feet), strenuous hike, 9 miles.

Starting Point: Parking area, Devil's Postpile National Monument.

Go to Beck Cabin as described in the preceding trail. Do not turn right (W) to Beck Lakes, but stay on the main trail for about another half-mile. Then turn right, cross King Creek, and follow it upstream. The stream's right fork goes to Holcomb Lake, its left to Ashley. Both lakes are in barren but spectacular country, Ashley being just below the glacier of Iron Mountain.

★**Devil's Postpile (7559 feet) to Soda Springs and Minaret Falls (7650 feet).**—Easy hike, 1 mile.

Starting Point: Parking area, Devil's Postpile National Monument.

Take the wide path through the meadow, then turn right and cross the bridge over the San Joaquin River. Just beyond the bridge, a few steps off the trail, several soda springs bubble forth from a gravel bar in the river. Such springs are not uncommon in areas of recent volcanic activity. Molten magma, cooling far below the earth's surface, may give off gases for thousands of years. Carbon dioxide, often one of the last to be given off, may be absorbed by spring water, thus producing the carbonated water of a soda spring.

From the Soda Springs proceed along the left (W) side of the large meadow, along an unsigned but well-defined trail. It leads generally upstream along the west bank of the river, then swings left through the forest to the base of Minaret Falls. In June and July the broad foaming cascade may be more than a hundred feet wide. In late summer, the falls are reduced to several streams, flowers growing abundantly among the rocks between them. The falls were created during the Ice Age by glaciers. As the enormous Middle Fork glacier scoured out its canyon, the smaller tributary glacier in Minaret Canyon cut its valley at a slower rate. As a result, when the glaciers melted away, the mouth of Minaret Creek's valley was perched several hundred feet above the main canyon. Such a valley is called a "hanging valley."

★**Devil's Postpile (7559 feet) to Johnston Lake and Minaret Lake.**

Johnston Lake (8100 feet), intermediate hike, 2 miles.

Minaret Lake (9800 feet) and mine (10,000 feet), strenuous hike, 8 miles.

Starting Point: Parking area, Devil's Postpile National Monument.

Follow the wide path across the meadow, then turn right and cross the bridge over the San Joaquin River. Proceed through deep pumice along the well-marked Minaret Lake trail to Minaret Creek, Johnston Lake, and Johnston Meadow—lush with varied wildflowers, including the rare giant shooting star. Above Johnston Lake, named for a promoter of the old Minaret Mine, much of the present trail follows the old mining road—recognizable by its width and by the young lodgepole (3–6 feet high) which have sprouted up in the roadbed since the mine closed in 1930. To reach the Minaret Mine—

worked 1928–30—watch for a small sign and for the mining road which turns off right from the trail.

In winter, the dozen men working at the mine were completely dependent on the Mammoth dog teams for supplies, mail, and transportation. Though the 20-mile trip usually took two days, on one emergency run to rescue a badly burned miner, a team made it from Old Mammoth, over Mammoth Pass, down to the Postpile and up to the mine in the record time of 4½ hours.

Several miles above Johnston Lake, the trail leaves dense forest and follows the rushing, noisy cascade of Minaret Creek a short way. Nearing the dramatic spires of the Minarets, beyond the mine junction, the trail passes many excellent camping spots near Minaret Creek, which cascades and meanders through a forest of unusually large mountain hemlock and lodgepole pine. An unsigned but recognizable trail branches left to Deadhorse Lake (10,000 feet). The main trail climbs on to deep, clear Minaret Lake, cupped in a rock basin at the very base of Clyde Minaret. Alpine wildflowers abound above the lake, where the ground is saturated with melting snow water. From the far (NW) shore of Minaret Lake, a faint, steep trail (the last pitch requiring a little rock climbing) ascends to Cecilᴕ (Upper Iceberg) Lake (10,300 feet).

Devil's Postpile to Trinity, Castle, Vivian, and Rosalie lakes.
Strenuous hikes.

Hikers wanting to reach these lakes are advised to start at Agnew Meadow rather than the Postpile, in order to avoid 3½ miles of uphill hiking in deep pumice above the Postpile. (See trail below, "Agnew Meadow to Rosalie and Vivian Lakes.")

Devil's Postpile (7559 feet) to Lake Olaine (8080 feet).
Intermediate hike, 5 miles.

Starting Point: Parking area, Devil's Postpile National Monument, or join the trail from any of the campgrounds up-river from the Postpile. Starting from Upper Soda Springs Campground, it is 3 miles to Lake Olaine.

Before the John Muir Trail from the Postpile to Shadow Creek was routed via Vivian and Rosalie lakes, it followed the San Joaquin River, and is so marked on old maps. For its first two miles the river trail is hard to follow, for it is obscured by the numerous campgrounds along the river. Beginning at the Postpile Ranger Station, however, simply follow the river upstream, staying close to its right (E) bank. Above Upper Soda Springs Campground, the trail is well-defined even though numerous fallen trees have made it unsuitable for stock. It follows the river closely, which here flows quietly in its deep canyon— past meadows and gravel beaches, and through small rock gorges. At Lake Olaine, named for Charles Olaine who prospected here around 1910, there are bright yellow pond lilies, which can be seen best by following around the lake's right shore.

As an alternative to hiking the river trail back to the Postpile, take the trail to Agnew Meadow which branches right (E) about ½ mile below Lake Olaine and arrange to be met by car there.

★ Agnew Meadow (8335 feet) to Shadow Lake, Lake Ediza, and Iceberg Lake.

Shadow Lake (8750 feet), intermediate hike, 3 miles.
Lake Ediza (9300 feet), strenuous hike, 6 miles.
Iceberg Lake (9800 feet), strenuous hike, 7 miles.

Starting Point: About 3 miles down the dirt road from Minaret Summit, turn right into Agnew Meadow and park just north of the pack station. You'll find the trail skirting the south side of the meadow. In early summer plan to cross the San Joaquin in the morning, when the water is lower.

From Agnew Meadow, the trail drops 400 feet to the San Joaquin River, then remains almost level to the river crossing. Along the way it passes Lake Olaine, where brilliant yellow pond lilies can be seen if you make a short detour around part of the lake. In the dense wood there, the low *whoomp* of the grouse can be heard in early summer. From the river crossing, the trail zig-zags up a hot, dry slope. Watch for the old wind-battered juniper trees along the way, their bark shining red-golden in the early morning sun, and notice the fine view back toward Mammoth Mountain. Just below Shadow Lake is a good viewpoint for seeing the roaring falls of Shadow Creek.

Shadow Lake is considered by many one of the jewels of the Sierra, particularly because of its setting below the peaks of the Ritter Range. A favorite spot for photographers is the outlet of the lake, across the stream from the trail, where the view west is especially striking. If the crossing is blocked by high water, reach this spot by circling the lake. From the upper end of Shadow Lake, the trail follows Shadow Creek to Lake Ediza, often the base camp site for mountain climbers who come from all parts of the country to scale the peaks of the Minarets. The glacier-polished canyon walls and the rounded rock ridges are evidence that glaciers hundreds of feet thick once filled much of Shadow Creek Canyon. If you wander cross country up the ridges, you may wonder about the trenches and cores and foundations that you come across. As far as we know, David Nidever was the first to locate claims in this canyon, in the early 1900s. He built a log cabin at Cabin Lake and another about half a mile below Lake Ediza.

This cabin was headquarters in 1956 for extensive mining exploration by the Climax Molybdenum Company. Though all the heavy equipment necessary for diamond-drilling was brought in, there is no road scar destroying the wild beauty of Shadow Creek Canyon as there is in Laurel Canyon. Both of these canyons were classified as wilderness by the Forest Service because of their natural beauty and their outstanding wilderness quality. To preserve their primitive character, commercial development and roads are prohibited. Yet by law any miner with a legitimate claim has the legal right to build a road on

National Forest land, even if it is a Wilderness Area. Often the claim proves to be of little value and all is abandoned—lumber, pipes, and empty oil drums left strewn on the slopes, the landscape bearing the scar for fifty years or more. Yet at Shadow Creek, where deposits proved to be noncommercial, the process of exploration destroyed none of the canyon's wildness. The supplies for such a large operation were taken in by helicopter and mule, and neither miner nor wilderness was the loser.

To reach Iceberg Lake, named for the ice sometimes still floating on it in late summer, go around the left (S) side of Lake Ediza and follow the footpath which goes up the left bank of a small stream. This is one of the best places in the region to see alpine plants, the meadows supporting a cover of dwarf, brilliantly colored alpine flowers. Across the lake and below the Minarets are some small glaciers. Though these may look like snowfields, they are masses of glacial ice—dirty gray on top, bluish within—moving slowly downward and cracking open into crevasses where they flow over cliffs. Upper Iceberg Lake (sometimes called Cecile Lake) lies 500 feet above. An indistinct path crosses the steep talus slope above Iceberg Lake and then follows the stream dropping out of Upper Iceberg.

★ **Agnew Meadow (8335 feet) to Rosalie and Vivian lakes to the Devil's Postpile.**

Rosalie Lake (9350 feet), strenuous hike, 5½ miles.
Gladys Lake (9600 feet), strenuous hike, 6 miles.
Devil's Postpile (7559 feet), strenuous hike, 12 miles.

Starting Point: Same as for previous trail, and proceed as described there to Shadow Lake.

At the inlet of Shadow Lake, cross the creek and follow the John Muir Trail. It switchbacks up a steep, densely forested slope above Shadow Lake. This part of the trail was constructed with the help of a small bulldozer—30-inch tracks, 4-foot blade—which bulldozed its own way from Minaret Creek. However, even this well-built trail is deteriorating, because hikers, by short-cutting across switchbacks, have helped gullies get started.

Rosalie, Gladys, Vivian, Lois, Emily, Castle, and a number of ponds and smaller lakes are in a little world of their own on the high broad shoulder of Volcanic Ridge, named for the old recrystallized volcanic rocks composing it. To the west the lakes are walled in by somber cliffs; elsewhere they are completely encircled by rounded rock slopes or dense forest. From the grass-rimmed lakes of the Trinity group, a side trail leads to Castle Lake, about ½ mile up a steep 700-foot slope. The Muir Trail zigzags down to Minaret Creek in the canyon below. The two slopes of Volcanic Ridge support different kinds of trees—hemlocks and western white pine on the shaded Shadow Creek side, red fir on the sunny Minaret Creek side, and lodgepole on both. The trail crosses Minaret Creek over a large log, and continues on to the Postpile. Arrange to be met by car at the Postpile parking area.

Agnew Meadow (8335 feet) to Thousand Island Lake (9834 feet), strenuous hike, 9 miles.

Thousand Island Lake, with its many small tree-studded islands, is the birthplace of the Middle Fork of the San Joaquin River. It lies in a broad rock basin dominated by massive Banner Peak, named for the cloud banners that sometimes stream from its summit. The rounded ridges on either side of the lake, worn low by grinding, moving masses of ice thousands of years ago, are typical of glaciated country. Scratches, or striations, are so well preserved on the rocks it is easy to trace the direction of the glacier's movement. The Thousand Island Lake country is barren, windswept, and harshly beautiful—wonderful for cross-country hiking. The rock is hard and smooth, the forest sparse, and small streams and lakes surprisingly numerous. Flowers often bloom until late September in the large alpine meadows at the lake's inlet.

There are three trails from Agnew Meadow to Thousand Island Lake, all about the same mileage but differing markedly in scenic beauty. The river trail is the most gradual, though it provides none of the glorious views of the other two. The High Trail offers exceptional views across the Middle Fork Canyon toward the lofty peaks of the Ritter Range, their glaciers and canyons; it also passes through acres of wildflowers, growing shoulder-high. The most strenuous route, which starts on the Shadow Creek trail and then follows the Muir Trail, traverses varied high-mountain country close to the base of Mount Ritter and Banner Peak. For an outstanding—though very strenuous—loop trip to Thousand Island Lake, go by the Shadow Creek trail and return by the High Trail to Agnew Meadow.

Via the River Trail.

Starting Point: About 3 miles down the dirt road from Minaret Summit, turn right into Agnew Meadow and park just north of the pack station. You'll find the trail skirting the south side of the meadow. This trail is particularly beautiful in early summer when the river is high.

The section of the river trail described here could better be called the "canyon trail," for though it is often within sound of the river, seldom is it within sight of it. However, to see its foaming cascades, small waterfalls and gorges, you need to make only small detours to the river's banks. From Agnew Meadow, follow the trail down to the bottom of the canyon, where it joins the river trail coming from Reds Meadow; stay on the river trail, passing the turnoff to Shadow Lake. At the Garnet Lake turnoff an old trail branches right, connecting with the High Trail east of Badger Lakes and with another old trail to Agnew Pass. The river trail continues leisurely on, following close to the infant Middle Fork for half a mile and then climbing up the slope to meet the High Trail swinging in from Agnew Meadow. Turn left and proceed to the inlet of Thousand Island Lake.

Or, if there's no hurry, pause a bit at the Badger Lakes. Some years, if they are too marshy and full of mosquitoes, you may have to wait until late August to explore these grassy lakes. A small, bare rock ridge west of the deepest and largest lake, two hundred yards or more south of the High Trail, provides a 360-degree view of the Middle Fork Canyon—a fine place for lunching and studying maps and getting acquainted with the landmarks.

★ Via Badger Lakes and the High Trail.

Starting Point: About 3 miles down the dirt road from Minaret Summit, turn right into Agnew Meadow. The trail starts a few yards beyond the Agnew Meadow Pack Station, to the right of the road.

The first mile up the High Trail is a steep, dusty pull through red fir forest, gaining five hundred feet without wasting time. Emerging from the forest, the trail climbs more gradually. Just before making its first descent, about 2½ miles from Agnew Meadow, the trail passes a point offering a good view directly across to Shadow Lake and Shadow Falls. Those not wishing to make the strenuous trip to Thousand Island Lake are urged to hike this far, however—for the view as well as the wildflowers. Along the numerous streams which cross the trail, plant growth is luxuriant even in fall—lupine, tiger lilies, delphinium, paintbrush. The streams come from springs above the trail where a mass of porous lava overlies dense metamorphic rock. At their contact, the rain and snow water stored in the lava gushes forth. Feed and water being abundant, animal life is abundant also. A silent hiker is sure to see deer, quail, hummingbirds, and hawks. The trail contours along the slope of San Joaquin Mountain, sage slopes alternating with flower-filled ravines. About a mile east of Thousand Island Lake there are junctions with the river trail and the Agnew Pass trail.

★ Via the Shadow Creek Trail, the Muir Trail, and Garnet Lake.

Starting Point: Agnew Meadow. Go to Shadow Lake (see p. 61).

About a mile above Shadow Lake, turn right and follow the Muir Trail. At the top of the 1300-foot ridge separating Shadow and Garnet Lakes, before dropping down to Garnet Lake, leave the trail for a few minutes to climb one of the higher points a few hundred yards away on either side. There are sweeping views not only of the Ritter Range, but also of peaks far to the south. Possibly Garnet Lake was named for the small garnet crystals that are locally abundant. In rocks north of the lake fossil clams were found recently, and have been dated as having lived 190,000,000 years ago. From the lake, the trail climbs over the 500-foot ridge separating Garnet and Thousand Island lakes.

Agnew Meadow (8335 feet) to Agnew Pass, Clark Lakes, and Silver Lake.

Agnew Pass (9900 feet), strenuous hike, 5½ miles.
Clark Lakes (9850 feet), strenuous hike, 6 miles.
Silver Lake (7223 feet), strenuous hike, 11 miles.

Starting Point: Follow the directions given above for the High Trail. Proceed along the High Trail for about 5 miles, until the trail leading to Agnew Pass forks to the right.

A short, steep climb leads to Agnew Pass, Summit Lake, and the meadows around the Clark Lakes. Before dropping down to Spooky Meadow, go a few yards to the left of the trail for an excellent view to the north and west—Gem Lake and the large drainage basin of Rush Creek, with towering Mount Lyell (13,114 feet) at its head. The famous Lyell glacier, second largest in the Sierra, is on the mountain's north slope and hence not visible from here.

The rest of the way to Silver Lake is all downhill, on a steep, rocky, dusty, but well-engineered trail. The grind is alleviated somewhat by the sparkle of a little stream that crosses the trail many times, and by the variety of the precipitous canyon walls—red and black lava, gray granite, and metamorphic rocks of white, rust, black, and gray. As the trail follows the shore of Agnew Lake, watch for a rare gentian with a large blue flower almost two inches long. A good bridge crosses Rush Creek below Agnew Lake dam, and the trail joins the main Rush Creek trail leading to Silver Lake. Arrange to be met by car near the pack station at the outlet of Silver Lake.

★ **Agnew Meadow (8335 feet) to Carson Peak and San Joaquin Mountain.**

Carson Peak (10,909 feet), strenuous hike, 7½ miles.

San Joaquin Mountain (11,600 feet), strenuous hike, 8½ miles.

Starting Point: To reach Agnew Pass, follow the directions given in the preceding trail. Be sure to carry water and a wind jacket on this trip.

This is the best-defined "trail" to these two mountains. Poor as it is, the others shown on some maps (coming from Yost Lake or Deadman Creek) are much worse, almost impossible to follow. From Agnew Pass, a good trail climbs southeast about a mile to a high pumice flat, then peters out. Not enough people come to this wind-swept pumice country to keep a trail trampled. From the pumice flat turn left (N) and walk up the gentle slope to Carson Peak, the highest point on a cliff that rises 3500 feet from June Lake basin. To reach San Joaquin Mountain turn right and walk southeast across the pumice flat, then circle around to its gentle, easily-climbed northeast slope. The view is unequalled anywhere in the area. There is a full-circle panorama—west to the Ritter Range, north to Koip and Parker peaks, east across domes, craters, blocky lava cliffs and square miles of pumice to the White Mountains, and south to the Silver Divide. (See figures 7, 8, and 10 for identification of peaks.)

Agnew Meadow (8335 feet) to Garnet Falls, Garnet Lake via the River Trail.

The foot of Garnet Falls (9100 feet), intermediate hike, 4 miles.

Garnet Lake (9680 feet), strenuous hike, 5 miles.

Starting Point: Follow directions given above for the river trail, "Agnew Meadow to Thousand Island Lake," to the Garnet Lake turnoff.

Leave the river trail here and take the trail to the left, which follows the river about ½ mile to the foot of Garnet Falls. There, at the first sight of the cascading falls, the trail forks again. Take the left fork, a footpath only, which crosses the river over a large log and then ascends the left (S) bank of Garnet Falls to the outlet of Garnet Lake. This is the shortest route to Garnet Lake, but is only for those who do not mind clambering up a very steep fisherman's trail, close to dashing water. Return to Agnew Meadow is possible by two routes from Garnet Lake (both longer but more scenic than the river trail)—either the Shadow Creek Trail or the High Trail (see above, "Agnew Meadow to Thousand Island Lake").

JUNE LAKE BASIN

The June Lake Basin contains four large lakes, all accessible by paved road. The area is bordered by ridges and peaks rising two to four thousand feet above the floor of the basin; consequently all trails leading from the area are unusually steep. Rush Creek, which empties into Silver Lake, drains an immense basin of fifteen streams and their tributaries, fifteen good-sized lakes, and dozens of small ones.

Topographic map needed: Mono Craters quadrangle.

Fern Creek (7350 feet) to Fern Creek Falls and Fern Lake.

Fern Creek Falls (8080 feet), intermediate hike, 1 mile.

Fern Lake (8900 feet), strenuous hike, 1½ miles.

Starting Point: Drive west from Gull Lake, pass the June Mountain ski area, and turn left into the Fern Creek Group Campground. Head generally up hill toward the sharp-pointed peaks and look for the trail sign.

The short but steep trip to Fern Lake is a good introduction to the trees of the eastern Sierra. Nine of the ten trees described in the tree section are encountered on the way. The trail climbs gradually through a grove of aspen and then across a sagebrush slope, the cliffs of Carson Peak rising sheer to the right (SW). The tumbling cascades of Fern Creek are an exciting sight in June or early July.

The trail leading to Fern Lake branches off to the right (S) just before the falls. This is a very steep unblazed trail that parallels the cascading creek about half the distance to the lake, which rests in a small, steep-sided cirque. The main trail continues on to Yost Lake, described in the following loop trip from June Lake to Fern Creek. June Lake is recommended as the starting point because the ascent is more shaded as well as more gradual, and because the starting point is 300 feet higher than at Fern Creek.

June Lake (7680 feet) to Yost Lake and Fern Creek.

Yost Lake (9100 feet), intermediate hike, 4½ miles.

Fern Creek (7350 feet), intermediate hike, 7 miles total.

Starting Point: Drive 2¼ miles down the June Lake road from its junction with Highway 395. Just beyond a narrow place in the road, opposite the Fire House, a small parking area indicates the start of the trail. Arrange to be met by car at Fern Creek Group Campground (see previous trail).

The trail angles up the slope for about two miles, then follows along the nearly level crest of a moraine to the large meadows above Yost Lake. Sheep are often driven here from Deadman Creek in late summer. Beyond the lake the trail follows Yost Creek downstream to a small meadow. If the trail crossing the meadow and the creek is difficult to follow because of criss-crossing sheep trails, watch for tree blazes. Just after the falls of Yost Creek there is a good view north. Reversed Peak lies directly across the canyon; Mono Craters are to the right (NE); and Mount Wood is the high red peak to the left (NW) rising behind Silver Lake. The trail slants down a steep forested slope, crosses Fern Creek Falls, and continues on down to the roadend at Fern Creek.

Flower-filled meadows high on the slope of June Mountain may come as a surprise on this trail. After crossing the June Mountain ski slope (tree blazes mark the trail) you come to the first of them; Yost Meadow, the largest, is half a mile long. Early in July they may be yellow with buttercups; later on, blue and lavender with wet-meadow flowers such as shooting stars and elephant heads.

Silver Lake (7212 feet) to Agnew, Gem, Weber, and Waugh Lakes.

Agnew Lake (8508 feet), intermediate hike, 2½ miles.

Gem Lake (9052 feet), strenuous hike, 3½ miles.

Weber Lake (10,000 feet), strenuous hike, 8½ miles.

Waugh Lake (9424 feet), strenuous hike, 7 miles.

Starting Point: Behind the pack station, near Silver Lake.

Start early; otherwise the 1300-foot climb to Agnew Lake Reservoir can be a hot, unpleasant pull. The trail crosses the tramway and penstock of the Southern California Edison Company several times. Buildings, wires, roads, and other construction are much in evidence all the way to Gem Lake. Where the switchbacks end and the trail heads into the narrow mouth of Rush Creek canyon just below Agnew Lake, notice the rounded, smoothed, striated rock just across the stream—striking evidence of glaciation and especially well preserved. The trail climbs on up past Agnew Lake to a high point which offers the first view of Gem Lake and of Mount Lyell (13,114 feet), the highest peak on the skyline to the right, large snowbanks lying in a cirque just to its left. Gem Lake received its name in the early mining days from Tom Agnew, who called it "Gem-o'-the-Mountains."

About half-a-mile beyond the Gem Lake dam, the trail goes through a 3-foot-wide trough gouged in solid rock—an outstanding example of a large glacial groove. Many parallel scratches (striations) can easily be seen, though the glacial polish has weathered away. The trail from here on is more gradual and stays in deep forest, with only occasional glimpses of Mount Davis and Rodgers

Peak to the west. Above Gem Lake the trail continues along an old tractor road which was used for maintenance of the Waugh Lake dam (called by old-timers Rush Meadows Dam), named for E. J. Waugh, chief construction engineer. Just below the dam, the trail to Weber Lake takes off to the left (S). The main trail follows the north shore of Waugh Lake and then joins the John Muir Trail two miles farther on. On the return trip, when nearing the inlet of Gem Lake, watch where the trail branches left from the tractor road. It is easy to overlook this and to continue on the road, which dead-ends at Gem Lake.

★ **Silver Lake (7212 feet) to Clark Lakes and Thousand Island Lake.**

Clark Lakes (9850 feet), strenuous hike, 5½ miles.
Thousand Island Lake (9834 feet), strenuous hike, 7½ miles.
Starting Point: Behind the pack station, near Silver Lake.
Start very early from Silver Lake, otherwise this grind can be oppressively hot. Proceed as above to the outlet of Agnew Lake, then take the trail which crosses a good bridge below the dam and zigzags relentlessly up a 1500-foot shadeless rocky slope to Spooky Meadows, nestled in a cirque of red and black lava cliffs marking the end of San Joaquin Mountain ridge. From Spooky Meadows the trail climbs again but less steeply. Just as it starts its descent to the first Clark Lake, there is a fine view a little to the right of the trail, of the whole Rush Creek drainage, walled in on the west by the Ritter Range which culminates at Mount Lyell. The trail to Thousand Island Lake follows the right (W) shore of the largest Clark Lake, crosses a gentle saddle, and then joins the trail coming from Agnew Meadow. (See trail above, "Agnew Meadow to Thousand Island Lake," for details on the lake.)

Silver Lake to Carson Peak and San Joaquin Mountain.

These peaks can be reached via Agnew Pass from either Silver Lake or Agnew Meadow. The distance from both starting points to Agnew Pass is the same, 5½ miles. However, since Agnew Meadow is a thousand feet higher than Silver Lake, it is recommended as the starting point. (See trail above, "Agnew Meadow to Carson Peak and San Joaquin Mountain.")

★ **Silver Lake (7212 feet) to Gem Pass (10,700 feet), Alger Lake (10,640 feet).**

Strenuous hike, 9 miles.
Starting Point: Behind the pack station, near Silver Lake.
Proceed to the north shore of Gem Lake as described in trail above "Silver Lake to Agnew, Gem, etc."). Just after crossing Crest Creek the trail to Alger Lake branches to the right (N). As it switchbacks up the forested slope to Gem Pass, it enters the high country of mountain peaks, snow, and timberline lakes. Looking back you see impressive views west toward the Ritter Range, and south

Mountain stream   Bev Steveson

Jeffrey pine bark   Gerhard Schumacher

Mountain hemlock cone   T J Johnston

Melting snowbank   Sierra Club photo

Rabbit and chipmunk tracks   Bev Steveson

Rabbit tracks in dust   Bev Steveson

Mosaic!

Pumice from the craters, sand washed down by the streams, gravel dumped by the glaciers — this is the raw material that supports all life here today. On the few inches of topsoil that have evolved depend all the living things — sagebrush, grass, trees, insects, deer, nutcrackers — in wondrous ways depending on each other. Upon them all, we too depend.

Thistle poppy   Bev Steveson

Willow 6 - 20 feet tall   Bev Steveson

Corn lily, Queen Anne's lace   Bev Steveson

Alpine willow 1¼ inches tall   Bev Steveson

Cow parsnip   Bev Steveson

Evening primrose   Bev Steveson

Swamp whiteheads 2 - 5 ft. tall   Bev Steveson

Pyrola   Bev Steveson

Golden-mantled ground squirrels   Bev Steveson

Sage grouse courtship display   Bev Steveson

Coyote   Bev Steveson

Marmot   David J. Dunaway

toward San Joaquin Mountain and the imposing lava cliffs surrounding Spooky Meadow. Beyond Gem Pass the trail winds around rocky cliffs of many colors—purple, red, black, rust—and then drops into the Alger Lakes basin, which is encircled by the high peaks of Mount Wood and Parker, Koip, and Blacktop peaks. Looking north from Alger Lake you can make out where the trail crosses the saddle between Parker and Koip peaks on its way to Tuolumne Meadows.

Silver Lake (7212 feet) to Parker Lake.

Intermediate hike, 3 miles to top of ridge (9050 feet).

Starting Point: The pack station, near Silver Lake.

At this writing a trail goes only as far as the top of the high sagebrush-covered ridge just north of Silver Lake. From the pack station go right, heading directly toward the high slope, and pick up the trail among the sagebrush at the base of the slope. The trail angles across the ridge, passing a surprising number of small streams. Wild rose and yellow mule's ears provide color in early summer; sage hen, quail, and deer are likely to be seen. The top of the ridge is an open, gently rolling area on the shoulder of Mount Wood, used as a sheep camp in August and as a deer hunter's camp in fall. In a grove of the largest, straightest aspen, vandals have disfigured most of the silver-barked trees.

PARKER AND WALKER LAKES

Parker Lake and Walker Lake lie in two small canyons between June Lake and Lee Vining. They are less popular than some of the other areas, possibly because there are no camping facilities.

Topographic map needed: Mono Craters quadrangle.

Parker Creek (7950 feet) to Parker Lake (8400 feet).

Intermediate hike, 2 miles.

Starting Point: From Highway 395 follow the paved road toward Grant Lake for 1½ miles, then turn right (SW) onto the Parker Lake road. This graded but rough road, though it winds a bit through the sagebrush, heads directly toward the mountains for 2½ miles. Do not turn off onto intersecting roads.

From the road end the trail climbs over Parker Canyon's sagebrush-covered moraine, an immense pile of loose material pushed down-canyon by an advancing glacier during the close of the last Ice Age. This is the only terminal (front) moraine in the region which remains whole and perfect, just as it was deposited thousands of years ago. The others, as near Grant Lake and Convict Lake, have all been cut through and partly washed away by streams. In Parker Canyon the stream cut through a lateral (side) moraine, leaving the terminal unchanged. Over the moraine the trail levels off and enters the forest surrounding Parker Lake, which lies in a U-shaped glacial canyon cut in highly colored rocks.

Walker Lake (7935 feet), Bloody Canyon, Mono Pass (10,600 feet).

Strenuous hike, 5 miles; or 7 miles from Walker Creek.

Starting Point: There are two approaches to Walker Lake: a short steep trail from the south to the lake's inlet; and a long but gradual walk from Walker Creek to the lake's outlet. Signs and maps may be confusing; follow these directions precisely. From Highway 395 follow the paved road toward Grant Lake for 1½ miles. Turn right (SW) onto the Parker Lake road and follow it ½ mile until it crosses a wide, graded, relatively straight road. This is the aqueduct road. Turn right (W) and follow the aqueduct road for one mile. Turn left (W) and drive two miles up a rough but passable road to its end. From this road end, a rocky trail climbs over the moraine bordering Walker Lake on the south, makes a steep traverse down to the lake, crosses the creek above the inlet, and there joins the Mono Trail.

The Walker Creek approach is at least two miles longer. Drive on the aqueduct road about 2½ miles. Just beyond Walker Creek, turn left and drive to the locked gate which marks the boundary of private land. Proceed on foot to the lake (named for a William J. Walker who settled near the lake, not for the famous Joseph R. Walker) and follow its right (N) shore to the beginning of the trail. This is part of the historic Mono Trail (see section on Roadsides for its history). The trail climbs steeply up a narrow, highly colored canyon to Lower Sardine Lake (9840 feet). About 600 feet higher is Upper Sardine Lake, and a gradual half-mile beyond is Summit Lake and Mono Pass. The old log cabins near the pass remain from the Ella Bloss Mine, contemporaneous with the May Lundy and the Mammoth mines. The *Mammoth City Herald,* fall 1879, predicted that thousands of men soon would be working at the adjoining Golden Crown Mine. But like so many other prospects, they never produced.

TIOGA

The Tioga Pass area is reached by the highest paved road across the Sierra; trails near the pass begin only slightly below timberline. Since all of the trails west of the pass are within Yosemite National Park, they are not discussed in this book. Information on park trails to places such as Gaylor, Young, Cathedral, and Elizabeth lakes or to peaks such as Mounts Lyell, Dana, Gibbs, and Conness can be obtained from the Tuolumne Meadows Ranger Station, about 30 minutes drive from Lee Vining.

Topographic maps needed: Mono Craters and Tuolumne Meadows quadrangles.

★ Saddlebag Lake (10,051 feet) to the high lake basin beyond (10,400 feet).

Intermediate hike, 3–4 miles.

Starting Point: West of Ellery Lake a graded road leads to the outlet of Saddlebag Lake reservoir.

From the road's end follow the trail going along the left (W) shore of Saddle-bag Lake,* then follow the mining road leading to a tungsten prospect at Steel-head Lake. Beyond the lake is a vast high-alpine meadow, open and gently sloping—ideal for cross-country wandering. Short-stemmed flowers bloom from August into late September. Evidence of glaciation is plentiful and well-preserved here—the rocks rounded, grooved and highly polished. The highest peak on the ridge to the southwest is Mount Conness; below it is Conness Glacier, one of the larger Sierra glaciers. East of Steelhead Lake is a low broad ridge which divides the streams flowing into Saddlebag Lake from those flowing north into Lundy Canyon. For a striking view into colorful, steep-sided Lundy Canyon follow one of the north-flowing streams down to the top of Lundy Falls (10,000 feet). Rock slides have obliterated the trail which once led down to Lundy Canyon.

LUNDY

Of all the canyons, Lundy Canyon, north of Lee Vining, has the most beautiful fall coloring. Red-gold and brilliant yellow aspen, their color intensified by the Jeffrey pine's deep green, gleam against Lundy's steep reddish cliffs in late September and early October.

Topographic maps needed: Bodie, Matterhorn Peak, and Tuolumne Meadows quadrangles.

★ Mill Creek (8050 feet) to Lundy Falls (8700 feet).

Easy hike, 1½ miles.

Starting Point: From the settlement at the west end of Lundy Lake the road continues 1¼ miles, rough but passable, and then forks. Park here. The left fork dead-ends at a nearby mining prospect. Walk up the right fork, which soon becomes a trail.

The trail follows the main stream of red-walled Lundy Canyon, through flower-filled meadows to the foot of Lundy falls. To see these five-hundred-foot falls in their glory, make this trip in June or early July.

Lundy Lake (7800 feet) to May Lundy Mine (9500 feet).

Intermediate hike, 3 miles.

Starting Point: About 3 miles after leaving Highway 395, the Lundy Canyon road forks. Take the left fork, which crosses the stream below the dam, and park near the gate.

Choose a cool day for this trip, enjoyable mostly for its historical interest. The rocky mining road, now abandoned, leads to the famous May Lundy Mine (see Background; also Roadsides, "Sideroad to Lundy Lake"). From the top of the cascades on, along the trail and also in the brush near the stream, watch for evidence of the old mining days—flumes, shacks, pipes, an old water-

---

* *Or arrange at the store for motorboat taxi service across the lake.*

wheel. Activity centered in a small settlement near Crystal Lake. No doubt the lake was named before milling processes had sullied its clear waters. Here were boarding houses, bunkhouses, cabins, and the 20-stamp mill. Though probably all the standing buildings date since 1900 (between 1898 and 1914 the mine was worked intermittently, and in 1937 tailings re-worked), there are remains of the very early days too. Machinery and stamps of the mill lie in a twisted mass near the largest mine dump. High up the canyon's west wall are several small dumps, timbers from the tramway, and several partly collapsed buildings. Just beyond the settlement is sparkling Lake Oneida, an old log and rock dam at its outlet. This is Lake Canyon; over the cliffs beyond Lake Oneida eight tons of machinery were hauled by sled to the Tioga Mine during the winter of 1882.

BEYOND CONWAY SUMMIT

Brief description of some trails north of Conway Summit is included; they can be reached easily and quickly enough for one-day trips.

Virginia Lakes basin is reached by a paved road which turns off from Highway 395 at Conway Summit. From the end of the road (9750 feet), eleven lakes are within an hour's hike. From the highest, Frog Lake (10,400 feet) a good trail leads to Summit Lake, connecting with the Green Lakes trail described below.

Green Lakes trail begins in a shaded, moist canyon and is reached by a dirt road turning west from Highway 395 about 9 miles north of Conway Summit. The trail passes Green, East, Nutter, Gilman, and Hoover lakes, ending at Summit Lake (10,203 feet), which is on the northeast boundary of Yosemite National Park. A park trail goes on down Return Creek and joins the Matterhorn Canyon trail in a beautiful and relatively little-traveled portion of the park.

Twin Lakes (Bridgeport). The commanding Sawtooth Ridge towers 5,000 feet above Bridgeport Valley. Pinnacles and small glaciers crown its summit. Famous among mountaineers for its clean, granite climbs, Sawtooth country has good trails for hikers. Horse, Tamarack, and Robinson creek trails all start from Twin Lakes (7096 feet). Another trail swings in, round and about from Buckeye Creek. Over the passes the trails drop down into the wild northern portion of Yosemite Park.

RECOMMENDED READING

Backpackers' trail guides are flooding off the presses at such a rate that any listing here would soon be out of date. Send yourself for the catalogues of the better publishers: Sierra Club Books, P.O. Box 7959, Rincon Annex, San Francisco 94020; Wilderness Press, 2440 Bancroft Way, Berkeley 94704. The Sierra Club classic, *Starr's Guide to the John Muir Trail,* has an old-fashioned quality—a loving approach to the mountains, less wordy, leaving more for you to discover for yourself—that I find refreshing and admirable. Its *Mountaineer's Guide* (1972) and *Climber's Guide* (1976) are the authoritative peak-climbing guides to the High Sierra. Wilderness Press guides cover the Sierra Nevada, other mountains in California, and the Pacific Crest Trail from Canada to Mexico. They are accurate, reliable, and blessed with exceptionally good maps. Two superior books on general backpacking are: *New Complete Walker* by Colin Fletcher, 1974; and *Backpacking One Step at a Time* by Harvey Manning, 1973.

Geologic Story

THE DARK GRAY AND brown cliffs encircling Convict Lake have been looked at and tramped over by several generations of people, as have the similar rocks of McGee Mountain and near the mouth of McGee Canyon. A few geologists guessed that these rocks were unusually old, but did anyone else imagine that they are the very oldest in the entire Sierra Nevada? Such they proved to be when, several years ago, fossils were discovered in them and dated as about five hundred million years old. Perhaps such great age becomes more meaningful if we consider that man has existed on earth for less than two million years.

Much of the story explaining the Sierra's rugged setting can be deciphered from its rocks. Picture a vast shallow sea—those five hundred million years ago—a part of the Pacific Ocean covering much of the West, including what is now eastern California. Salt water covered the region for at least one hundred million years. During that time mud, silt, and sand were deposited on the ocean floor in horizontal layers or beds (figure 14, *a*), finally accumulating to a thickness of more than twelve thousand feet. Today this same process takes place as rivers carry dirt and sand grains to the ocean; ocean currents distribute and winnow them into the layers of mud, silt, and sand now accumulating on the ocean floor. The formation of sedimentary beds can be simply illustrated by putting a handful of mixed silt, sand, and gravel into a jar of water and shaking it. The sediments will settle out in layers according to the density and size of the particles.

Evidence obtained in the Mammoth Lakes area—also in the Hawthorne-Tonopah area and the Inyo Mountains—indicates that the land then rose above the sea and remained so for a long time. Accompanying this period of uplift, the sediments—now compacted and hardened into mudstone, siltstone, and sandstone—were subjected to great stresses that squeezed the layers into folds (figure 14, b). The land, now standing above the sea, was vulnerable to erosion. Rain, creeks, and rivers wore away the rocks. Water and gravity transported the rock particles from the higher altitudes to the lower and eventually deposited them far away in the ocean. Similarly, the rocks of the Ritter Range are at this moment being slowly worn away and their constituents carried by the San Joaquin River to the ocean through San Francisco Bay. Actually only the finest particles reach the Bay, the pebbles and gravels being deposited upstream where the current is not swift enough to carry them farther. The coarse materials eventually break down into smaller and smaller particles until nearly all is finally swept to the sea.

Again the region sank beneath the sea, remaining submerged seventy-five million years. The sea floor was blanketed by new layers of sediments, this time mostly silt, totalling a minimum of six thousand feet (figure 14, c). Crinoids, or sea lilies (see figure 12, trail section), lived in this ocean, their remains constituting a significant part of a thick limestone bed exposed today in Laurel and

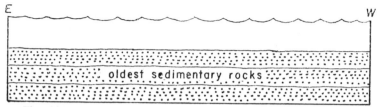

a. The oldest sedimentary rocks (Ordovician) in the Mammoth Lakes area were deposited in the sea about 500 million years ago.

b. 400 million years ago the land rose above the sea. The oldest sedimentary rocks were folded, and were tilted to the west.

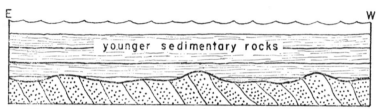

c. Younger sedimentary rocks (Pennsylvanian-Permian) were deposited in the sea about 300 million years ago.

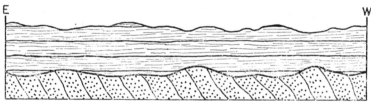

d. About 225 million years ago the land again rose above the sea, and some of the younger sedimentary rocks were stripped off by stream erosion.

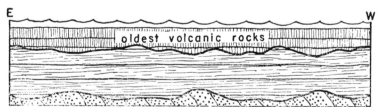

e. The oldest volcanic rocks (Triassic?-Jurassic) were deposited in the sea about 190 million years ago.

Figure 14. Geologic history of Mammoth Lakes region.

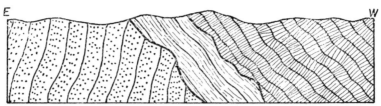

f. About 100 million years ago the land rose above the sea for the third time. The rocks were folded, and again were tilted westward.

g. After the folding shown in the preceding figure, fluid granitic rock invaded the folded sedimentary and volcanic rocks. Heat given off by the granitic rock metamorphosed the older rocks.

h. Streams cut through the older rocks and exposed much of the now-cooled and crystallized granitic rock, leaving disconnected remnants of the former "roof" as islands in a sea of granitic rock.

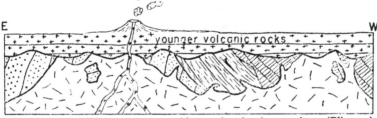

i. About 3.5 million years ago, widespread volcanic eruptions (Pliocene) commenced to blanket the area with lava flows and showers of fragments. Eruptions continued sporadically, the most recent being the explosion that ripped out the Inyo Craters about 1400 A.D.

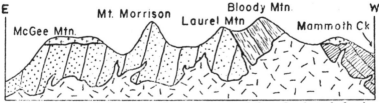

j. Streams and glaciers removed vast amounts of the volcanic rock, leaving only remnants scattered through the mountainous areas. This is a diagrammatic cross-section of the local terrain today, as seen by an observer at Mammoth Lakes looking south.

upper Convict canyons. The remains of brachiopods, clamlike contemporaries of the crinoids, also are found in the crinoid-bearing beds and in other rocks deposited during this submergence.

The sea floor was elevated once again, but this time stresses did not develop enough to fold the rocks and they remained essentially horizontal. Subsequent stream erosion washed away part of the newly formed sedimentary rock (figure 14, *d*). Accompanied by widespread volcanic eruptions, the land for the third time again sank beneath the sea. The eruptions persisted intermittently for perhaps ninety million years, depositing layer upon layer of volcanic material —a mass nearly five miles thick (figure 14, *e*). Much of the material erupted as dust or sand-sized particles, although some fragments two to six inches across were intermixed, and was deposited directly in the sea. When the land rose again and the sea retreated once more, the volcanic rock layers and all the older sedimentary rocks beneath them were subjected to enormous stresses that squeezed and folded them until all the layers were tilted nearly on edge (figure 14 *f*).

After the rocks were folded, a great mass of molten granitic material invaded them tens of thousands of feet below the surface, in some places shouldering aside the rocks to make room for itself, in others dissolving its way into the folded rocks by dislodging huge fragments and partially or wholly assimilating them (figure 14, *g*). The molten material remained at such great depth that it took a very long time to cool and solidify; recent laboratory work suggests that it required several million years. The solidified material is called granitic rock or granite, the commonest rock of the Sierra. The great heat absorbed by the overlying sedimentary and volcanic rocks was sufficient to cause new minerals to crystallize in them at the expense of their original minerals, locally changing completely the appearance and character of the rocks. This is essentially the process of metamorphism; the resulting rocks are called metamorphic rocks. The preceding events (folding, invasion of molten granitic rock, metamorphism of the folded rocks, and cooling of the granitic rock) occurred during an interval of perhaps seventy million years. All during this time, streams and rivers were eroding away the deformed metamorphic rocks until the region finally became an area of low, gently rolling hills, and much of the now-solid granitic rock was exposed at the surface. Remnant patches in a mass of granitic rock were all that remained of the original metamorphic "roof" (figure 14, *h*).

After the granitic rock was exposed, widespread volcanic outbursts again occurred, covering the area with flows and showers of fragments (figure 14, *i*). Though there is little evidence left of the total thickness of these deposits, near San Joaquin Mountain a section more than two thousand feet thick still remains. As the frequency of the eruptions diminished, the range we now call the Sierra Nevada began to rise along fractures, or faults, chiefly along the eastern margin of the range—a tilting westward of a 430-mile-long, 70-mile-wide block of the earth's crust.

Early in the uplift of the Sierra, the earth's climate became cooler and more moist. Each winter brought snow that fell on deep snows remaining from preceding seasons. As a result of continuous accumulation, the deeper snow was compacted into ice and finally began to creep or flow slowly, as glaciers, down the canyons. Thus was the Ice Age born, the time when ice covered half of

Figure 15. Simplified diagram showing how the Sierra rose along faults that mark the east boundary of the range.

North America and many other parts of the world. Before the development of glaciers, the Sierra probably consisted of rolling hills separated by rather narrow, shallow stream valleys (figure 16, *a*), in contrast to the sharp ridges and deep, wide canyons of today. The stream valleys that guided the first glaciers were widened and deepened eventually by glacial scouring, until the topography resembled that shown in figure 16, *b*. At least four and possibly six times during

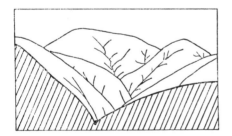

Figure 16. *a*. Narrow stream valleys before glaciation.
b. Widened by glaciation, valleys become characteristically U-shaped.

the Ice Age the glaciers melted back to their sources or cirques—theater-shaped basins at the head of glaciated valleys—in response to climatic changes. Following each of the melt-backs, or recessions, the climate apparently became cooler and moister again and the glaciers again advanced down the valleys. A record of these retreats is preserved in the forms of the huge arc-shaped piles of rock debris, or moraines, deposited by the glaciers at the mouths of each of the major canyons along the range front (see photo section). Other traces of the glaciers can be found throughout the area—the rounded form of ridges and canyon walls, the grooves and scratches ground into them, and boulders of all sizes deposited by the glaciers as they melted back.

ROCKS

All the rocks that constitute the outer shell of the earth are classified into three great categories: *sedimentary rocks*—those composed of clays, sands, and gravels that were once transported by running water, ice, wind, or gravity and then accumulated in oceans or in basins on land; *igneous rocks*—once-molten rocks that welled up from the earth's interior; *metamorphic rocks*—those which, because of heat and pressure, were recrystallized from original sedimentary, igneous, or earlier metamorphic rocks. Examples of all three classes abound in the Mammoth region.

SEDIMENTS AND SEDIMENTARY OR "LAYERED" ROCKS

In the area depicted on the geologic map, most of the sedimentary material is unconsolidated. It includes the loose silt, sand, and gravel that are the floors of the large valleys, and also the gravel and boulders comprising the impressive glacial moraines which block the mouths of all the major canyons.

Most sediments eventually harden into rocks. A good example of sedimentary rock can be found throughout a large area west of Alkali Lakes, toward Benton Crossing. The area is underlain by sandstone long ago deposited in a lake as sand by streams flowing from the Sierra. The western edge of the sandstone marks the shoreline of a prehistoric lake that filled Long Valley during the middle of the Ice Age. The lake basin was similar to the present form of Long Valley, its deepest part being near the present course of Owens River as evidenced by the conspicuous mounds of grayish white clay (some of them containing tiny shells of organisms which lived in the ancient lake) near Benton Crossing. The same streams that deposited the sand (now sandstone) close to the shore also carried the clay, but because clay particles are so small and light they drifted out to the deeper, quiet water before settling out. Most of the clay has since been stripped from the valley by erosion, only remnant mounds remaining of a once-extensive layer.

The same processes involved in the formation of these ancient lake deposits are active today. If, say, Convict Lake could be sliced in two lengthwise so that a cross-section of the sediments on the bottom could be seen (figure 18), the coarse gravels would be found near the small delta at its inlet, grading outward into finer material in the deep center of the lake.

Figure 18. Segregation of lake deposits.

Igneous Rocks

Igneous rocks occur as two distinct kinds—volcanic and granitic (or plutonic). Though most granitic rocks are commonly called granite, *granitic* (or *plutonic*) refers to a family of related rocks, true granite being only one of its many members. Although many volcanic rocks have nearly the same chemical composition as granitic rocks, their appearance is strikingly different, chiefly because of the size of their minerals. Granitic rocks are composed entirely of interlocking crystals averaging at least one-sixteenth to one-eighth inch long; volcanic rocks typically contain only a small proportion of such crystals, their remainder consisting of natural glass or of material so fine-grained that its particles cannot be distinguished even with the aid of a microscope.

To understand the dissimilar appearance of the two kinds of igneous rocks, granitic rock can best be considered as volcanic rock that failed to reach the earth's surface. Both are believed to have originated as a fluid deep within the earth. But unlike the volcanic rocks which erupted on the earth's surface and then cooled quickly as earth and air conducted heat away from the flowing rock, the plutonic "magma" was unable to force its way through the earth's crust and consequently cooled and crystallized slowly at depths measurable in tens of thousands of feet. The slow cooling process allowed crystals to form and grow until the molten rock was completely transformed into the solid mass of interlocking crystals we see today in granite and other plutonic rocks. Recent laboratory research suggests that the time involved in the cooling process is measurable in millions of years. Granitic rock is visible today only because erosion eventually removed the great thickness of overlying rock.

Volcanic Rocks—Most of the volcanic rocks occupy a large area north and east of Mammoth Lakes. Their color often tells much about the nature of their eruption.

Dark-colored volcanic rocks are exposed at numerous places along the road from Highway 395 to the Mammoth Lakes Post Office. The rough black rock projecting jaggedly above the sagebrush once flowed as lava from vents probably less than a mile from the Post Office and since buried under the great thickness of glacial debris which covers most of Mammoth Creek's valley. Lava of this type, called basalt, commonly erupts with less violence than the light-colored varieties. Close inspection of the basalt reveals many features typical of dark-colored volcanic rock. The surface of the flow is full of bubbles, or "vesicles," and is ropy, somewhat similar to taffy in appearance. Many of the vesicles are lined with a hard white material, which was deposited there by gases streaming up through the lava before it cooled completely. On a freshly broken surface glass-clear feldspar crystals, some nearly an inch across, can be seen within a mass of extremely fine-grained material. These crystals grew while the fluid rock was still deep within the earth, long before there were any signs of eruption.

Eruption of the light-colored volcanic rocks, which formed at a lower temperature than the basalt, commonly resulted in the formation of symmetrical protrusions called *volcanic domes* (see photo section). Although many of the domes stand hundreds of feet above the immediate landscape, they are dwarfed by the towering peaks of the Sierra and consequently many of them go unnoticed. Perhaps the best place to examine light-colored volcanic rocks is at the dome about three and three-quarter miles west of Highway 395, on the Deadman Creek road. This dome, formed of a light gray rock called *rhyolite,* is probably one of the youngest in the area. Erosion has not yet modified its shape nor has vegetation become established. The light weight of this rock shows it to be of a much lower density than the basalt, partly as a result of its spongelike texture. Some of the rocks look much like solidified froth, while others are solid glass ranging in color from light to dark gray. Some of the glass is black and is called *obsidian.* Including such a dark rock as obsidian in the light-colored group may seem inconsistent. Obsidian, nevertheless, is typically associated with light-colored volcanic rocks and is similar to them in chemical composition; it rarely occurs with the dark-colored rocks such as basalt. Rhyolite often has a layered appearance, a relic pattern developed when the rock was fluid. Obsidian generally occurs as layers, streaks, or pods in the light-colored, frothy rhyolite. There may be a few very small white or clear crystals of feldspar and clear quartz, and much of the rock may be sprinkled with tiny black flakes of mica.

Unlike basaltic lava, which flows readily from its vent, rhyolitic lava is extremely viscous and is often semiplastic or solid by the time it emerges at the surface, thus readily plugging its vent much like a cork in a bottle. This allows gas pressure below to build up a tremendous head, which may be relieved by violent explosions and the eruption of showers of pea- to walnut-size pumice fragments and fine ash which may blanket the country for miles. The pumice, found almost everywhere in this area, resembles the frothy rhyolite seen in some of the large blocks around the dome's base, although it is generally lighter weight and will even float for a time on water. During the active life of a rhyolitic volcano, the viscous lava may become sufficiently fluid to flow sluggishly for short distances; much of the light colored volcanic rock just north of the Mammoth Post Office formed in this way. There are similar stubby flows associated with the Mono Craters, which are also rhyolite domes. Often the formation of domes marks the last activity of rhyolite volcanoes, although sometimes domes may succeed each other many times, each time being destroyed by violent explosions. The explosions frequently develop large craters, within which a new dome may arise—as at Panum Crater, the northernmost of the Mono Craters.

The Mono Craters, the Inyo Craters, and the young domes in the Mammoth area are in almost perfect north-south alignment. It is likely that all of the domes and craters along this line were formed at about the same time and from the same subterranean lava reservoir. The remarkable alignment suggests that a large fracture, or a narrow zone of fissures, provided channels through which the fluid rock reached the earth's surface.

Granitic Rocks—Granitic rocks are exposed in the canyons of Sherwin, Hilton, and Rock Creeks and on Mammoth Crest; they become progressively more abundant toward the west, near the core of the Sierra Nevada. Though exposures of granitic rock in place are not easily reached without hiking, granitic boulders abound in nearly all the glacial moraines and can also be seen around Rock Creek, Tom's Place, and along the road from Highway 395 to Mammoth Lakes. Nearly all the granitic rocks in this area are light gray, some almost white. They are readily distinguished from the light-colored volcanic rocks because they are composed entirely of visible crystals, while the volcanic rocks consist of very fine-grained material and glass, with only a scattering of crystals that can be seen with the unaided eye. The rock's gray color is caused by a sprinkling of small black crystals of mica and the mineral hornblende, which occur among the cloudy quartz and light-gray to pale flesh-colored feldspar crystals.

METAMORPHIC ROCKS

Metamorphic rocks—rocks which have been changed (metamorphosed) from their original state—in the Mammoth Lakes area originated from the older sedimentary and volcanic rocks that covered the intruding molten granitic rock and that were subjected for a long time to intense heat and pressure. Today, most of the metamorphic rocks have been removed by stream and glacial erosion; those that remain appear as islands in a sea of granitic rock. To distinguish these rocks from their younger, unmetamorphosed relatives, they will be referred to below as *metasedimentary* and *metavolcanic* rocks.

Metamorphic rocks, widespread in the Mammoth Lakes area, form most of the high peaks that define the local skyline. Many are conspicuously layered, with beds a few inches to several feet in thickness. They range in color from the light gray metamorphosed limestone (marble) of Mammoth Rock, through shades of brown and brownish red as those exposed on the aptly named Bloody Mountain, to the typical dark gray of the metavolcanic rocks that form the southern two-thirds of Mammoth Crest. Although all these rocks originally accumulated as nearly horizontal layers of sediments, enormous forces preceding and accompanying the granitic rocks' emplacement metamorphosed and slowly deformed them until the beds now stand nearly vertical. The metamorphic rocks are in two distinct bodies, the metasediments to the east and the younger metavolcanics adjacent to the west. To understand why the rocks are arranged so regularly, examine the sequence of cross-sections (figure 14). Prior to their last folding, the layered rocks were stacked up very much like a deck of cards. The major effect of the folding was to tilt the entire pile toward the west (figure 14, *f*) with the top (younger) layers west of the bottom (older) layers. Regardless of where one stands on the metamorphic formations, the younger rocks always lie to the west.

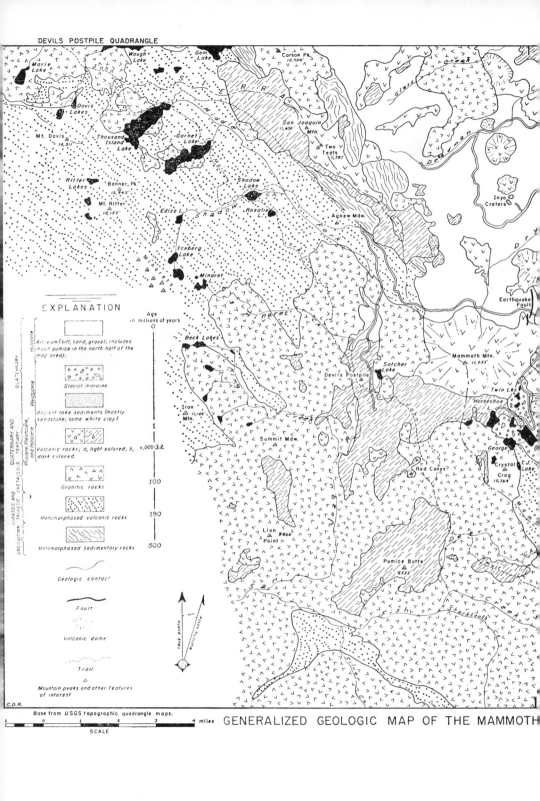

EXPLANATION

Age
in millions of years
0

Alluvium (silt, sand, gravel; includes
much pumice in the north half of the
map area).

Glacial moraine

Ancient lake sediments (mostly
sandstone; some white clay).

1

Volcanic rocks; a, light colored; b,
dark colored.   <.001-3.2

100

Granitic rocks

190

Metamorphosed volcanic rocks

500

Metamorphosed sedimentary rocks

Geologic contact

Fault

Volcanic dome

Trail

Mountain peaks and other features
of interest

HOLOCENE
PLEISTOCENE
QUATERNARY
PLIOCENE PLEISTOCENE,
QUATERNARY AND TERTIARY
and HOLOCENE
JURASSIC, TRIASSIC CRETACEOUS
ORDOVICIAN

TRUE NORTH
MAGNETIC NORTH

Base from USGS topographic quadrangle maps.

SCALE

0   1   2   3   4 miles

GENERALIZED GEOLOGIC MAP OF THE MAMMOTH

LAKES-DEVILS POSTPILE AREA, CALIFORNIA

Geology of the Mt. Morrison quad. by C.D.Rinehart & D.C.Ross,
1955; Devils Postpile by C.D.Rinehart & N.K.Huber, 1958.

Most of the metasediments are very fine grained, having been deposited as mud and silt in a shallow seaway covering eastern California and Nevada.

The metavolcanic rocks are unlike most of the younger volcanic rocks described above. Only a very few originated as molten lava. Instead, the material of which they are made exploded from volcanos and vents, and fell to the earth as fine ash laden with small feldspar and quartz crystals and with rock fragments. At least some, and perhaps much of this material fell into a generally quiet body of water, for many of the resulting rocks are bedded—showing the action of gentle currents which winnowed the volcanic material and sorted it into thin laminations of fine and coarse material. Also, beds of limestone a few feet thick, some containing fossil clams, occur here and there within the metavolcanics, further indicating the existence of an ancient sea.

The most common metavolcanic rock is a dark gray fine-grained rock, inset with abundant white or gray feldspar crystals averaging slightly less than a sixteenth of an inch across and with dark rock fragments averaging an inch or less across. Rock of this type is well exposed along the trails to Duck Lake and Shadow Lake. Probably the most spectacular rock in the area, common between Shadow Lake and Lake Ediza, is the metavolcanic breccia (pronounced "bretchia") which occurs in beds measurable in tens to hundreds of feet thick. This breccia consists of many angular rock fragments, an inch to more than a foot across, cemented together by a very fine-grained material. It is likely that the fine-grained material erupted explosively as ash while the large fragments were ripped from the throat of a volcano and hurled out. The large size of the fragments suggests that they were deposited near the site of eruption.

Since the changes wrought by metamorphism are often obscure, they can best be seen with the aid of a microscope. The principal change is the growth of new minerals, mostly microscopic in size, in response to heat and pressure; the chemical composition and the general appearance of most of the rocks is essentially unchanged.

RECOMMENDED READING

Hill, Mary. *Geology of the Sierra Nevada*. Berkeley: University of California Press, 1975. Cloth and paper. With this one little book in hand and time to hike and drive to suggested locations, one can happily learn much about Sierra geology.

Pearl, Richard M. *How to Know the Minerals and Rocks*. New York: McGraw Hill, 1955. Cloth and paper. Superbly illustrated guide to 125 minerals and rocks.

Pough, Frederick H. *A Field Guide to Rocks and Minerals*. Boston: Houghton Mifflin, second edition, 1955. The standard, authoritative guide.

The excellent booklet on the Devils Postpile, revised by Wymond Eckhardt, is scheduled for publication in 1976. New, authoritative information on the Postpile's origin and on nearby explosions and eruptions. Available at the Postpile.

Climates and Life Zones

EXTREME CLIMATES—THE heat and dryness of the high desert, the cold and snow of the arctic—are only a few miles apart on the Sierra's steep eastern slope. Annual snowfall at the Mammoth ski tows averages over forty feet (water content over 48″); nearby Long Valley is lucky to have ten inches of rain. On the first of June it is still winter at the lakes above nine thousand feet— willows bare, lakes frozen, and few birds nesting. Yet only twenty minutes by car to the east and three thousand feet lower in Long Valley, spring has already gone and the hot summer begun— some flowers gone to seed and young birds already out of their nests.

The Sierra Nevada is one of the world's great mountain ranges, in height as well as length. Its crest towers nearly two miles above Owens Valley, more than one mile above Long Valley. Twelve peaks exceed fourteen thousand feet, rising almost three miles above the Central Valley to the west. Such a colossal mountain range has not one, but *several* climates.

A basic fact governing climate is that air becomes colder the higher one goes. At high altitudes ice forms on airplane wings; in the high mountains, rain often falls as hail or snow. Daily temperatures in the High Sierra may be thirty to eighty degrees colder than in the Central Valley. The ground itself is colder, slowing down plant growth. Snow covers the ground seven to nine months, making a short growing season. Rainfall too is affected, for as clouds heavy with water vapor are blown eastward from the Pacific, they are deflected upward several miles to cross the Sierra. Increasing coldness makes more and more of their moisture condense; rainfall increases up the western Sierra slope until it reaches a maximum at about 6500 feet in altitude. Above that, rainfall (measured as water content of the snow) decreases, for the clouds have already dropped much of their moisture. As the clouds soar over the Sierra crest and cross the eastern slope, they have little moisture left. Consequently the eastern slope is more arid, and the desert ranges and desert valleys beyond are said to be in the "rain shadow" of the Sierra. All this causes tremendous climatic variations up the Sierra slope.

Each climate has its own assemblage or community of plants and animals that can live only under the special conditions of temperature, moisture, and soil found there. These conditions result in "life zones," ranging from the desert of Owens Valley to the arctic cold of the Sierra crest. Among plants there is a regular progression from the heat-tolerant forms at the low altitudes to the cold-tolerant at the high altitudes. For example, sagebrush flourishes in the desert, and a four-inch dwarf willow above timberline. One is adapted to heat, the other to cold; neither survives in the other's climate. The progression of climates and plant communities can be recognized readily by the changes of tree species. A generalized profile of the eastern Sierra slope shows the following changes.

85

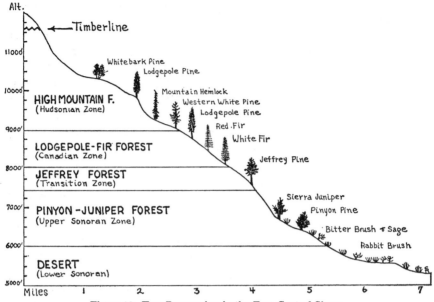

Figure 19. Tree Progression in the East Central Sierra.

Animals too distribute themselves according to climatic zones. For example, in the typical Lower Sonoran life zone as at Lone Pine and Manzanar—open desert prairie country with creosote bush, where summer temperatures are high—certain mammals such as the antelope ground squirrel and the desert coyote live, but in no other zones. Along Sherwin grade, where the juniper and pinyon pine grow, is the Upper Sonoran zone. Typical Upper Sonoran mammals are the black-tailed jack rabbit, the Panamint kangaroo rat, and the Townsend ground squirrel. Look for them again among the pinyon at Casa Diablo. A little higher is the Transition life zone, marked by mountain mahogany and Jeffrey pine. Here the least chipmunk lives.

As the higher elevations of Mammoth Lakes, Crestview, or June Lake are approached, there will be fir trees, lodgepole pine, and quaking aspen, all characteristic of the Canadian zone. The climate of this zone is ideal for summer camping, not so chilly as the next higher zone yet cooler than the sometimes hot and dry Transition zone. The greatest variety of mammals occurs in the Canadian zone, among them the lodgepole chipmunk, golden mantled ground squirrel, chickaree, porcupine, and the Belding ground squirrel. Actually, more Belding ground squirrels will be seen in the next higher and still cooler Hudsonian life zone. Stands of lodgepole pine, mountain hemlock, and finally whitebark pine (which at timberline often consists of little else than low shrublike thickets) indicate fairly well the extent of the Hudsonian zone. Here also live the chickarees, white-tailed jack rabbits, pikas (especially in talus slides), marmots, golden mantled ground squirrels, Inyo mule deer, and the little Alpine chipmunks.

The barren areas and rocky slopes from timberline to the very crest of the Sierra are in the Alpine-Arctic zone which has scattered dwarf plants, seldom over four inches high. This is the coldest zone of all and has the shortest growing season; flowers must grow, bloom, and produce seeds all in a few weeks. Few mammals can survive the rigorous climate. During the summer months the Alpine chipmunk, pika, marmot, and white-tailed jack rabbit extend their range into the Alpine-Arctic zone. Occasionally the mountain coyote and Inyo mule deer also range into this zone. The latter two are wide ranging species and, on the east slope, range rather freely into and across Canadian, Hudsonian, and Alpine-Arctic zones all summer.

There are variations, of course, from the ideal progression. If the slope is abrupt as in the eastern Sierra, the zones may be so jammed together that one of them is missing. Most zones have fingerlike extensions upward and downward into the next zones. For example, in a forest of Jeffrey pine there may be a ribbon of lodgepole and aspen following down a stream. Since lodgepole live in a colder climate, they will be among the Jeffrey only if there is a cold pocket in the warmer Jeffrey climate. Such pockets or ribbons are often caused by cold air draining down canyon bottoms or by differences in exposure to the sun. Occasionally the sequence of trees may be upside down, as when a shady slope or ravine dominated by hemlock and lodgepole is topped by a sunny slope or ridge of juniper. Each zone, then, is actually a mosaic of microclimates—small areas having climates that differ from the general zonal pattern because of exposure to the sun, protection from wind, or unusual moisture. Despite these variations, the concept of life zones is very useful. The diagram represents the general elevations where the different trees grow abundantly, though locally some may range higher and lower.

Notice in the diagram that the distance from desert to arctic climate is only six miles. The same changes on the more gradual west slope of the Sierra may cover sixty miles. The steepness of the eastern Sierra slope accounts for the unique and often spectacularly contrasting variety of scenery and vegetation within short distances. The great variety of soils and climates accounts also for the great variety of flowers and the wide range of growing and blooming seasons. Growing seasons vary from six months at 6,000 feet to two months or less on the high slopes, and the length of the flowering season often depends on how long snow remains in spring.

Trees

FOLLOWING ARE THE TEN MOST COMMON trees of the eastern Sierra, grouped from lower to higher altitude, as on the diagram on p. 86. Other trees that may be encountered in the area are: copper birch, willow and cottonwood in the lower altitudes near water; mountain mahogany on hot, dry slopes; limber pine near timberline.

PINYON-JUNIPER FOREST. Trees scattered, ground covered with sagebrush and other desert shrubs.

Pinyon Pine (*Pinus monophylla*)

Needles single, about 1 inch long. Cones up to 3 inches long.

As you drive north from Bishop, there are few trees except in stream-beds or near houses. But as the road climbs Sherwin Grade, the high-desert country begins where short, squat, gray-green trees grow—the pinyon pines that produce the pine nuts sold in many stores in late fall. These nuts were the most important food of the Paiutes, each Indian band having its own pine-nut territory. Trespassing was resented, and was the most common cause of quarreling among otherwise peaceful Paiute groups. Pine-nut crops are irregular, however, and a poor crop meant a hard winter and even starvation for the Paiutes. In good years, some of the Paiutes moved from the valleys up to the pinyon belt to live during fall and winter, unlike most mountain Indians who *descend* to the valleys in winter.

Of all the pines of the world, only the pinyon has a single needle; that is, only one needle to the bundle. Its wood makes a quick and very hot fire.

Sierra Juniper (*Juniperus occidentalis*)

Leaves scalelike, ⅛ inch long. Bark light reddish brown, stringy. Berries ½ inch, blue-black with grayish bloom.

About a mile up the Valentine Lake trail is one of the few stands of tall, symmetrical junipers, beautiful examples of this tough rugged tree. More commonly it is short and scrubby looking. On exposed slopes where it has no protection against windstorms, often its trunk is exceedingly large for its height, its top splintered, and its thick limbs grotesquely twisted and broken with only a few tufts of green showing that it still lives. Its richly colored bark shining in the early morning sun, as below Shadow Lake, is a sight worth hiking for.

Quaking Aspen (*Populus tremuloides*)

Light green leaves that tremble in the slightest breeze. Bark white and smooth, though rough and black at the base of old trees.

This is the tree that comes into its glory in late September, when its leaves glow red and golden. Lundy, McGee, and Hilton canyons have particularly extensive displays of brilliant color. The French trappers of the west's early days had a legend that the Cross was fashioned from aspen wood, and that all aspens have trembled since that day. Less colorfully, perhaps, science explains the aspen's quaking in the nature of its leafstalk. Besides being longer than the leaf, it is

89

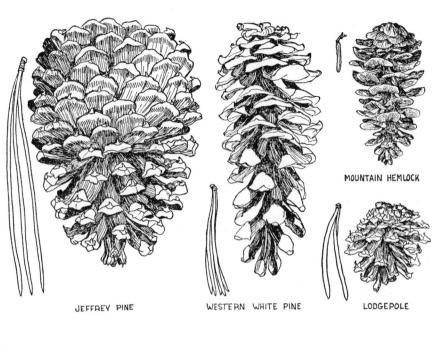

JEFFREY PINE   WESTERN WHITE PINE   MOUNTAIN HEMLOCK

LODGEPOLE

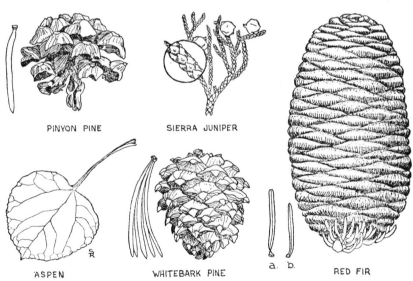

PINYON PINE   SIERRA JUNIPER

ASPEN   WHITEBARK PINE   a. b.   RED FIR

flattened perpendicular to the leaf's plane, thus acting as a pivot and causing the leaves to quiver in the gentlest wind.

Aspens prefer damp areas, but since they can tolerate a variety of climates, they are not good indicator trees (of altitude or forest progression). From the sagebrush country, where they often grow large and straight along streams, they range to the upper limit of the lodgepole–fir forest, where usually they are scrubby and bent from heavy snows. Near campsites, the bark of many aspens is rough and black with irregular scars, rather than a shining white—the trees' attempts to heal the deep wounds inflicted by pocket knives.

Aspen have a peculiar ability to reproduce by means of root suckers, which gives them a temporary advantage when a forest is swept by fire.

JEFFREY FOREST. Open forest of tall trees. Trunks of mature trees clear
   of branches for many feet above the ground. Little underbrush.

Jeffrey Pine (*Pinus Jeffreyi*)
   Needles 3 in a bundle, up to 6 inches long. Cones measure 6–10 inches. Bark
   of mature trees cracked into irregular reddish brown plates, like very large
   jigsaw pieces.

The vanilla-bark pine, as the Jeffrey is called sometimes, is the three-needle pine of the eastern slope; its counterpart on the western Sierra slope is the ponderosa or yellow pine, familiar to Yosemite Park visitors. The differences between the two are slight. The bark of the Jeffrey has a distinct vanilla or pineapple odor. Its cone is larger. Holding both hands around a cone is a simple test. If the prickles hurt, probably it is a ponderosa cone; if they curve in and consequently do not hurt, it is a Jeffrey cone.

LODGEPOLE-FIR FOREST. The densest forest, with crowded young trees
   shouldering their way up toward the sunlight.

White Fir (*Abies concolor*)
   Needles single, usually more than 1 inch long. Cones upright on top branches,
   up to 5 inches long. Bark of young trees silvery; of older trees, ashy gray.

Many summer campers find the climate of the Jeffrey-white fir forest most to their liking. It is cooler and greener than the lower sagebrush country, yet warmer than the sometimes nippy red-fir climate. At about 7500 feet in elevation, white fir gives way to red fir. If the trees are large, the two can be distinguished readily. Break off a small piece of bark; if the fresh surface is tan

Figure 21. Comparison of white fir needles, left, and red fir needles, right.

it is white fir, if deep red it is red fir. Determining young firs requires close examination of their needles. A white fir needle has a half-twist at its base, where it joins the twig; a red fir needle is curved but *not twisted* at its base.

Lodgepole Pine (*Pinus Murrayana*). Also called Tamarack Pine.

Needles 2 in a bundle. Cones up to 2 inches long. Bark thin, ¼ inch.

The needles of this tree, the only two-needle pine in the area, are broad and stiff. Since lodgepole cones are both pitch-free and small they are ideal for decorating Christmas packages. The dead lower branches remain on the tree a long time, hence a lodgepole forest looks more scraggly than most others. For the same reason, it is usually easy to find dry lodgepole wood even in wet weather. Old fallen pine trees also provide good firewood. Much of the trunk may be decayed but the pine "knots" where the limbs branched out are usually hard and full of pitch. The knots pull out easily and make a quick, very hot fire. The Plains Indians used lodgepole trunks for their teepee poles; the pioneers for their log cabins. It was valued because its trunk—in some varieties—is straight and tapers little, it has few large branches, and its thin bark is easy to peel.

Red Fir (*Abies magnifica*)

Needles single, up to 1¼ inches long. Cones upright on top branches, up to 8 inches long. Bark of mature trees up to 6 inches thick, deep red inside, red-brown outside.

Beware of camping under a dead fir-snag, for firs are very susceptible to rot. A little wind may topple over a thirty-foot length. Foresters sometimes refer to fir snags as widow-makers and make a point of clearing them out of campgrounds. A dead pine is much less dangerous, its pitch helping to resist decay. During severe storms, pines may crash down roots and all, but they very seldom break off as do the firs.

The bark of a dead red fir giant is a prize well worth hunting for. It burns slowly, and makes glowing long-lasting coals. (The famous Yosemite firefall fire was made of red fir bark.) Fir cones (red or white) seldom are found on the ground. They disintegrate on the tree, the scales peeling off and the seeds dropping down, leaving the center stems standing upright on the top branches like candles. It is sometimes hard to distinguish red from white fir (*which see*). The red fir is often called silver-tip (prized as a Christmas tree), after the silvery green new growth on the tips of its branches.

HIGH MOUNTAIN FOREST. Much of the ground bare, occasional low shrubs and flowers. Near timberline, most trees are twisted and stunted by wind and snow.

Western White Pine (*Pinus monticola*)

Needles 3–5 in a bundle, slender, 2–4 inches long. Cones up to 8 inches.

This pine, also called the silver pine, is most easily identified by its cones, which hang from the tips of its branches like bunches of bananas. On a mature tree, it is often impossible to get a sample of the needles, for the trunk is clear of branches for many feet above the ground. In the Sierra, the western white pine intermingles with lodgepole and red fir and is not abundant. The match industry has found its even-grained, soft, strong light-weight wood ideal for making matches and uses this wood almost exclusively.

Mountain Hemlock (*Tsuga mertensiana*)

Needles single, up to ¾ inches long. Cones 2–3 inches.

Above 9500 feet the mountain hemlock is in its element. Occasionally it is found lower, but then always on shaded north slopes or in cold canyons. It can be identified easily by its bent and drooping tip (fir and pine tips are stiff and erect). Hemlock limbs grow down to its base, and the ends of its branches droop.

It is a fascinating experience in June to see a young hemlock, bent over at right angles under the packed snow of winter, suddenly be released from the weight as the sun melts the snow and then straighten up in a few hours.

Whitebark Pine (*Pinus albicaulis*)

Needles 5 in a bundle, up to 1½ inches long. Cones on the trees purple, up to 3 inches long, with conspicuous drops of shiny pitch. Bark silver, or reddish silver if wind-whipped, except at the base of old trees, where it is rough and black.

This is the creeping pine of timberline, often dwarfed and misshapen, yet surviving in a climate where few other trees and only a few small plants live. It usually grows in a cluster, with several trunks coming from a common center. Its flexibility helps it survive storms and snows which would break the branches of a less pliable tree. If you choose to camp or sleep under a whitebark's low branches, which can give amazingly good protection in timberline's wind-swept country, treat it kindly. The foot-long twig you snap off carelessly may have taken twenty years to reach its stubby length. Covered with snow seven months or more, withstanding gale winds, and blessed with few days warm enough for growth, a whitebark may grow less than one-half inch a year. Mature cones seldom are found on the ground intact, for nutcrackers and chipmunks shatter them while they are still on the tree. Their remains litter the ground beneath— single thick scales, thumbnail-size.

RECOMMENDED READING

Peterson, Victor P. and Victor P. Jr. *Native Trees of the Sierra Nevada*. Berkeley: University of California Press, 1975. Cloth and paper.

Wildflowers and Shrubs

MORE THAN ONE THOUSAND kinds of flowering plants have been collected in this region. Thirty-eight of the more common and colorful flowers are described here. To make identification easier, they are grouped according to their color—white, yellow, red, lavender, blue. Flowering periods may vary considerably from summer to summer, and from place to place.

With each road, each new building, each new campsite, living places for plants are reduced. To make up for the millions of flowers destroyed by acres of asphalt, perhaps we can give greater care to those remaining. Mountain plants are sturdy, surviving ice, snow, and winds; but they cannot survive constant trampling and picking. Many of them are perennial, needing several summers free from human interference to reach maturity and to bloom. Even if there were no state law forbidding the picking of many flowers, common sense and true appreciation of wildflowers would keep many people from gathering them, for they wither and die disappointingly soon. As a sign reads in a St. Louis botanical garden, "Let it be said of these flowers that they died with their roots on." A permit for making botanical collections may be obtained at ranger stations. The scientific plant names in this book conform to Philip Munz's and David Keck's *A California Flora* (Berkeley: University of California Press, 1959).

WHITE FLOWERS

Corn lily or **false hellebore:** *Veratrum californicum* Durand; Lily Family. This plant with its 3–6-foot stem and large leaves dominates the marshy meadows, where it is common. The tall stems resemble cornstalks and are oftener seen without the bloom, for they do not bloom every summer. When this plant first comes up in the spring, it resembles the "skunk cabbage" of the Northwest.

Mariposa lily: *Calochortus Leichtlinii* Hook.; Lily Family. These one-inch flowers have creamy-white petals with a dark spot at their base. They grow in dry areas (6,000–8,000 feet) and bloom from late June to early July. "Mariposa" is from the Spanish for "butterfly."

Sierra rein orchis: *Habenaria leucostachys* (Lindl) Ames; Orchid Family. The thick, hollow stem, 10–15 inches long, is sheathed in plain long leaves. The ¼-inch flowers have a delicate sweet-spicy perfume. Though few people expect to find orchids in the mountains, this one grows in damp meadows (6500–9500 feet) throughout the region, blooming in late July.

Thistle poppy or **chilcote:** *Argemone munita* Dur. & Hilg. Prain; Poppy Family. Flowers 3–4 inches broad, showy, white with yellow center and fragile petals. It is named for the stiff spines that cover the entire plant except the petals. The stems are 1–3 feet long, several arising from the base of each plant. Common along edges of roads (5500–8500 feet).

Nude buckwheat: *Eriogonum nudum* Dougl. var. *deductum* (Greene);

S. Stokes; Buckwheat Family. Very small flowers grouped into compact round heads up to ½ inch in diameter; blue-green stems. Leaves, sometimes red, cluster in a circle at the base of the plant. Common in dry places up to 9,000 feet.

Cow parsnip: *Heracleum lanatum* Michx.; Parsley Family. What appears to be a 6–10-inch flower actually is a group of umbrella-like heads of tiny white flowers. An unpleasant odor is characteristic of the plant. Stems are coarse and hollow, 4–6 feet tall. Grows in damp meadows and along stream courses up to 8500 feet.

Swamp Whiteheads: *Sphenosciadium capitellatum* Gray; Parsley Family. A robust plant 2–5 feet tall, blooming in wet meadows in July and August. Pinhead sized flowers make up marble-like balls arranged in open, round clusters.

White or **bell heather:** *Cassiope mertensiana* (Bong.) G. Don.; Heath Family. Bell-shaped flowers less than ¼ inch across nod on red threadlike stems. Grows in low, dense mats, 2–4 inches high. It is found only at elevations above 9,000 feet in forest areas. This plant has close relatives in arctic regions throughout the world.

Prickly phlox (see Purple Flowers).

Yarrow: *Achillea lanulosa* Nutt.; Sunflower Family. Flowers ⅛ inch or less, dull white with greenish centers, forming flat-topped clusters. Stems 1–2 feet tall; leaves finely divided, resembling carrot leaves. Foliage and flower both have a strong acrid odor. Common in dry areas.

YELLOW FLOWERS

Little tiger lily: *Lilium parvum* Kell.; Lily Family. Flowers 1–2 inches across, yellow-orange with purple spots and delicate sweet scent, the curved outer part of the petal red-orange. The stems sometimes exceed six feet in height and support one to twenty-five flowers on a stalk. May be seen in wet, boggy places from 6500 to 10,000 feet.

Sulphur-flower: *Eriogonum umbellatum* Torr.; Buckwheat Family. Flowers a brilliant sulphur yellow to chartreuse, fading to deep orange or brick-red, many very small flowers forming spherical clusters. Small gray to reddish leaves form a mat around the base of the plant. Flower stalks 3–9 inches long. When in full bloom, this plant makes a colorful display on dry hillsides from 6,000 to 9500 feet. Growing at higher elevations are several smaller close relatives with yellow, white, or red blossoms.

Western wall flower: *Erysimum asperum perenne* (Wats. ex Cov.) Abrams; Mustard Family. Bright lemon-yellow fragrant flowers. The slender stem unbranched, 1–2 feet high.

Cinquefoil: *Potentilla gracilis* ssp. *Nuttallii* (Lehm.) Keck; Rose Family. The yellow roselike flowers (*a*) are ½ inch or more across. Two or more types of this plant grow commonly in the dry woods and drier meadows throughout the area. The yellow variety is more often found in meadows; its creamy white relative, *Potentilla glandulosa*, (*b*) in forests, especially of lodgepole pine.

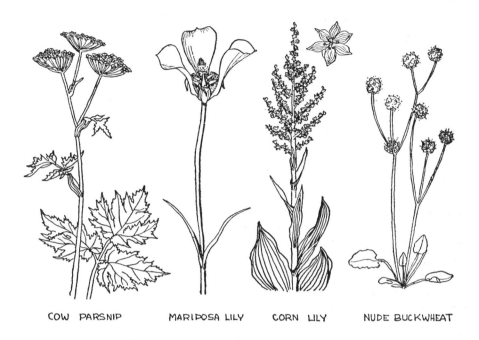

COW PARSNIP   MARIPOSA LILY   CORN LILY   NUDE BUCKWHEAT

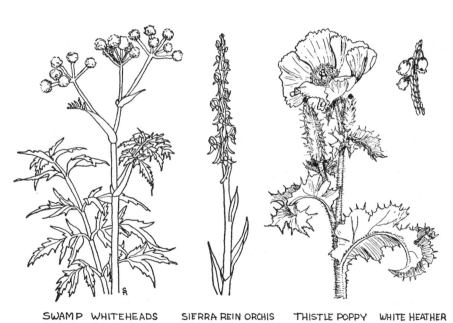

SWAMP WHITEHEADS   SIERRA REIN ORCHIS   THISTLE POPPY   WHITE HEATHER

Evening primrose: *Oenothera Hookeri* T&G; Evening Primrose Family. Flowers 2–3 inches, lemon-yellow, opening toward evening and closed during the day. Stems tough, 2–5 feet long; leaves strongly influenced by light direction, following the sun throughout the day. Very common along stream-beds and in sandy meadows from 4,000 to 8,000 feet.

Mullein: *Verbascum Thapsus* L; Figwort Family (not pictured). Flowers ½ inch across, light yellow-gold, many of them crowded on a single robust stalk, 3–5 feet long. Woolly leaves sheath the tall heavy stalk. A mass of leaves forms a rosette at the base. Very common along highways at lower elevations in the region especially near Mono Lake, becoming very conspicuous in August. The seeds of this plant were used by Indians for food.

Common monkey flower: *Mimulus guttatus* Fisch. ex DC; Figwort Family. Flower 1 inch across, brilliant yellow with brown spots in the throat. Stems fragile, leaves delicate, wilts almost immediately when picked. This plant grows in or near running water from 7,000 to 10,500 feet. A very tiny yellow monkey flower is seen in meadows, and a miniature rose-purple one grows on dry slopes at high elevations. A larger sturdier plant with a pink flower striped yellow and white, grows in damp places, *M. lewisii*, Pursh.

Woolly wyethia: *Wyethia mollis* Gray; Sunflower Family. The flower head is 2–3 inches across, showy, with deep-yellow flowers arranged in a circle around the outside of the head; the inner flowers are greenish. Several flower stalks 1–2 feet long rise from among large woolly leaves. These plants are very conspicuous in sagebrush areas, especially in late June when they are in full bloom.

Golden groundsel or **old man's beard:** *Senecio triangularis* Hook.; Sunflower Family. Deep yellow flowers ¼–½ inch across cluster to form ragged looking heads. Common in meadows at all elevations, blooming by late August.

PINK AND RED FLOWERS

Red columbine: *Aquilegia formosa* Fisch. in D.C. (Greene) Boothman; Buttercup Family. Flowers 1 inch broad, red with yellow centers, hang on slender stems. These bright flowers are great favorites of hummingbirds. Common in drier parts of meadows of the lodgepole–hemlock woods. A rare relative, *A. pubescens* Cov., is a delicate flower with creamy white petals tinted yellow, pink, or less commonly blue. It is found in rocky areas above 8500 feet and is a true alpine plant.

Red heather: *Phyllodoce breweri* (Gray) Hel.; Heath Family. Rose-pink flowers, ½ inch across, are held on delicate threadlike stalks. Leaves that look like pine needles cover the low-growing evergreen stems. This plant grows in low dense mats in pine forests (9,000–10,000 feet). It may be confused with the bog laurel described below.

Alpine laurel: *Kalmia polifolia* Wang var. *microphylla* (Hook.) Rehd.; Heath Family. Soon after snow melts from high mountain meadows, this plant

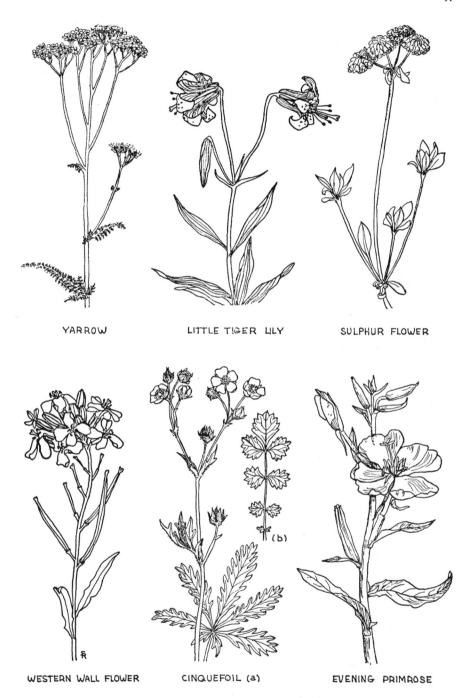

YARROW

LITTLE TIGER LILY

SULPHUR FLOWER

WESTERN WALL FLOWER

CINQUEFOIL (a)

(b)

EVENING PRIMROSE

blossoms with pink, ½-inch flowers. The tips of the pollen sacs are lodged in tiny pits at the center of the petals when the flower opens. When an insect lights on the flower to get nectar, the stamen springs up, and pollen is dusted over the body of the insect, which then transports the pollen to another flower.

Scarlet penstemon: *Penstemon Bridgesii* Gray; Figwort Family. Bright red, tube-shaped flowers line stalks 10–15 inches long. Many stalks grow from one root crown, making a flash of color along rocky banks and roadsides (7,000–9,000 feet). Several other members of this group are common to the area—a larger, bright blue penstemon on dry slopes, magenta "pride-of-the-mountains" in high, rocky places, and a tall delicate pink penstemon in the sagebrush flats.

Scarlet gilia: *Ipomopsis aggregata* (Pursh) V. Grant; Gilia Family. Flowers brilliant, 1–2 inches long. Numerous blossoms line a single stem, 8–20 inches long. Though the gilia's tube-shaped flower opens into a five-pointed star, it may be mistaken for the scarlet penstemon described above. Slender, finger-like leaves form a rosette at the base; many of these rosettes may be seen among blossoming plants, for this plant grows one year, then blooms the next. Common on dry hillsides (6500–9,000 feet). A color variation in rich salmon pink is sometimes seen in meadows (6500–7500 feet).

Indian paintbrush: *Castilleja miniata* Dougl. ex Hook; Figwort Family. Vivid red-orange, 1–1½ inches long in a dense cluster at the end of the stem. The actual flower is a green tube hidden inside the colorful bract and not easily seen. This plant common in moist places. Several other varieties—including one deep pink, one light yellow, and one light orange—grow on dry hillsides. A brilliant purplish-red, short paintbrush grows in moist alpine meadows. A smaller paler variety grows on high, rocky slopes.

Lewis' monkey flower (see common monkey flower).

LAVENDER FLOWERS

Wild onion: *Allium validum* Wats.; Lily Family. Small flowers are packed into a flat cluster atop a leafless triangular stalk 1–3 feet long. The entire plant emits a distinct onion odor; it is an excellent substitute for domestic onions, although much stronger. Common in wet meadows, especially above 8,000 feet. Different varieties may occasionally be found on dry sagebrush slopes.

Pussypaws: *Calyptridium umbellatum* (Torr.) Greene var. *caudicifera* (Gray) Jepson; Purslane Family. Rose-lavender flowers, smaller than ¼ inch, are sandwiched between two white papery structures, which persist long after the flower has gone, making the round heads look like soiled white fur. These clustered heads resemble the bottom of a cat's paw. The stems radiate out from a circle of dark leathery leaves that lie flat on the ground. Grows in dry, open places above 8500 feet.

Fireweed: *Epilobium angustifolium* L.; Evening Primrose Family. Many rose-purple flowers less than an inch across line a single red-stemmed stalk. The

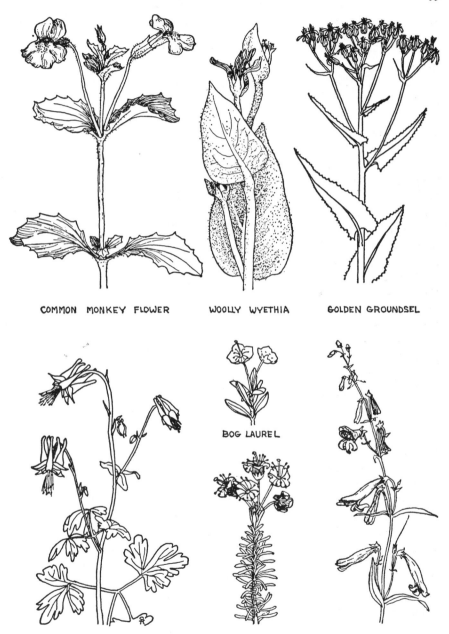

COMMON MONKEY FLOWER   WOOLLY WYETHIA   GOLDEN GROUNDSEL

BOG LAUREL

RED COLUMBINE   RED HEATHER   SCARLET PENSTEMON

leaves turn bright red in fall. Its name comes from the fact that in many areas this plant is the first to grow on a burned-over area.

Prickly or **Douglas phlox:** *Phlox diffusa* Benth.; Gilia Family. Cushions of light lavender to white catch the eye on dry hillsides in early summer. The small flowers, less than ½ inch across, bloom all at once, covering up the prickly leaves of the plant. Common on dry slopes from 7,000–11,000 feet. Many forms of this occur in the Sierra.

Sierra shooting star: *Dodecatheon jeffreyi* Van Houtte; Primrose Family. Lavender petals with a yellow band at the base turn back from black anthers that form the point of the shooting star, on ruddy stalks 1–2 feet tall. Common in moist meadows from 7,000 feet in spring. Later, in summer, as the snow disappears from high meadows, the related miniature alpine shooting star, *D. alpinum* (Gray) Greene, can be seen.

Mustang mint or **pennyroyal:** *Monardella odoratissima* Benth; Mint Family. Many very small lavender flowers form rounded clusters on stalks less than a foot long. The leaves give off a pungent minty smell. Grows on dry hillsides (6500-9500 feet).

Elephant heads: *Pedicularis groenlandica* Retz.; Figwort Family. The deep reddish purple flowers, less than ½ inch across, resemble the head of an elephant. This plant can be seen in the higher meadows (7500–10,500 feet) in July and August. Elephant's ears or snouts, *P. attollens* Gray, a near relative, can be distinguished by its lighter color. Its petals do not form an elephant's head, but are more like ruffles.

Mountain daisy: *Erigeron peregrinus* (Pursh) Greene; Sunflower (not pictured). Flowers 1–2 inches broad with yellow centers grow singly or in twos and threes on slender leafy stalks. It is common in drier meadows and shaded forests (7,000–10,000 feet). There are numerous other daisy-like flowers in the region, but this is by far the most common.

BLUE FLOWERS

Western blue flag: *Iris missouriensis* Nutt.; Iris Family. Flowers 3–4 inches broad, sky-blue with yellow ribs on the inner petals. This flower—also called mountain iris—blooms early; in June, meadows from 6,000 to 8,000 feet may turn blue with its blossoms.

Larkspur or **delphinium:** *Delphinium* species; Buttercup Family. One larkspur of the region is a magnificent plant up to 7 feet tall, which blooms in late July and August (6,000–9,000 feet). Stalks with medium blue flowers crowded along them rise 2–4 feet above masses of leaves. Another larkspur is smaller, 2–4 feet high. It has several stalks of deep blue-violet flowers, less than an inch across. Lush, round, many-lobed leaves form a bushy growth around the base of the plant. It is frequently found along watercourses, 7,000–10,000 feet. A much smaller variety is found in forests and dry hillside areas.

Monkshood: *Aconitum columbianum* Nutt.; Buttercup Family. This plant

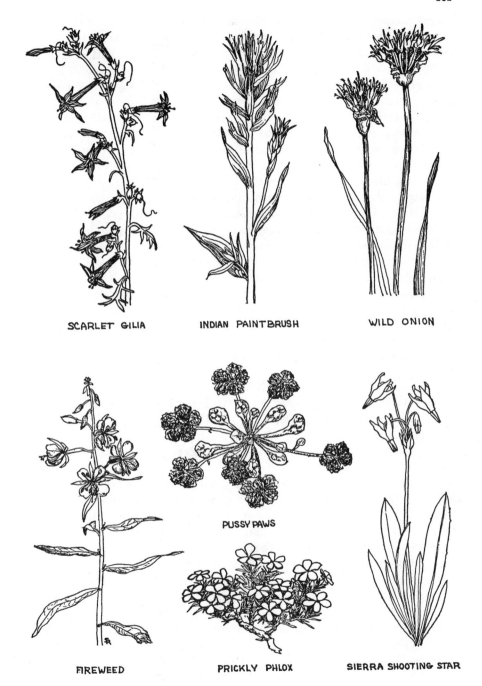

SCARLET GILIA   INDIAN PAINTBRUSH   WILD ONION

PUSSY PAWS

FIREWEED   PRICKLY PHLOX   SIERRA SHOOTING STAR

is often mistaken for those described above, but closer examination reveals the distinctive shape of the flowers, which are like the hoods of monks. In all other respects this plant is very similar to the larkspur but is considerably less common.

Lupine: *Lupinus* species; Pea Family. There are five or more similar species of lupine common in the region. The flowers are like small, deep blue sweet peas crowded together on erect stems. The most common species, drawn here, grows in damp meadows. Others prefer the shaded forests, some the dry hillsides, and still others grow on wind-swept ridges. All are long-blooming.

Gentian: *Gentiana holopetala* (Gray) Holm; Gentian Family. The common species is a deep blue flower on a short stem, often hidden among the taller grasses in damp meadows in early autumn. Two other types of gentian are occasionally found in the region—one a much larger plant with two-inch brilliant blue flowers, the other a tiny white one restricted to high mountain meadows.

Blue stick-seed or **forget-me-not:** *Hackelia floribunda* (Lehm.) Jtn.; Borage Family (not pictured). Flowers sky-blue with white centers, ¼ inch across. Small clumps of this plant are common along the edges of forests (7,000-9500 feet). The name comes from the fact that the seed is covered with tiny hooks that cling to anything with which they come in contact. Occasionally a group of plants will have pure pink blossoms. A relative with much smaller, lighter blue flowers grows in meadows.

Blue penstemon (see under Red Flowers).

SHRUBS

Mountain alder: *Alnus tenuifolia* Nutt.; Birch Family. This shrub is 4–10 feet high and grows above 7,000 feet. The flowers are like tiny pine cones, persisting on the branches long after the seed is shed. The bark varies from silver to rich brown. Dense stands grow in wet places and form nearly impassable thickets.

Willow: *Salix* species; Willow Family. There are a number of willows in the region, typically growing where there is an abundance of water. Large ones, reaching tree proportions, line creeks at lower elevations; smaller bushy forms cluster in thickets at higher meadows; above timberline, the dwarf willow carpets the moist ground near snowbanks. The characteristics of all are similar, despite their great variation in size. The leaves are long and narrow, the stems covered with a smooth golden to rose-toned bark that is especially striking in winter after the leaves have fallen. The typical catkins, coming just as soon as the snow frees the branches, are not often seen by visitors.

Wild rose: *Rosa woodsii* Lindl. var. *ultramontana* (Wats.) Jeps.; Rose Family (not pictured). This scraggly shrub is common in lower meadows (6,000–8,000 feet). In late May and June it is covered with delicate pink blossoms having a rich perfume. The fruit turns scarlet in August, and in late autumn the leaves turn a rich red-brown.

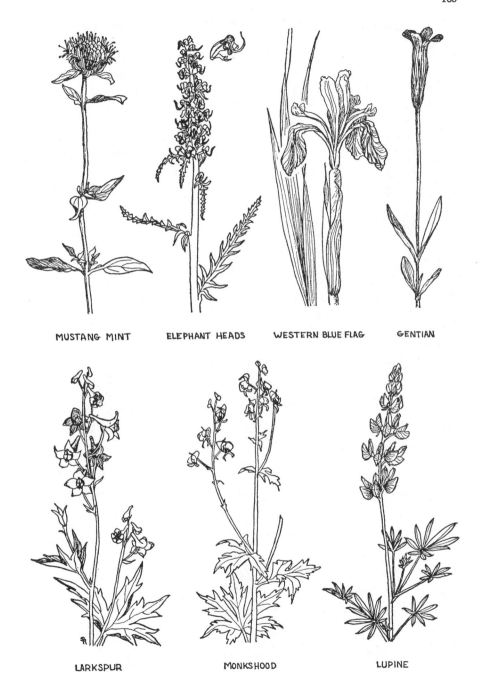

MUSTANG MINT   ELEPHANT HEADS   WESTERN BLUE FLAG   GENTIAN

LARKSPUR   MONKSHOOD   LUPINE

Bitter brush or **antelope brush:** *Purshia tridentata* (Pursh) DC; Rose Family. This shrub forms dense masses 1–4 feet high in sagebrush country and in open parts of Jeffrey pine forests. It is a preferred food of deer, antelope, and sheep, and in some places is conspicuously angular in form owing to intense browsing. Only a certain portion of each year's tender young shoots can be eaten without seriously damaging the plant. If they are overbrowsed they die, and the range becomes virtually useless. When the population of any deer herd exceeds the capacity of its winter range, three things may happen: (1) many deer may die of starvation, especially a large proportion of fawns; (2) some may migrate into unaccustomed and often inhabited areas, where they can cause serious damage to orchards and crops; or (3) the deer barely manage to survive, mainly on the food stored as body fat, but the vigor and well-being of the herd decreases markedly.

Bitter cherry: *Prunus emarginata* (Dougl.) Walp.; Rose Family. This graceful shrub has a red-brown glossy bark. In spring it is covered with delicate white, sweet-scented flowers. Small bright red cherries, bitter and inedible, ripen later in the summer. Its habitat is similar to that of bitter brush.

Service berry: *Amelanchier pallida* Greene; Rose Family. This plant is known in some regions as "sarvus berry." It resembles the bitter cherry and grows in similar localities, but has round rather than slender leaves.

Sierra snowbush or **tobacco brush:** *Ceanothus velutinus* Dougl. ex Hook.; Buckthorn Family. This shrub is often called "wild lilac," a name shared by some forty plants in the state. The more appropriate name of Sierra snowbush comes from the mass of white, sweet-smelling flowers which blossom in early summer. The plants grow up to 5 feet high, forming dense hillside stands, especially in the Jeffrey pine and red fir forests (6500–9,000 feet). The evergreen leaves are sticky and appear freshly varnished on the upper surface. When broken, they give off a strong, spicy odor.

Green-leafed manzanita: *Arctostaphylos patula* Greene; Heath Family. Often mixed with the Sierra snowbush, manzanita is distinguished by its smooth red-brown bark and very gnarled branches. It is said that a reward of one hundred dollars was once offered to any person who could find a piece of straight manzanita branch 12 inches long—and that the reward has never been claimed. The evergreen leaves are leathery in texture. In late June, bunches of delicate pink, bell-shaped flowers blossom. The early Spaniards named this plant *manzanita* ('little apple') for its small apple-shaped berries. Above 8,000 feet a smaller relative, *A. nevadensis* Gray, carpets the forest floors.

Wax currant: *Ribes cereum* Dougl.; Saxifrage Family. This relative of the domestic currant lives on dry hillsides from 7,000–9,000 feet elevation. It is 3–5 feet high, covered with small, toothed leaves having a waxy surface (*a*). The stems are without spines and have a smooth silvery bark. The small red fruits which ripen late in August are pithy and quite unpalatable. In moist shaded places, *R. montigenum* McCl. is found, sometimes in large nearly impenetrable

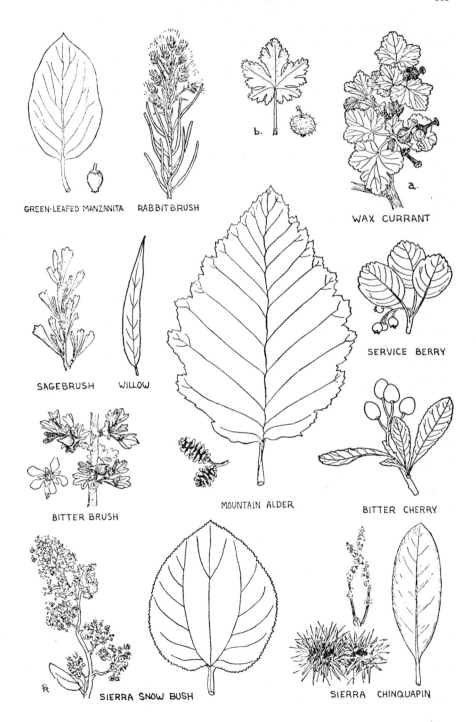

GREEN-LEAFED MANZANITA   RABBITBRUSH

WAX CURRANT

SAGEBRUSH   WILLOW

SERVICE BERRY

BITTER BRUSH

MOUNTAIN ALDER

BITTER CHERRY

SIERRA SNOW BUSH

SIERRA CHINQUAPIN

patches. This "gooseberry currant" (*b*) has many stiff yellow spines on its branches. Its juicy, tart fruit makes excellent jelly.

Sagebrush: *Artemisia tridentata* Nutt.; Sunflower Family. Although large expanses of the eastern Sierra are covered with this common shrub, nearly to the exclusion of all other plants, its growth stops abruptly at the edge of forested areas, for it cannot survive the forest's moisture and lack of sun. The name and odor of "sage" are deceiving, for this plant is not at all related to seasoning sage of the mint family, but is more closely related to goldenrod. In late fall, slender flower stalks bear tiny greyish yellow blossoms.

Sierra chinquapin: *Castanopsis sempervirens* (Kell.) Dudley; Oak Family. This plant is found in localities similar to those of manzanita and Sierra snowbush. Its evergreen leaves are backed with rusty fur. Clusters of spine-covered fruits remain on the plant for several years.

Rabbitbrush: *Chrysothamnus nauseosus* (Pall.) Britt; Sunflower Family. This 2–5-foot shrub, growing commonly on sagebrush flats, is easily mistaken for sagebrush because it is the same color, except in fall when masses of brilliant golden yellow blossoms cover the tops of the plants. A smaller species of rabbitbrush, called ragweed, is seen along the roadways at higher elevations.

Other common plants of the region (mountain mahogany, grass of Parnassus, western roseroot, Labrador tea, mountain penstemon, alpine willow, Sierra primrose, etc.) are described and illustrated in *Deepest Valley: Guide to Owens Valley.*

RECOMMENDED READING

Bakker, Elna. *An Island Called California.* Berkeley: University of California Press, 1971. Cloth and paper. The marvels and differences of California's biological communities. These chapters refer to the eastern Sierra: "Mountain Meadow," "The Bluest Sky," "The Other Side of the Mountain," and "The Short Forests." Highly recommended.

Crittenden, Mabel and Dorothy Telfer. *Wildflowers of the West.* Millbrae: Celestial Arts, 1975. Paper. If you can count a flower's petals, you can identify it—this book shows you how. Excellent introduction to keying out plants.

Storer, John. *The Web of Life,* 1972, and *Man in the Web of Life,* 1968. New York: New American Library. Paper. Two fascinating books about "everything"—the interrelationships of all living things and their environments.

These excellent, knapsack-size books—published by the University of California Press in cloth and paper—include plants of the eastern Sierra. Well illustrated with both sketches and color photographs.

Munz, Philip A. *California Desert Wildflowers,* 1962, and *California Mountain Wildflowers,* 1963.

Niehaus, Theodore F. *Sierra Wildflowers: Mt. Lassen to Kern Canyon,* 1974.

Thomas, John H. and Dennis Parnell. *Native Shrubs of the Sierra Nevada,* 1974.

Mammals

FOLLOWING ARE BRIEF DESCRIPTIONS of some of the more conspicuous mammals of the region. Although they are grouped roughly according to the life zones which they prefer, there are no sharp lines or boundaries between the zones, and animals will range into higher or lower zones whenever they can find food and suitable habitat. The accompanying diagram illustrates the progression of life zones and some typical mammals to look for.

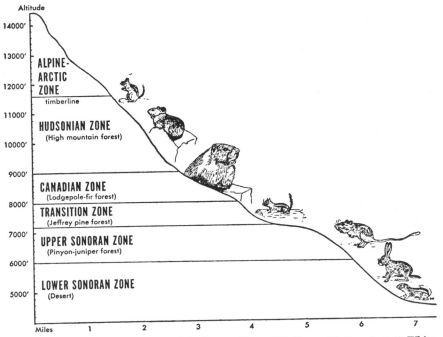

Figure 28. Progression of Mammals in Eastern Sierra Life Zones. (*Bottom to top*) White-tailed antelope squirrel, black-tailed jackrabbit, Panamint kangaroo rat, least chipmunk, yellowbellied marmot, pika, Alpine chipmunk.

LOWER SONORAN ZONE

White-tailed antelope squirrel: *Ammospermophilus leucurus.* A small ground squirrel about the size of a chipmunk, but has a shorter tail and seldom climbs trees. Has a single white stripe down each side. Total length about 8½ inches.

A small chipmunk-like ground squirrel with conspicuous white tail arched over its back may scamper in the early morning or evening across Highway 395 between Lone Pine and Independence or on Sherwin Grade. Beyond the highway shoulder, it may stop beneath a shrub to take a quick look before going on. This is a desert squirrel and feeds on grains, seeds, and green plants—and on meat when it is available (animals and insects killed on the highway).

107

UPPER SONORAN ZONE

California ground squirrel: *Spermophilus beecheyi.* Larger than a house rat, about the size of a gray squirrel but the tail not bushy as in a tree squirrel and only about three-fourths of the body length. General coloration dull yellowish brown with grizzled white patches on the sides of the neck and shoulders. Total length about 17 inches.

In Inyo-Mono the California ground squirrels are not abundant, as they are in the foothills of the San Joaquin and Sacramento valleys. Primarily ground dwellers, single squirrels may be seen atop fence posts, rocks, or even in the low branches of the brush just south of Casa Diablo. Look also for these "digger" or Beechey squirrels and their workings in the dry sandy ground beneath sage and bitterbrush at Rush Creek Ranch and just north of Lee Vining. Like other ground squirrels their diet is varied—seeds, grains, green plants, insects, meat, and the eggs and young of birds when available.

Black-tailed jackrabbit: *Lepus californicus.* A large slender yellowish brown rabbit with upstanding ears about 5 inches long; upper side of the tail black. About the size of a small house cat. Total length about 22 inches.

In the early morning or evening, jackrabbits are commonly seen in Long Valley. If you see one ahead of you along the highway, slow down for a better look; chances are that if you stop he will dart into the sagebrush cover. Occasionally, one will race beside the road ahead of the car, leaping into the air in a characteristic spy hop to get a better look at the whole situation. Pressed harder, he will stretch out—into a speedy overdrive—until overtaken, then dash for cover. Jackrabbits feed on grains, seeds, grasses, green plants, and some shrubs. Apparently they can exist for long periods without water, obtaining enough for their needs from their food, though they take water readily and regularly when it is available. It is reported that jackrabbits are quick to find and use guzzlers, devices for collecting and storing rain water below the ground in arid regions. A built-in ramp enables mammals, birds, and even reptiles to use this kind of water supply.

Panamint kangaroo rat: *Dipodomys panamantinus.* Smaller than a common rat; very small front feet and large kangaroo-like hind legs and feet; coat silky soft; tail longer than head and body, with a pronounced hairy tuft. General coloration light brown above and pure white below. Total length about 12 inches.

Near Casa Diablo the Panamint kangaroo rat can often be seen at night in the beam of headlights hopping jerkily across the highway.

Striped skunk: *Mephitis mephitis.* About the size of a house cat but very chunky, with short stocky legs and a big bushy tail almost as long as the head and body. The general color is black, with a broad white patch across back of head and nape which splits into a very wide stripe down each side of the back and onto the base of the tail. Total length 28 inches.

CHIPMUNK

GOLDEN-MANTLED GROUND SQUIRREL

CHICKAREE

BELDING GROUND SQUIRREL

WHITE-TAILED JACKRABBIT

PIKA

Figure 29.

Look for the striped skunk in early morning, at dusk, or at night shuffling across Highway 395—particularly just south of Mammoth Creek, at Convict Creek, or at Rock Creek below Paradise Camp. Often its tail will be arched behind. If you stop the car and attempt to press him he'll hurry up to a point, then raise his tail stiffly like a warning flag, the tail appearing much broader as the hair also stiffens. He will stand his ground in partial reverse, ready for action if further pressed. If not, the flag will slowly descend as he ambles off for cover with no harm done. Skunks are valuable mousers; they also eat pounds of insects and their eggs and larvae each season. Their diet also includes small mammals, frogs, snakes, birds and their eggs, and carrion from highway kills. In sum, skunks are widely and beneficially omnivorous.

TRANSITION ZONE

Least chipmunk: *Eutamias minimus.* A typical chipmunk but very small, only a little larger than a house mouse. Shoulders and top of head gray, sides reddish brown, body with nine alternately light and dark brown stripes. Total length about 7 inches.

In large open sage and bitterbrush flats, as in Long Valley, virtually any chipmunk dashing across the highway or scampering about the brushy cover will be the least, or painted chipmunk. If he is badly frightened, the dash may be accompanied by a staccato call as he heads for a dense brushy clump in which to hide. As he travels, he often holds his tail nearly vertical or with a slight arc forward. Foraging and alert spying regularly takes individuals to the very tips of sage or bitterbrush twigs; there they may perch quietly feeding with tail draped over foliage or hanging downward. If alarmed, the chipmunk may utter a single call at short intervals with frequent flicks of the tail. Since the least chipmunk hibernates for only a short period, they can be seen from about mid-February until mid-November. The usual chipmunk diet of seeds, grains, green herbage and browse, and petals of flowers is varied from time to time with meat. One least chipmunk at Gull Lake in late winter fed avidly on bits of cooked beef remaining on a bone placed in a bird-feeding station.

CANADIAN ZONE

White-tailed jackrabbit: *Lepus townsendii.* A large jackrabbit with white feet and large fluffy, all white tail. In summer light brownish gray above with mostly white underparts; in winter the coat is pure white except for the black-tipped ears. Total length about 25 inches.

In winter or early spring along Highway 395 north of Rock Creek you are almost certain to see at least one of these beautiful snow-white jackrabbits (or Sierra hares). In spring, during the change to summer coat, any large grayish jackrabbit with pure white tail seen along the highway will be a white-tail. The best time to see them is in the late evening or at night. The normal summer range of the white-tailed jackrabbit is from Canadian through Hudsonian into Alpine-Arctic zones. In late fall, severe frosts and snow drive the rabbits to better habitat at the lower elevations, hence their relative abundance during the winter months. These jackrabbits are often, but incorrectly, called snowshoe rabbits. The true snowshoe does not occur in Mono County.

Porcupine: *Erethizon dorsatum.* Larger than a house cat, with a long wiry brownish and yellowish black coat overlying many sharp yellowish white spines on the upper parts of the tail, body, and head (except the face). Total length about 36 inches.

Occasionally streamside campers near aspen and willows are awakened at night by the sound of paper rattling or something shuffling about. A flashlight beam reveals not a cub bear but a fat, woolly (and spiny) rodent snooping about, possibly for the vegetable sack. If he finds a sweaty shoe or belt, a porcupine will gnaw such items for their saltiness. Undisturbed, porcupines are generally harmless; but if aroused, they will quickly bristle, and if pressed hard will attempt to strike with flicks of the tail. Porcupines cannot throw their quills, but many a dog has felt the pain of a cluster of barbed spines driven hard into its muzzle by the tail of a porcupine he molested. Look for them slowly shuffling across the highway in fall and again in spring when they are migrating. Many are killed by cars, especially in the evening.

There are occasional cries of alarm about damage done to forests by the porcupine's habit of eating bark and often girdling a tree in the process. The alarm is caused by an old, but dying, human habit of trying to classify animals according to how good they are or how bad. The ecologist knows that many of the natural forces which man has chosen to call destructive are in reality constructive. Predators, for example, although lethal to individuals, enhance the vigor of the herd as a whole upon which they prey. Fire, through the ages, has been a forest-building force, favoring fire-resistant species and thinning out fire-vulnerable species, which, because they have certain other advantages, would otherwise take over a range. Disease weeds out mutations toward weakness.

Thus it is probably fire that has made it possible for man to look upon—and enjoy—a slope of aspens, golden in the autumn. It is probably the lodgepole needle miner that has kept the lodgepole from taking over much of the forest and has given the graceful mountain hemlock a chance instead. Mountain lions and other predators kept the deer population in balance with the range. All these are fairly obvious examples and natural cycles that exist in nature, that led to John Muir's observing that when you try to pick out something by itself you "find it tied to all the universe." Aldo Leopold put it this way: "Who but a fool would ask, What good is it"?

And so the porcupine, among other things, may be one of the forces that tend to keep a forest an open forest rather than a thicket.

Perhaps the porcupine is like the termite, which has the scavenger role of eating, or cleaning up wood that has been attacked already by some fungus. Perhaps the porcupines single out trees that need singling out. Whatever their role may be, they played it for millions of years before man began to fret about it, and the forests survived nevertheless—and *perhaps even improved.*

Belding ground squirrel: *Spermophilus beldingi.* About the size of a common rat, with a short tail (less than half the length of head and body) and small ears. The general coloration is light yellowish brown above, the underparts lighter.

These ground squirrels are known also as picket pins, undoubtedly from their habit of sitting or standing stiffly erect, with forelegs pressed closely to their chests, in mountain meadows or open flats. Persistent watching will reveal that they often pivot in place or melt to the ground as individual squirrels resume feeding. They eat succulent bits of grass, herbs, seeds, a little browse where it can be reached from the ground, and meat (animals killed on roads). Each season hundreds of Belding squirrels are themselves killed crossing the highway. They are an important prey of hawks, badgers, coyotes, and weasels. Belding squirrels appear from hibernation usually about mid-March, and are active until November.

Lodgepole chipmunk: *Eutamias speciosus.* The lodgepole chipmunk is slightly larger than the least chipmunk, and has more reddish brown and dark brown in its body color and less gray. It is distinguished from the golden-mantled ground squirrel by its smaller size, larger ears and more pointed nose, and the white stripes on its head as well as on its body. Total length 8½ inches.

The lodgepole chipmunk is predominantly arboreal, and is most abundant in the Inyo-Mono region about lodgepole pines, and in forests in which lodgepole, western white pine, and hemlock are mixed. Like most chipmunks, it is very active and alert. When frightened, it will often dash for the nearest tree, ascending on the far side out of sight. Alarmed or angry, it will often scold sharply from a limb, flicking its tail with each call. Seeds, grains, nuts, and often meat (insects, eggs, nestling birds) are among the foods eaten.

Golden mantled ground squirrel: *Spermophilus lateralis.* A small, brilliantly colored ground squirrel, resembling a chipmunk except that its body is stockier, the nose blunter, and the tail shorter. Head and neck rusty red. There is a broad white stripe on each side sandwiched between two dark stripes. This white stripe extends from hip to neck, but never onto the head as in chipmunks. Size a little smaller than a house rat; total length 9½ to 11½ inches.

Although predominantly terrestrial, these ground squirrels will climb trees and shrubs for short distances. They are common in sun-swept rocky areas. Campgrounds are often their food centers; various and sundry items including meat are crammed into their bulging cheek pouches, then stored in burrows or buried in odd places in the forest duff. Many of the seeds planted then germinate, adding to the forest cover. Look for golden mantled ground squirrels from late February until November.

Each year dozens of squirrels and chipmunks are captured or handled by campers, and attempts made to tame them. The State Department of Public Health earnestly cautions against this hazardous practice, for these animals may carry the germs of relapsing fever, bubonic plague, or even rabies. Feed them if you must, but do not fondle or touch them lest a scratch or sharp bite cause injury or serious illness.

Chickaree: *Tamiasciurus douglasii.* A small, dark brown, tree-climbing squirrel, about the size of a common rat; brushlike tail, about two thirds the length of head and body; buff-colored beneath. Total length about 12½ inches.

Also called pine squirrel and Douglas squirrel, this is the little tree squirrel of the high mountain forests, ranging to timberline. It seldom lingers for long on the forest floor, except to travel between widely spaced trees, to water, to investigate, or to "work" and scale a cone it has severed from aloft. Few travelers get by without being seen by a watchful and vocal chickaree, who will sound off the alert with his calls. The approach and position of many a hunter has been quickly revealed by the chickaree. Chickarees are active the year around and, helped by their stored supplies, are able to find food throughout the long winter. Probably their most feared enemy is the pine marten, who is able to pursue them relentlessly through the tallest trees.

Shasta beaver: *Castor canadensis shasta.* A large, husky, and powerfully built mammal, largest of North American rodents; broad flat tail; short inconspicuous ears on a rather boxy head with squarish muzzle. Color usually rich chestnut brown above, somewhat lighter beneath. Total length 43 inches; tail 4½ inches wide, 16 inches long.

The first trial transplant of Shasta beaver from Modoc County was made in August 1941, when five animals were placed in Robinson Creek near Bridgeport. Basic purposes were water conservation, formation of a lake for fishing, and more beaver for fur. Later, other transplants were made. The resourceful beaver took hold and, with ideas of their own, individuals began "bud colonies." Beaver will eventually explore and settle an entire drainage; and a really eager beaver will follow water courses and even cross over into other drainages twenty-five to thirty miles away. This was the origin of the Mill Creek colony above Lundy Lake.

Five beaver were planted in the shallow lake on McGee Creek in 1955. These beaver are thriving and their work is much in evidence—gnawed aspen stumps, and a large mound of branches (the beaver lodge, housing the whole family) at the upper end of the lake. Though these remarkable rodent engineers are wary, watchfulness in early morning, at dusk, or on cloudy days will likely reward the patient observer. Preferred foods of beaver include stems and roots of aquatic plants, bark, twigs, and wood of cottonwoods, willows, and especially aspen. Because of the limited groves of fine aspen and streamside cover along Inyo-Mono streams, serious question has been raised regarding the value of beaver introductions in some areas. On McGee Creek, for example, the beaver may eventually destroy most of the aspen trees within their range; many other trees and much streamside cover will be killed by flooding. The entire area, monumented by an impenetrable tangle of trash and dead standing cover, may then be abandoned.

Inyo mule deer: *Odocoileus hemionus.* In summer, tannish or tawny above, grayer in winter. The rump is white to buffy; the narrow tail constricted at the base, white with prominent black tuft. Fawns are generally light chestnut with buffy spots. Length up to 5½ feet, weight up to 200 pounds.

The Inyo Mule Deer of the eastern Sierra, the California Mule Deer of the western slope, and the Black-tailed Deer of the Coast Ranges are all races of the same species with minor distinguishing characteristics. The Inyo mule deer— which ranges from Walker Pass as far north as Yosemite, and east to the White and Inyo Mountains— is slightly larger and heavier than its close relative on the western slope. Deer migrate with the seasons, to the high country in summer and back down to the snow-free valleys in late fall. Since their foods are chiefly tender herbs, grasses, new twigs, buds, and leaves, they follow spring as it advances up the mountain slopes. Thus they are found at various times of the year in the Jeffrey pine, lodgepole-fir, and high mountain forests, and occasionally even above timberline. Their fawns are born in June and July, in a healthy herd often as sets of twins.*

For your own protection, do not feed or try to touch the deer. They are easily frightened; an enraged deer can tear deep gashes with its sharp front hooves. Never pick up a fawn because it seems to be an orphan. Forest rangers are often brought young animals by well-meaning people who think them abandoned. The mothers are only hiding—watching and waiting for the humans to leave, to resume care of their young. Since it is usually impossible to find the place from which the baby was kidnaped and to return it there, it must then be raised artificially, which is often unsuccessful.

HUDSONIAN ZONE

Alpine chipmunk: *Eutamias alpinus.* About the size of a house mouse; smallest of the Sierra chipmunks, with head and body about 4 inches long, tail barely 3 inches long. Typical chipmunk color pattern but much paler, tail more buff than black.

The agile Alpine chipmunk is characteristic of the more rocky areas of the Hudsonian zone. You will see them snooping about scrubby timberline pines, often with short quick movements punctuated by a flick of the tail. One might think that at the higher elevations chipmunks would be relatively safe; this is not the case. Their arch enemies are least weasels and pine martens; occasionally they fall prey to sharp-shinned, Cooper's, and red-tailed hawks.

Yellowbellied marmot: *Marmota flaviventris.* A large woodchuck about the size of a broad house cat, heavy set, with short legs and bushy tail. Dark brown above grizzled with white; underparts yellowish; a narrow white cross band in front of eyes. Total length 22 to 28 inches.

---

* *See page 143, 10.*

Other common names for the marmot are rock (or granite) chuck, mountain chuck, or whistler (from the sharp whistling note often uttered by an alarmed marmot from his boulder lookout). This big fellow often sprawls flat atop a sunny promontory or a large boulder. As you approach he may flatten even more, with just the head and shoulders showing. If closely approached, he will appear to slither or slide from his lookout into the talus out of sight. If surprised while feeding on tender grass in a small meadow patch, he will hastily gallop like a small roly-poly bear to the safety of his rocky home, stopping squirrel-fashion for a last look before disappearing. Coyotes, eagles, and red-tailed hawks are among their common enemies. Although typical of the Hudsonian zone, marmots descend into rocky areas to their liking in the Canadian and even the Transition zones, as in the basaltic lava near the junction of the Mammoth Lakes highway with Highway 395.

Pika or Cony: *Ochotona princeps.* Resembles a small guinea pig, or a tiny gray rabbit with very short ears. Total length 7½ inches.

You may be travelling a high mountain trail near a talus slide when suddenly a cony, or pika, sounds off with a sharp series of calls echoing among the rocks (sounding a little like two rocks struck together) and difficult to pinpoint. Careful scrutiny of every boulder in the general direction of the calls may reveal what appears to be a little rock rabbit, which may betray itself as it runs from its vantage point toward its den beneath the talus. Usually near the entrance, the cracks of the rocks will be crammed with various kinds of hay brought in for curing by the busy cony. Enough is stored during summer to last the winter. Enemies of the pika include weasels and martens.

ALPINE-ARCTIC ZONE

All the mammals characteristic of the Hudsonian also range upward above timberline into the Alpine-Arctic zone. Generally speaking, the higher one travels the fewer individuals will be seen, owing to the increased severity of living conditions. The most common mammal will probably be the Alpine chipmunk. The Sierra marmot probably ranges the highest; marmot signs have been found at the very top of Mount Ritter.

RECOMMENDED READING

Burt, William H. and Richard P. Grossenheider. *A Field Guide to the Mammals.* Boston: Houghton Mifflin, second edition, 1964. Beautifully illustrated field guide to all mammals found north of Mexico.

Ingles, Lloyd G. *Mammals of the Pacific States.* Stanford: Stanford University Press, 1965. Comprehensive, authoritative.

Murie, Olaus. *A Field Guide to Animal Tracks.* Cambridge: Riverside Press, 1954. Cloth. Boston: Houghton Mifflin, 1975. Paper. A more personal narrative than most field guides. Crammed with field observations.

The DFG, see p. 120, publishes these excellent booklets on mammals: *Big Game of California* by William P. Dasman, 1958; *Upland Game of California* by Robert D. Mallette, 1969; *Furbearers of California* by George Seymour, 1960.

Fish

TWO GENERAL TYPES OF FISH ARE FOUND IN the east-central Sierra region—game fish and rough fish.

Rough fish are nongame species, most of which contribute to the habitat in which they live, often by providing forage in one way or another for the game species. Several kinds of rough fish have been used for many years in Inyo-Mono waters as bait for large trout; lake chubs, a species of minnow, are perhaps best known. Other kinds of rough fish are dace, suckers, sticklebacks, and carp. The latter two were introduced many years ago into certain Inyo-Mono waters and, fortunately, have never become widely distributed. Carp, especially, have frequently destroyed important game fisheries by competing for food and muddying the water. Many thousands of dollars have been spent by the Department of Fish and Game in rough fish control work directed primarily at carp. The work is done most economically with chemicals that suffocate the carp as well as all other fish. The fishery is restored by replanting when the chemicals have disappeared from the water, usually after several weeks.

The most important game fish in the Inyo-Mono area are the trouts. Some are native to California and some were introduced many years ago from the eastern United States. Prior to settlement of the Inyo-Mono area by white men there were no trout fisheries south of Conway Summit on the east side of the Sierra crest. To the north, in the East and West Walker River drainages, there were cutthroat trout in abundance. It is believed that these were introduced in the Mono Basin and Owens River basin shortly after 1850, the trout having been carried over the summit in water barrels fastened to freight wagons. Abundant cutthroat trout fisheries were present in Rush Creek and Bishop Creek by 1900.

Golden trout, which are native to waters at the head of the South Fork of the Kern River, were first introduced into Inyo-Mono waters in 1893 by cattlemen. A few of the trout were carried from Mulkey Meadows in a coffee can and planted in the Cottonwood Lakes. From these lakes have since come most of the golden trout stock planted in hundreds of High Sierra lakes and streams. The other nonnative trouts—rainbow, eastern brook, and brown—were introduced soon after 1900 and were planted from state hatcheries established on Oak Creek near Independence and on Fern Creek near Silver Lake. Nearly all the high lakes and streams accessible from Inyo-Mono were originally planted with fingerling trout raised in these hatcheries.

As the number of anglers fishing the more accessible waters increased, the resident stocks of trout were rapidly depleted. The fisheries were supplemented with larger and larger hatchery fish. Thus was developed the catchable rainbow —a special hybrid trout of fast growth and high egg yield which could be produced in great numbers at such tepid volcanic springs as Hot Creek, Black Rock, and Fish Springs, where ample water of fairly constant temperature was available. Plants are made at intervals throughout the fishing season in order to distribute the trout as equitably as possible and, at the same time, prevent excessive drain on the resident fisheries. Catchable rainbow are planted where a return to the angler of at least fifty per cent may be expected. In one Inyo-Mono stream returns of ninety-two per cent from catchable rainbow planting were recorded. The four-year average recorded return was eighty-five per cent. In 1975 it cost about 28 cents to produce and plant a catchable rainbow.

Prior to 1947 back country lakes were planted by pack train or back pack. Since then, more and more such waters have been planted by airplane. Fingerling trout are released in free fall 200-600 feet above the water surface. The little trout sound like heavy rain drops as they hit the water. They are momentarily stunned, but quickly recover and disappear. Within a few minutes hundreds of them may be seen swimming about the margin as they get acquainted with their new home. Tests have shown the accuracy of planting to be about 99 per cent; the loss of fingerlings in planting is usually less than 2 per cent. Airplane planting takes only a fraction of the time and expense of the old method.

By far the greatest effort in management of California fisheries is devoted to rainbow trout, for several reasons. First, rainbow trout are the predominant native species of California. Second, experimental culture from 1930 to 1940 revealed that more could be obtained economically in terms of growth rate, egg production, flexibility of stock, and desirable sporting qualities than from any other species. And third, rainbow trout could be used in greater numbers over a much wider range of habitat than any other species. Over the years two principal strains have been used—spring-spawned and fall-spawned. From spring-spawned stock come the fingerlings planted in High Sierra lakes or streams where fisheries have been depleted through natural causes. Rainbow spawn naturally in spring, when nursery areas are provided with ample water of favorable temperatures for eggs and young fish emerging from the gravel. Fall-spawned stock were developed in order to provide large numbers of catchable rainbow trout for planting in the lower-altitude roadside waters just before and during the summer fishing season. Usually the "aged" trout are planted in greatest numbers just ahead of the principal holiday periods in order to offset seasonal peaks of angling pressure.

The golden trout is the State fish. Anglers prize it for its brilliant coloration, fighting qualities, and delicate taste (stemming from rich body fat). For these reasons, golden trout have been reared and planted to maintain the species within its present range. The major part of at least one entire drainage in the central Sierra has been dedicated to golden trout. In a number of other drainages where other trout species predominate, it has been the aim of fish management to maintain where possible one or more good golden trout fisheries in order to provide a degree of variety for fishermen. Still, since comparatively few alpine waters are really suited for golden trout, their distribution will probably always be somewhat restricted.

TROUT IN THE CENTRAL SIERRA

Rainbow trout: *Salmo gairdneri.* Planted throughout Inyo-Mono in nearly all heavily fished roadside streams and lakes as catchables averaging 8 inches. Fingerlings are air-planted in back-country lakes where natural propagation is insufficient to maintain the fishery. Irregular black spots on the upper half of head and body, and on back and tail fins; bluish green to gunmetal gray back, silvery sides to pearly white belly and chin. Often conspicuous reddish band extending midway along sides from gill covers on head to narrow part of body in front of tail.

In large, deep clear lakes (Lake Mary, Duck, Garnet, and Thousand Island lakes) steelhead-like rainbow trout are frequently caught. In these the upper half of the body is deep bluish or gray blue, the lower half silvery to white. There are few spots and no reddish band, except for male trout in spring at spawning time. A granite-type rainbow has developed in certain high montane glacial lakes where the margin and bottom is mostly granite talus or rubble. Such rainbow have a pale grayish to silvery white ground color and are profusely spotted over the head, body, and fins.

Golden trout: *Salmo aguabonita.* Originally from headwater streams tributary to the South Fork of the Kern River; now most abundant in alpine regions of Fresno and Tulare counties. Good golden trout fisheries also found in upper Fish Creek and in alpine Inyo-Mono waters from the Cottonwood Lakes near Olancha northward to Sonora Pass, as in the Shadow Creek drainage. Some golden fisheries sustained by annual or biennial air-plants of fingerlings. Many waters self-sustaining and no planting required since suitable spawning areas provide ample new stock.

A brilliantly colored trout with olive green on the upper areas of the body giving way to pale lemon-yellow sides, then golden-yellow and vermilion or cherry red on the lower sides and belly. Gill covers and lower body fins often bright red. Large back fin, belly and anal fins are often white-tipped bordered with black. Relatively few round black spots are generally confined to the back fins and tail with a scattering of spots forward onto the head. A typical golden has a row of roundish blotches (called parr marks) on the sides from the head to the tail through which extends a bright red band. Golden and rainbow trout cross readily in nature, and where the two have intermingled every variation may be found between the typical rainbow and the typical golden.

Lahontan cutthroat trout: *Salmo clarkii henshawi.* Once widespread in

Inyo-Mono; now restricted to a few rather isolated waters. A large number of cutthroat fingerlings are planted each year in Crowley Lake, where perhaps the largest number of Inyo-Mono cutthroat exist. Elsewhere only a few persist in waters wherein isolated or not driven out by other species. Like golden, the cutthroat does best where not mixed with other trout. Body usually yellowish-olive with a wide ruby band along each side from gill covers to tail. Gill covers are usually ruby to rose red. Body and unpaired fins typically covered with numerous black spots (hence the common name "black-spotted trout"). Look for two bright red stripes, one on each side of the midline beneath the lower jaw.

Eastern brook trout: *Salvelinus fontinalis.* Probably more widespread and more abundant than any other species, owing to hardiness and adaptability to rigors of high mountain lake and stream habitats. Planted in High Sierra lakes and streams from Haiwee north to Sonora Pass and eastward to certain small streams in White Mountains. Prefers relatively shallow, weedy, timbered lakes with mud or silt bottoms; has done fairly well in a few large deep clear rock-bound lakes. Chiefly a marginal or shoal feeder and readily rises to a wet or dry fly cast from shore; therefore more easily caught than any other species. Spawns in the fall from late September to December. Eggs refrigerated by a blanket of winter ice and snow, hatching from March to May, when the spring thaw occurs. Back and sides usually dark olive green with the back, head, back fin, and tail marked by wavy lines. Sides punctuated by round light spots with scattered red spots or small red spots with blue halos. Paired and unpaired belly fins have conspicuous white edges bordered with black. Black markings or blotches inside mouth. At spawning time the lower sides and belly in male eastern brook are bright orange to cherry red, while lower sides and belly of female are opalescent silvery.

Brown trout: *Salmo trutta* (also called loch leven). Widely distributed from stock cultured at Mount Whitney Hatchery near Independence. Many high mountain streams and lakes planted with them but they prefer lower altitude. Now common to abundant only in such waters as the Owens River, Crowley Lake, Convict Lake, Bridgeport Reservoir, and Grant Lake. In Grant Lake they quickly crowded out the former cutthroat fishery and for years supplied enough eggs for planting throughout the Inyo-Mono area. Good self-sustaining brown trout fisheries still persist in many high lakes and in several lower streams.

The brown trout is more wary and less easily caught than any other trout; a fisherman can be justly proud of catching one. Spawns from October to December. Eggs lie dormant in the gravel, under snow and ice, and hatch from March to May or soon after spring thaw.

Color usually dark brown or olive brown on the back, more golden brown or bronzed on the sides and lower fins; yellow or yellow to white on the belly. Large, dark spots on head and gill covers, upper part of body, back fins and tail. In the so-called loch leven variety, red spots along the sides of the body are set off by a light halo and there are relatively fewer large dark spots on the body. Brown trout from large lakes such as Bridgeport Reservoir, Grant Lake, Crowley Lake, and Convict Lake are often silvery on the sides and belly.

RECOMMENDED READING

The booklet and folders listed below are published by the California Department of Fish and Game. Copies may be obtained from any of the department's regional offices (Los Angeles, Fresno, Yountville, Sacramento, Redding) or from Office of Procurement, Documents Section, P.O. Box 20191, Sacramento 95820.

Ehlers, Robert R. *Angler's Guide to the Lakes and Streams of the Mono Creek Area.* California Department of Fish and Game, 1962. Folded angler's map 18 by 27 inches with description of 47 waters of the Mono Creek Area, Fresno County.

Wales, Joseph H. *Trout of California.* California Department of Fish and Game, 1964. A superbly illustrated pocket-size booklet. Includes distinguishing characters, distribution, and habit highlights on all native and introduced trouts.

Birds

IN THE SIERRA HIGH COUNTRY, WHERE winter temperatures go below freezing and the ground is snow-covered for many months, few kinds of birds are able to find enough food year-round. Some which are not ground-feeders—such as chickadees, nuthatches, nutcrackers, and water ouzels—remain in the mountains in winter, but even they come down from the high country they frequent in summer. Most birds come to the mountains in late spring, nest, raise their young during summer while the insect population is at its height, then in fall migrate back to lower altitudes and warmer climates where their particular foods—berries, seeds, worms or insects—are more plentiful during the winter months.

Following are descriptions of fifteen birds easily identified and commonly seen in much of the eastern Sierra.

Additional birds common in the mountains of this region are the fox sparrow, pine siskin, and several varieties of warblers, woodpeckers, and hummingbirds. Persons particularly interested in birds will do well also to explore the desert marshes and lakes east of Highway 395. Ducks, grebes, pelicans, terns, avocets, willets, and phalaropes are among the water birds there. The sagebrush country has its birds also—shrikes, nighthawks, Brewer's sparrows, thrashers, magpies, horned larks, towhees, kingbirds, and marsh- and sparrow-hawks.

Sage hen or **sage grouse:** *Centrocercus urophasianus.* The size is about that of a chicken. The upper parts are mottled brown and gray, the under parts whitish, the belly black.

The sagebrush country east of the Cascades and Sierra is the home of the sage hen. Look for it in sage flats and swales, usually less than a mile from water. When startled, the birds take flight with the loud whirring of wings characteristic of grouse, pheasant, and quail. The sage hen can be distinguished in flight from the quail by its larger size and particularly by its long tail of stiff pointed feathers; the quail has a rounded tail. The female grouse is smaller than the male and has a shorter pointed tail. Her nest is a shallow depression in the ground hidden under shrubs. The half-grown young, seen occasionally in early summer, are scrawny birds resembling young turkeys.

Mountain quail: *Oreortyx picta.* About twice the size of a robin. Body blue-gray, sides barred with black and white, throat red-brown.

This bird is plump and has a straight black plume on its head. It lives in open country, often in the sagebrush. It nests on the ground, in dense brush. An amusing sight in summer is a brood of quail chicks (up to fifteen) scurrying after their mother, their legs moving so fast they seem to be on wheels. In fall, flocks of mountain quail migrate downhill to avoid the deep snows which cover the berries, seeds, leaves, and flowers on which they live. They travel chiefly on foot, seldom flying except to escape danger.

California gull: *Larus californicus* (not pictured). About the size of a crow. Gray above, white below. Under side of wing tipped with straight edge of black. Yellow bill, greenish legs.

Thousands of California gulls fly inland in April to nest on Negit Island in Mono Lake, returning to the coast in October. The rookery is faced with changes that may be fatal. Perhaps by the time you read this, Negit is an island no longer but a peninsula (see Mono Lake). The question is whether the gulls can protect their nests from predators and people, or whether they will abandon the site entirely.

Gulls are one of the so-called "predator" birds who eat the eggs and very young of other birds. Perhaps predation among animals would be less abhorrent to us if we remembered that man is the greatest predator of all, killing other living things not only that he may eat, but also for sport and for the trophies, furs, and feathers he displays. Predation is one of nature's vital mechanisms which prevent any animal from becoming too abundant and out of balance with its food supply. Nature is prolific, producing each year many more young of all kinds than there is food or shelter for. This is her insurance that the species will survive, despite the death of many individuals. Should *all* young water birds survive and reproduce for only a few years, the lakes of the earth would be crowded with birds who could find neither room to swim nor food to eat.

Remove the predators—such as hawks, coyotes, and mountain lions, as man has done in many regions—and in only a few years mice, rabbits, and deer will multiply out of all proportion to their natural food supply, eventually causing great damage to farmers' crops and ranchers' grazing lands. Many birds and animals have managed to survive predation, and to flourish, for thousands of years. Since predators often catch the crippled, the sick, the slow and the old, they also may contribute to the health of a species by encouraging the survival of the fittest—the most alert and vigorous.

Steller's jay: *Cyanocitta stelleri.* Slightly larger than a robin. Wings, tail, and most of body deep blue. Foreparts and crest blackish.

Jays are in the same family as crows and magpies, including some of the most intelligent of all birds. The bold, saucy Steller's jays frequent campgrounds and resorts, where they have learned to take advantage of the plentiful picnic scraps. Their calls are many and varied, the most common one being harsh and raucous. But near their own nests, which they build of twigs and mud, they are quiet and secretive. They will rob other nests when they can, but their main foods are nuts, grains, and insects. One female jay, killed while foraging for her five nestlings in Sequoia Park, was found to have twenty-two pine beetles in her mouth and throat. With nestlings demanding food many times an hour, how many insects destructive to trees will just one pair of birds kill in a season! No wonder many foresters consider birds among a tree's best friends.

Clark's nutcracker: *Nucifraga columbiana.* Slightly larger than a robin. Head and body light gray. Tail white with black center-feathers. Wings black with conspicuous white patches, bill black.

SAGE HEN (GROUSE)

MOUNTAIN QUAIL

STELLER'S JAY

HERMIT THRUSH

MOUNTAIN CHICKADEE

WATER OUZEL

CLARK'S NUTCRACKER

MOUNTAIN BLUEBIRD

WESTERN TANAGER

CASSIN'S PURPLE FINCH

OREGON JUNCO

WHITE-CROWNED SPARROW

The sleek, gray nutcracker, like its relative the Steller's jay, is noisy, conspicuous, and smart. It has many unusual behavior patterns quite unlike the jay, however, all associated with its preference for pine seed. During late summer most nutcrackers feed near timberline on the whitebark pine, exchanging raucous calls with each other and whacking open the cones with their sturdy, black bills. Then in fall they begin to store seed. Each bird, filling its throat pouch with over a hundred seeds, makes many trips a day to a storage site, where it buries small caches of seed in the ground. In late fall nutcrackers continue storing seed but at lower elevations—seed from the Jeffrey and pinyon pine. These lower-elevation, snow-free caches enable them to nest during late winter and feed their young in early spring, months earlier than other Sierran birds. By mid-summer most nutcrackers have returned to timberline, feeding on seed they stored the previous fall until new cones are ripe. Some of the buried seeds are never eaten and eventually sprout. Although most pine seeds have large "wings" to catch the wind, whitebark seeds are wingless and must be scattered some other way. It is the nutcracker, caching seeds, that is the major agent in scattering as well as planting whitebark pine.

Sometimes during nesting season, a nutcracker may be seen flying to the top of a tall tree, pursued by a dozen or so scolding, excited small birds. They are mobbing him, defending their nests against a supposed or real attack. Hawks and owls are similarly mobbed, by small birds and by nutcrackers too.

Mountain chickadee: *Parus gambeli.* Smaller than a sparrow. Black cap and throat, gray back and tail. Underparts grayish-white.

This small friendly bird may be found almost everywhere in the forests above 7500 feet, constantly hopping from twig to twig, often hanging upsidedown as he hunts for tiny insects and their eggs under leaves and in the cracks of bark. His strong feet, a bit large for his size, enable him to perform the acrobatics necessary to his foraging.

Tie a piece of suet to a tree branch, and chickadees soon will come. They will eat some, but will also spend many hours storing bits in the crevices of tree trunks, which they may find again in winter. Other birds may take advantage of the chickadees' industry, as did a little brown creeper one of us saw who spiraled around a tree, picking out what the chickadees had just put in.

Imitating the chickadees' call is fun, for they respond readily. Learn to whistle their simple call—tsee-dee-dee—keep repeating it, and usually several will answer and come close.

Water ouzel or **dipper:** *Cinclus mexicanus.* Slightly smaller than a robin. Dark gray all over. Yellowish feet.

The ouzel is easily identified by his plain color and his habit of constantly bending his legs and dipping up and down. He is one of the most unusual of birds for he lives his whole life near and in the water of plunging, foaming streams, often below the outlets of lakes where there are waterfalls. He nests in rock crevices along streams, sometimes behind falls. Water insects and larvae are his main food, which he obtains by diving and walking under water.

Yet he is a songbird, related to the wrens and thrushes, rather than to any of the water birds whose habits he has adopted. Though he does not have the webbed feet and long bill characteristic of most water-birds, he does have other specialized equipment which enables him to live in an environment of constantly dashing water—large, strong legs and sharp-clawed feet for gripping slippery rock and walking under water, dense plumage, an oil-gland ten times larger than that of related land-birds which enables him to keep his feathers pliable and water resistant, a cover over each nostril which he can close underwater, and a silvery white inner eyelid whose function seems to be wiping spray and water away from his eyes.

The ouzel sings loudly and joyously, often covered with spray and in the midst of a roaring stream. Almost every evening for three weeks in late September and October, one of us heard an ouzel sing at the outlet of Thousand Island Lake. He seemed oblivious to bad weather; his warbling came through the sleet and snow just as clearly and brightly as on the crisp evenings of Indian summer.

Hermit thrush: *Catharus guttatus*. The size of a sparrow. Grayish brown head, back, and wings. Rusty tail. Speckled throat and breast.

This shy bird of the deep woods is more often heard than seen. His is one of the most beautiful of all bird songs. It is an arresting experience to hear his clear flute-like notes in the stillness of a forest. During the nesting season in June and July, he repeats the two phrases of his song over and over—the first consisting of three high notes, the second a slur down the scale. This is his warning to other thrushes to stay away from his nesting and feeding territory.

Hermit thrushes can almost always be heard in the woods east of Horseshoe Lake, along the Crystal Lake trail, and elsewhere in dense red fir forest from about 8500 to 9500 feet. They are hard to see because they spend much of their time in the shade, near cover. But they can be identified by their large eyes and slender bills, their habit of frequently raising and lowering their tails slowly, and their robinlike actions—running a few steps, then drawing themselves up and cocking their heads as they look for food. Insects comprise half their diet, but they also eat seeds and berries. They usually nest in deep shade in small trees.

The hermit thrush might be confused with the fox sparrow, because their coloring is similar. But the sparrow can be distinguished readily by his short broad bill, and his habit of jumping forward and scratching back vigorously with both feet at once in loose leaves.

Robin: *Turdus migratorius* (not pictured). Breast rusty-red, head and tail blackish, back gray, bill yellow.

The handsome rusty-breasted male and the lighter colored, duller female come to the mountains usually in June. They build their nest of twigs, grass, and mud, often in the fork of a tree branch. Robins are common around many of the lower mountain lakes and in meadows—wherever worms are plentiful and the grass not high enough to hide them. They feed also on berries and on insects such as caterpillars, beetles, and grasshoppers. In August, look for young robins with speckled breasts and fluffed out feathers, almost as big as their parents but still following them and begging for food.

Mountain bluebird: *Sialia currucoides.* Slightly larger than a sparrow. Rich azure blue all over except for whitish belly. Female paler.

The bluebird is one of the most brightly colored of the high-mountain birds. Watch for the male in flight, his rich sky-blue flashing in the sun. Bluebirds may be seen in the big meadows at Old Mammoth, sitting on fence posts or hovering in the air as they look for food. Insects make up 90 per cent of their diet. They are just as commonly seen 3,000 feet higher, at timberline. Often they nest in old woodpecker holes or natural hollows, high in dead snags.

Brewer blackbird: *Euphagus cyanocephalus* (not pictured). A little smaller than a robin. Glossy black, pale yellow eye. Female more brownish than black, dark brown eye.

This is the common blackbird of farms, city lawns, and parks that walks importantly rather than hops, while scavenging about the campgrounds and foraging for his natural food of ground insects and seeds. Blackbirds usually flock and prefer marshy places, where they nest in dense thickets of brush and small trees. There are many in the swamp areas along the road to Benton Crossing, where there are also red-winged blackbirds and the rarer yellow-headed blackbird.

Western tanager: *Piranga ludoviciana.* Larger than a sparrow. Orange-red head, bright yellow body, middle of back, wings and tail black. Female dull greenish above, yellowish below.

The western tanager is the most colorful bird of this region, often seen as a flash of bright yellow and black flying among the trees. Their call has been likened by some to the sound of dripping water. They live in the forest from about 7500 to 9,000 feet and build their nests toward the tips of branches. They are relatively unafraid of people and are quick to take advantage of a feeding tray. Watermelon, placed out of reach of ground squirrels, readily attracts them.

Cassin's purple finch: *Carpodacus cassinii.* The size of a sparrow. Rose-red patch on top of head. Neck, back, wings and tail brown. Rump, throat and breast pale rose. Female brown streaked with gray.

Small flocks abound in the forests from about 8,000 to 9500 feet in summer. They often build their nests at the tip of pine branches. They forage for buds, seeds, and insects in trees and bushes as well as on the ground. Since they are not ground-feeders exclusively, they can live in the mountains even in winter, though they may go to the lower slopes. They are commonly mistaken for the house finch or linnet, since their colorings are similar; but the linnet is never found at such high altitudes.

Another finch, the Sierra rosy finch, inhabits the even higher altitudes of timberline and above. His coloring is less bright; his head is dark and his wings, rump and belly are washed with a deep pink. The rosy finch nests on the crags, feeding in early summer on insects frozen on high snowfields. It has spectacular flight habits, sometimes diving one or two hundred feet before opening its wings.

Dark-eyed (Oregon) **junco:** *Junco hyemalis.* Sparrow size. Head, neck and breast black, bill whitish. Back and wings rusty brown, underparts gray. Tail black, bordered with white on each side. Legs and feet pink.

This chunky little bird seems to mind his own business as he hops about on the ground, sparrow-like, picking up the seeds which form the major part of his diet. He is most easily identified in flight by the conspicuous flash of white on the outer sides of his tail. He frequently nests on the ground, in shrubs, or in low branches of trees such as mountain hemlock or white fir. In June and July he often hops about on snowbanks, picking out insects that have landed there and frozen. In late summer and fall, juncos usually flock together. They are one of the more successful kinds of birds, for in most of the Sierra they outnumber any other bird species.

White-crowned sparrow: *Zonotrichia leucophrys.* Upper parts grayish brown, underparts clear light gray. Three prominent white stripes on head, separated by black.

The cocky white-crowned sparrow is found commonly in the willows of mountain meadows and lakes, from about 7500 to 9500 feet. He nests on the ground or in the low branches of willows. In summer, his chief food is insects; in winter, seeds and weed sprouts.

RECOMMENDED READING

Hoffman, Ralph. *Birds of the Pacific States.* Boston: Houghton Mifflin, 1927. A good companion book to Peterson, describing bird behavior, habitats, and calls.

Peterson, Roger Tory. *A Field Guide to Western Birds.* Boston: Houghton Mifflin, second edition, 1961. Cloth and paper. The most widely used field guide for beginner and expert alike.

Stebbins, Cyril A. and Robert C. *Birds of Yosemite National Park.* Yosemite National Park: Yosemite Natural History Association, revised edition, 1963. Excellent booklet on Yosemite birds, including most of the common eastern Sierra birds.

Background

DISCOVERY IS THE THEME of much of the Mammoth Lakes Sierra. Again and again you can have the feeling—once you are off the highway—that you are walking places where few have walked before. Chances are good that you will be right in thinking so, but the chances aren't improving. In the 1930s there were still dozens of High Sierra peaks that had not yet been climbed. No more. But there are still slopes and woods and streamsides that you can find where there will be no evidence of human passage—until you pick up a fragment of obsidian arrowhead.

For all the newness the high country still promises, there is oldness to think about too. And what has gone before, the vivid but fleeting vision of time past, adds greatly to the Mammoth country.

Suppose, for example, you have chosen to take one of the trails that is a little more than moderate (unless you elect to ride a horse) and have crossed McGee Creek Pass. You are dropping down the west side into a high granite world, with colorful peaks piling up around you in their metamorphic colors, spacious meadows sloping up to them, crags, snowfields, flowers, meandering stream, clean wind—all these things telling you about what *is*—then suddenly in a geological context where there has been no volcanic activity (you know this) you stumble upon a fragment of obsidian. Dozens of them, hundreds of them, *thousands* of them! They lie along the trail. They spread out into the meadow, all over! Suddenly, then, you find your alpine Shangri-La shared, shared by people who found this place just about as wonderful as you do—brown-skinned Paiutes sharing it, through century after century, coming up to this haven (or so it must have been) to chip and exchange obsidian for something else, something that time would not treat so well.

There they are in your mind's eye, through all time, or at least all the time that Indians had to travel this pass year after year, and you find that you look at the great peaks differently, see them in a new dimension.

What you saw there is *pre*history, and we can't tell you much about that here. No one thought to put it down. But it does help to look at the record that has been written, to glean from it the bits of condiment that can flavor your *today* for you, give it perspective, add to it what other hands have felt and thought, other feet have walked and worn down, other eyes have seen and have hated and loved; let you realize that off the Sierra and down to you comes the same cool, clean, fresh, and sage-perfumed air, promising a moon or two of pleasant days before winter again swirls in to wall you off.

HISTORY OF THE REGION

The "Cutza Dika," the Paiutes of Mono Lake

East of the Sierra and west of the Rockies, encircled by high mountains, lies a high desert land—the Great Basin. Its rivers sink into sand or drain into ever-saltier lakes. Its climate is harsh, its forests scrubby, its animals scarce. Along the western edge of this inhospitable land—in eastern Oregon, western Nevada, and eastern California—lived the Northern Paiutes, related by language and culture not to the California Indians west of the Sierra, but to the Shoshoni and Bannock and other Great Basin peoples. "Paiute" (spelled also Piute, Pah Ute, Payuches) was the name early explorers gave vaguely to many Great Basin Indians. There were many Paiute groups, collections of families living near each other, too loosely organized to be considered "tribes." Customs of the groups varied slightly, their dialects considerably. Among the Paiutes living along the eastern base of the Sierra, was a small group near Mono Lake. These Indians called themselves neither Paiutes nor Monos, but "cutza dika," meaning cuzavi eaters—cuzavi being one of their food staples, fly pupae resembling small white worms which were collected from Mono Lake and dried.

How many hundreds of years the Paiutes have lived in the Great Basin no one knows. Their petroglyphs—cut in the rock in many places in the west, including the Benton Range, Owens Valley, and Death Valley—are no help. Present day Indians know nothing of their meaning or origin. (Recent research suggests that they were a type of magic, located near deer trails to ensure good hunting.) Anthropologists agree that they were made by the Paiutes' predecessors, but some believe they may be only several hundred years old; another thinks that they are at least a thousand years old and possibly even twice that age. It is believed that the ancestors of the petroglyph makers developed in central Asia, then migrated to this continent via the Bering Strait twenty or thirty thousand years ago. They fanned out through the Americas, some descendants eventually locating east of the Sierra and developing the customs and languages now labelled "Paiute."

The cutza dika were acquainted with other Paiute groups. Their neighbors at Benton they called "ütü′ ütü witü" (hot-place people), in Owens Valley "pitana patü (south-place people). Among other nearby Paiutes were the "salt-place people" in Deep Springs Valley, the "alkali-eaters" in Soda Springs Valley and the "fish-eaters" at Walker Lake, Nevada. Paiute groups were generally peaceful with each other and with their eastern neighbors, the Shoshoni, sometimes intermarrying. The squabbles that occurred usually resulted from one group's trespassing on another's pine-nut or hunting territory; most often they were settled by shouting and hurling stones at the intruders. Each group had a head man who settled disputes and organized the few communal activities such as pine-nut trips and rabbit drives, when the old men held nets in a long crescent to catch rabbits the others drove in and clubbed.

Paiute customs

Boys when young hunted lizards and mice, or smudged out gophers and ground squirrels. They also caught fish with small bone hooks, or shot them with their small willow bows. Later the men would teach them hunting secrets;

they would learn also to respect their elders and not to boast. One morning an older boy would be awakened very early, just after the morning star had risen. After special songs had been sung to him, he would bathe in a creek, asking the Great Power for blessing and guidance. This was his initiation into manhood, after which he would be allowed to join the hunts for big game. His first kill he must neither skin nor eat, lest he have bad luck and poor hunting in the future.

Though the word "Indian" usually evokes a picture of a splendid feather-bonneted, war-whooping creature, the Paiutes little resembled this type. They lived not in wigwams, but in circular shelters made of poles covered with grass, small branches, and juniper or sagebrush bark. Their summer "house" was rather a sun shade, a roof of branches supported by four willow posts. They hunted deer and mountain sheep occasionally, but subsisted mostly on small game, insects, pine nuts, and seeds. Piüga (pee-ăg'-gee), a caterpillar that lived part of its life in the Jeffrey pines, was an important food. They collected them in steep-sided trenches encircling the trees (traces of these trenches can still be recognized in the Jeffrey forest), cooked them in a fire pit with hot coals, and then dried them. They raised no corn and did not plant or cultivate, though Owens Valley Indians diverted streams and irrigated some wild seed plots. The women gathered many kinds of seeds, which they added to a mush of ground pine-nut meal, the staple to which might be added a handful of cuzavi, piüga, other insects, or meat. They wore no feathered headdresses, rode no horses. They often went barefoot, in good weather the men and children going naked. There was no emphasis on warfare—no war paint or war dances, seldom a scalping. Surviving through a bitterly cold winter often depended on the year's pine-nut crop. With only simple tools of wood, stone, and bone, they were able to utilize what few materials were at hand for food, clothing, and shelter. They made bows from juniper wood, or occasionally mountain mahogany, arrows from willow—with greasewood foreshafts and obsidian points which they wrapped on with sinew and glued with a sticky substance from sagebrush. Traps for small animals were made from looped willow stems. They wove rabbit skins into capes and robes, fiber into nets for fishing and rabbit drives. From local clays they made smoking pipes and a little pottery. They wove beautiful willow baskets of many sizes and shapes—food containers, cooking baskets, hats, cradles, seed beaters, winnowing trays, water bottles (pitch-coated inside). A small group from Mono Lake occasionally crossed the Sierra to trade with Yosemite Indians. The men traveled with buckskin bundles slung over their shoulders, the women with large baskets on their backs, tumplines pulling against their foreheads. The baskets were crammed with pine nuts, pieces of obsidian, red and white powder for paint making, cuzavi, smaller baskets, and salt (which had been scraped up from alkali lakes and patted into flat cakes). In return, they brought back bead money, acorns, and manzanita and elder-berries.

Despite their rigorous life, the Paiutes had their jolly times. Gambling, their favorite amusement, took many forms—wrestling, running, ball games, throwing spears, and most popular of all, the hand game. In this game four small bone sticks, two marked, were hidden in the hands of two partners; an opponent guessed in which hands the unmarked sticks were, betting large amounts of shell beads or goods. After seeds were gathered in fall, Paiutes congregated at certain centers for week-long celebrations of dancing and gambling. On winter evenings there was story telling, often about the two favorite characters Coyote and Hai'nanu. Both got themselves into all sorts of scrapes, Hai'nanu being a rascal and a rogue, Coyote a trickster—greedy, disobedient, and boastful. As related by Jack Stewart, a very old Paiute from Big Pine: "The evil in the world came from Coyote. Wolf and Coyote settled things so that there would always be evil along with good. Evil is clever and talks well, always trying to get you. It makes people dishonest and lazy. But by following a good life, being kind, helpful, and generous, you have great power, as I have had."

White men west of the Sierra, 1542–1825

For some three hundred years after California was discovered by the Spanish explorer Cabrillo in 1542, the Paiutes continued gathering cuzavi, grinding pine nuts and living off the land as they always had. The ships of the Spanish explorers, the "rush" of fur ships to the northwest for sea otter pelts, the chain of missions established by the padres, the great ranchos of the Spanish land grants, the beaver trade developed by the Hudson's Bay Company in the Oregon Territory, the ships which took the rancho's cowhides and tallow to New England's boot and shoe factories and returned with manufactured goods—all these activities were confined to a few coastal pueblos and valleys, for ships were California's sole tie with the rest of the world. By 1825, when about seven thousand Spaniards and Mexicans (plus a few British, Americans, and Russians) had settled in California, no white man had yet crossed the immense mountain barrier of the Sierra Nevada nor the deserts of Nevada and Utah.

The mountain men, trail blazers of the West

When fashion decreed that the well-dressed man should wear a high-crowned beaver-trimmed hat, early in the 1800s, the sudden demand for beaver skins sent their price soaring. Lured by the profits to be made—prime furs brought four to six dollars a pound in St. Louis—the adventurous and the enterprising set out to trap in the vast wilderness west of the Missouri, roaming the Rocky Mountains and the far west wherever their search for beaver led them. These American fur trappers, known as Mountain Men, were the first to travel the immense distances still separating coastal California from the frontier towns along the Missouri River. It was they who explored the west and blazed the first trails, and who served later parties as guides and scouts. One of the most daring was Jedediah Smith, who was still in his twenties when he led the first trapping party to reach California overland in 1826 and when he made the first crossing of the Sierra on his return trip to Salt Lake. The central route across the Sierra was discovered in 1833 by another experienced frontiersman, Joseph Reddeford Walker, hired by a Captain Bonneville who was organizing a trapping expedition. Sent to explore west of Salt Lake and to visit California, Walker with his party of fifty crossed the desert by following the Humboldt River, then struck south to Bridgeport Valley, passing Carson and Walker lakes on the way. Crossing the Sierra divide, probably by one of the southern tributaries of the East Walker River, the party descended the western slope possibly near Virginia Canyon, then traveled through Yosemite country to the San Joaquin Valley. On his return trip Walker discovered the pass in the southern Sierra that Frémont later named in his honor.

The beginning of westward migration, 1840—1848

Mountain Men returning to the frontier towns were lavish in their praise of California—its temperate climate, game, fertile soil, the easy life on the ranchos. Sailing men, too, spread tales of the wonders of the Pacific Coast. Adventurous pioneers were settling west of the Missouri River, a few pushing all the way to Oregon. The first pioneers reached California in 1840, the thirty-some members of the Bidwell party. Traveling was so difficult, they abandoned their wagons in northeastern Nevada. They walked the rest of the way to the Sacramento Valley, crossing the Sierra over Sonora Pass with their goods strapped to oxen and mules. Pioneer migration steadily increased during the forties, most of the settlers going to the northwest over the well-established Oregon Trail, a few coming to California. The first to follow a route along the Sierra's east slope was the Chiles-Walker party, which descended the Humboldt River and then headed south past Walker Lake and through Owens Valley to Walker Pass.

Three years after the Chiles-Walker party, the first expedition charged officially with exploring and making maps entered Inyo-Mono country, Captain John Frémont's third expedition. Leader of five expeditions to the west, Frémont gathered his group at Walker Lake (Nevada)—among them the famous mountain men Joseph Walker and Kit Carson, and two others whose names are immortalized on Sierra maps, Dick Owens and Edward Kern. At Walker Lake, the party split; Walker guided the largest group south through Owens Valley and over Walker Pass.

The gold rush, 1849

The pioneer's steady parade westward was interrupted in 1848 by the spine-tingling news that gold had been discovered near John Sutter's Sacramento Valley rancho. Californians dropped whatever they were doing and raced to the Sierra foothills. As the news spread that miners were panning out $100 in gold a day, that a lucky one had found a twelve-ounce nugget, men streamed in from neighboring Mexico and Oregon. By the following year, California's magic name had crossed both oceans to Europe and the Orient, and men from every-

Historic water wheel

T J Johnston

Silver!
The discovery of blue-black silver ore at the Comstock

in 1858, east of Lake Tahoe, brought a torrent of men flooding east across the Sierra into lands the gold-seekers had passed by without a look. Among miners at the played-out placers of the Mother Lode, news of the Comstock's incredible riches spread like wildfire.

Stamp mill, May Lundy Mine   Frasher's Photo

Lundy about 1900   Frasher's Photo

Hotel, Benton   Genny Smith collection

On to Washoe!
Silver at the
Comstock!

By tens, by hundreds, across the Sierra to Washoe they surged, answering the cry of Silver at the Comstock! Rumors and dreams spurred them on farther, east into the desert ranges and south along the Sierra to prospect its eastern slope. And right behind the prospectors came hundreds of teamsters, merchants, cattlemen, and farmers to supply them.

The Paiutes and Washoes east of the Sierra had lived undisturbed longer than most western Indians. The massive Sierra effectively barricaded them from all the trappers, traders, padres, soldiers, and ranchers west of the mountains. But the torrent of white men lured by the Comstock disrupted their lives and overran their lands almost overnight.

News of gold near Mono Lake in 1859 brought seven hundred men racing to Monoville the first summer. Other strikes followed quickly. Aurora, northeast of Mono Lake, mushroomed into a camp of five thousand people. Silver was discovered at Blind Springs Hill near Benton, gold at the May Lundy, both silver and gold at Bodie, the wildest camp of all.

Prospectors   Eastern California Museum photo

Pack train early 1880s   Laws Railroad Museum photo

Freighting for the California-Nevada   Billy Young
Canal Water & Power Company

Church, Bodie

Philip Hyde

Boom, bust, ghost town, oblivion —

this is the story rusted wheels and weatherbeaten boards tell us at hundreds of old mining camps. For some the boom was brighter and lasted longer; for others the bust came sooner. But even the richest camps such as Bodie and Aurora, each producing thirty million dollars in gold and silver, had only brief years of glory. Few traces remain of most camps. Though fire destroyed much of Bodie, what survived is now preserved as a state historic park — not a restored tourist attraction, but a true ghost town.

Bodie   Philip Hyde

House, Bodie   Philip Hyde

Mammoth Camp in the 1920s

H.W. Mendenhall, Adele Reed collection

Old Mammoth took its name from the Mammoth Mine,

one bonanza that never materialized at all. In 1878 General George Dodge of Civil War and Union Pacific fame and associates bought five claims on Mineral Hill east of Lake Mary. Their Mammoth Mining Company built a flume, tramway, and 40-stamp mill. The mill was powered by the six-foot Knight wheel (similar to a Pelton) pictured on the first photo page. It's said a thousand people flocked to Mammoth that first summer (it was touted as the "largest bonanza outside of Virginia City"), but they soon flocked elsewhere.

Less than two years later, the mill shut down and company property was sold at a sheriff's sale.

Twenty years later, young Dr. Guy Doyle from Chicago hauled the old wheel up the hill to power a 10-stamp mill he built closer to the mine tunnels. But the bonanza eluded him too, and another twenty years later, its mining days over, the old wheel was sledded down to the meadows. There it generated power for Mammoth's first resort, the Wildasinn Hotel. Later Charlie Summers hooked it up to the new hotel and rooming house he built in 1918, Mammoth Camp.

Doyle mill early 1900s   Stephen H. Willard, Adele Reed collection

Mammoth Mining Company mill   Genny Smith collection

Hauling logs to Mammoth sawmill, about 1919   H.W. Mendenhall, Adele Reed collection

Mono County Courthouse, built in 1880

Julius Shulman

Mono County's first choice for county seat was the booming camp of Aurora. When Mono and adjacent Esmeralda (Nevada) counties were established in 1861, no one knew exactly where the state line was. Both counties claimed Aurora and both named it county seat. In fact, in a most unusual election in 1863, Aurorans voted twice, for two full slates of county officers — one for Esmeralda, one for Mono. But Mono lost its claim, when the boundary survey determined that Aurora lay east of the state line, and its voters then chose Bridgeport. The courthouse, built in 1880, continues to serve Mono County today.

where were embarking for the land of gold. The Gold Rush of '49 set in motion the greatest migration ever; in four years California's white population soared from 14,000 to 223,000. However, this was neither the first nor the last "rush" in the Americas. The discovery of northwest Mexico's great silver mines three hundred years before, the race for sea otter—and then, beaver—pelts, later gold and silver strikes in many western states, then copper, later oil, and most recently uranium—each caused a sudden, feverish movement of people.

Prospectors east of the Sierra, 1853

While all the world knew of the Mother Lode on the Sierra's west slope, no one bothered about the eastern slope. The first prospectors in this region were probably Leroy Vining and his companions, who about 1853 took the Mono Trail to prospect east of the Sierra. Shortly after Vining, other prospectors looking for new placers must have drifted south from the Mormon settlement of Genoa in Carson Valley. In 1857 rumor had it that Mormon miners were washing out gold at Brown's Creek (also known as Dogtown Creek, Dogtown Diggings), the general location still marked by the remains of stone cabins along the creek, about six miles north of Conway Summit. Two years later it was reported that Dogtown had a store and that seventy men lived along the stream. It is ironic that the first sizable group of miners on the east side should be predominantly Mormon, for of all groups the Mormons were about the only ones who did not heed the siren song of gold. Brigham Young threatened the Saints in Salt Lake Valley with damnation if they did; few disobeyed him.

It was along streambeds that these early prospectors searched, for they were looking for placers—stream deposits of sand and gravel, rich with particles of gold. Some of the placers were phenomenally rich; in seven weeks, fifty hired Indians washed out two hundred seventy-three pounds of gold at the Feather River diggings. Placer mining was essentially a settling process, washing away the sand and mud and retaining the heavier gold. And since placer mining required few tools, anyone became a miner simply by outfitting himself with a shovel, pick, and gold pan. But panning proved to be slow, back-breaking, and profitable only on the richest placers. Crude wooden devices were invented—rockers, sluices, long-Toms—which enabled several men working together to wash much larger amounts of river sand. Hydraulic mining—aiming a high-pressure stream of water, as through a fire hose, at stream banks—was a later development for removing much material quickly.

Gold at the Mono Diggings, 1859

Cord Norst, a Dogtown miner, discovered gold in a wash a few miles from Mono Lake in July of 1859. (The site can be seen from Highway 395, as it begins the climb to Conway Summit—the large wash to the east.) Dogtown miners rushed to the new diggings, and soon west-side miners came racing over Sonora Pass and Mono Pass. That summer, seven hundred men in the new camp of Monoville were washing out anywhere from ten to a hundred dollars a day; it is claimed their number reached two or three thousand. In the fall of the same year, Bill Bodey and four friends located placer ground while prospecting northeast of Monoville, but it caused no excitement.

Silver at Esmeralda, 1860

The same year as the Monoville strike, fabulously rich silver ore was discovered east of Lake Tahoe—the Comstock Lode, the biggest bonanza of them all, which eventually produced about $700,000,000 worth of gold and silver. Thousands of miners who had only recently come to California now poured back across its borders to Washoe, as Nevada was then called. Three prospectors who had been at the Comstock long enough to learn a little about silver, located rich quartz veins several miles east of Bodey's find the next summer. The miners there organized the Esmeralda District, and the wildly speculative camp that grew up was named Aurora. In their best days, the mines supported seventeen mills and a prosperous community of five thousand people. Hopelessly infected with "Washoe fever" and the "Esmeralda excitement," men surged to the new camps, each expecting to strike it rich. Along with them went just about as many others to supply them with food, liquor, clothing, and tools, and the mines with fuel, lumber, and machinery.

With Aurora booming, agitation began for a wagon road west over the Sierra. Supplies for the thousands of men at Monoville and Aurora had to come all the way from Carson Valley, or over Mono and Sonora passes by pack train— long, precarious, and expensive trips. Most "roads" were just tracks in the sand, but over mountain passes and in rough country, roads had to be built. Usually they were constructed as private business enterprises, their owners collecting toll from all who passed. Construction started in 1864; in 1868 the Sonora Pass Toll Road was completed. In these few years, ironically, Aurora had passed her peak and was on the way to becoming a ghost town.

The Paiutes' land was theirs no longer. Cattle grazed on the best wild-seed lands, sheep on the deer's brush slopes. Pine-nut trees were cut for fuel. Game and fish, never abundant, became even scarcer. Some of the Paiutes fought back; many began working for the white man.

Creation of Mono County, 1861

The sudden influx into the land east of the Sierra, then eastern Calaveras County, led to a petition asking the California Legislature to create Esmeralda County. The bill was amended to read Mono County, and passed in 1861. Nine years later Mono County's first census was taken. Such are the fluctuations of mining prosperity that, instead of thousands, Mono County now had only 430! Of the two sizable communities existing when the county was created, Monoville was deserted and Aurora was found to be in Nevada (after the state boundary was finally established and after it had been chosen the county seat of

Mono). The 1870 census also mentioned Mono County's agriculture. Sixty farms and ranches had been settled and over nine thousand acres were producing wheat, oats, barley, hay, and potatoes; 35,000 pounds of butter and 4,000 pounds of cheese, besides local beef and pork, were produced yearly for local consumption.

The mining districts and unofficial self-government

In the absence of any effective county or state government in the scattered mining camps that sprang up, anarchy was effectively avoided by holding a meeting, attended by any miner in the area. At the first meeting it became customary to formally declare a "District," to name it, and to elect a committee for drawing up a set of regulations governing claims. The formalities over, a liquid celebration usually rounded out the evening. The regulations, adopted at another meeting, often provided that a miner could hold only one claim—of a specified length—that he could hold it only as long as he worked it, that he could add to his holdings by buying others, and that a specified procedure was to be followed when disputes arose, such as calling a mass meeting or choosing arbiters. A District Recorder was elected to register claims and make transfers of title. Sometimes at these public meetings a simple but effective criminal code was also adopted, such as: thieves were to be whipped in public, horse thieves and murderers hanged. Banishment from the camp was another common punishment (Git on yer horse an' git!). Justice was immediate, for there were no jails to hold the accused. The district served its purpose remarkably well, though if the recorder was stupid or careless, claims might be recorded incorrectly or the whole book of claims might be lost; it became superfluous when County, State, and Federal government ultimately assumed the regulation of mining.

The Lost Cement Mine

In 1864, several mining districts were formed southeast of Aurora, the only one of importance being the Blind Springs Mining District with its camp of Benton. Over a period of twenty years, this district produced about $4,000,000 worth of silver. For the next thirteen years nothing of any importance was discovered in Mono County. The center of excitement shifted south to the Coso and Slate ranges beyond Owens Lake. The Cerro Gordo mines proved to be of lasting importance, producing an estimated $13,000,000. Other strikes, mostly silver, were being made in Nevada.

Prospecting continued in Mono County during the '60s and '70s, however, much of it stimulated by the widely spread tale of the "Lost Cement Mine." Lumps of gold "like raisins in a pudding" had been found in a reddish "cement" somewhere on the headwaters of the Owens River, according to one version. Another version is that a prospector took ore samples from an unusual rock with him across the mountains to the western foothills. Later when he became very ill and knew he could never make it back to his find, he gave to a Dr. Randall in San Francisco as payment for his services some ore, a map, and a detailed description of the site. Arriving in Monoville in 1861, Dr. Randall hired men to go with him to Pumice Flat (supposedly eight miles north of Mammoth) and there located a quarter-section of land. The next summer Dr. Randall returned to his location, and employed eleven men with a Gid Whiteman as foreman. They found some reddish lava or cement, and though the story is vague on whether this reddish rock contained any gold or not, hundreds of others began searching for red cement. Possibly the golden studded cement was found but kept a secret; possibly the whole story was the raving of a deranged prospector; possibly the tale was true and the reddish cement is there still, waiting to be uncovered. Indians who brought gold to Benton, never saying where they got it, were suspected of knowing the mine's whereabouts. Whiteman searched for over twenty summers, believing until his death in 1883 that he was near the lost mine. The legend lives; occasional prospectors still search for the Lost Cement Mine.

Mining excitement returns to Mono County

In the late 1870s, mining excitement returned to Mono County as new discoveries were made, one after the other. Four men prospecting for the Lost Cement Mine in 1877 located the Alpha claim on Mineral Hill, now known as Gold or Red Mountain. A month later the nearby Mammoth claim was filed, then dozens more. The next spring the Lake District, as it was called, was visited by General George Dodge of Union Pacific and Civil War fame and pronounced "good enough for a stock deal." General Dodge bought the Mammoth claim for $10,000 in cash and $20,000 in company stock, and organized the Mammoth Mining Company. Work was started, eighteen other companies entered the area, and the rush to Mammoth was on. Flumes, a tramway, and a 20-stamp mill were constructed, another twenty stamps added shortly. The population grew to a reported 2500. Mammoth's boom also stimulated road building, routes later important to settlers and stockmen—the Sherwin Toll Road south to Bishop, a wagon road to Benton, and the French (toll) Trail which led west across the mountains to Fresno Flats.

But the Mammoth bonanza never materialized. The mill's shutdown early in 1880 was attributed by a Mammoth newspaper to a lack of quicksilver and chemicals; a more likely report blamed disagreement among the stockholders.

Bodie, 1878

A few months after making his placer find in 1859, Bill Bodey had perished in a blizzard on his way to Monoville for supplies. Other prospectors staked quartz claims nearby over a number of years. Companies succeeded each other but all failed financially, including one headed by Governor Leland Stanford. An accidental cave-in uncovered a rich ledge, which was bought eventually by the newly organized Standard Company in 1877. The company erected a mill, the ore proved to be very rich, and within a year the rush was on to Bodie. Bodie's production record far surpasses that of any other Mono County mine, an estimated $30,000,000 in gold and silver. The Standard Company paid almost a million dollars in dividends to its stockholders during a single year. Bodie also boasted more gambling, drinking and shooting than any other lawless mining camp. A favorite story is of a child being taken to Bodie, who prayed, "Good-bye God! I'm going to Bodie." A Bodie editor replied that the little girl had been misquoted, that what she really said was, "Good, by God! I'm going to Bodie." High living and speculation dominated the camp of eight (possibly ten) thousand people, until the stock market crash of 1881. One by one Bodie's mines closed until by 1888 only four or five hundred people remained. Bodie's notorious days were over, though the two most profitable companies—The Standard and The Bodie—merged and operated successfully for a number of years more.

Promoters' hey-day—the mining companies

During the twenty years separating Dogtown and Bodie, mining methods had changed considerably. Prospectors no longer explored only stream beds; mostly they tramped the mountains looking for gold-bearing quartz veins. Few prospectors worked their claims; instead, they looked for a company to sell to. Most "miners" were day laborers working for companies at about four dollars for a ten-hour day; few remained as independent as the Forty-niner with his burro and a few tools. These changes were due to the exhaustion of the rich placers and to the nature of quartz mining. Extracting gold from quartz is difficult. First the ore has to be blasted and hauled out, then broken to free the gold particles, and finally the gold has to be separated from the crushed rock. To do all this by hand yielded so little gold that few tried it. To be worthwhile, quartz mining required big-scale operation. Tunnels had to be driven into mountains, tramways and railroads constructed to move the ore. Three-story stamp mills were needed for crushing it, water or steam power for running the mills. Skilled men, expensive machinery, buildings, roads—all required thousands of dollars of capital.

With the development of the all-important Company, the promoter and the financier came into prominence. Many fortunes were made, not by producing gold, but by buying and selling mining stock at the right moment. Stock in the Bodie Mining Company jumped from 50¢ to $54 a share; Hale and Norcross Mine (Virginia City) stock slid from $2900 to $41.50 a share in six months. Promoters of 1870 were much like those of today—some honest, some dishonest, their mine always a sure thing. Many were the gullible investors who bought stock on the high assay value of a single ore sample.

Exact production figures for the early mines are impossible to obtain. Few records were kept (the income tax had not yet been invented), and of those few, most were lost or destroyed. Promoters' optimistic reports, quoted in early newspapers, are unreliable for they were often aimed at raising stock prices or enticing potential investors. The State Division of Mines was created too late (1880) to obtain current figures for the early mines. However, its estimates are more reliable than the inflated values of local rumor, for they are based on statistics of the U. S. Mint (gold received) and the U. S. Customs House (gold shipped). All production figures quoted in this book are taken from correspondence with or publications of the Division of Mines.

The Lundy and Tioga mines

In 1879, the year of terrific excitement both in Bodie and Mammoth, veins of ore were also discovered in Mill Creek (now Lundy) Canyon and the Homer Mining District was formed there. The small town of Lundy lived on for a number of years, the May Lundy Mine producing an estimated $2,000,000 in gold. Lundy's newspaper, the *Homer Mining Index*, is one of the most entertaining of the old mining camp papers. "Lying Jim" Townsend, its editor, aimed his news at faraway Britishers with money invested in the Lundy mines—printing time tables for a nonexistent Lundy railroad, advertising two imaginary banks and several large grocery stores, and describing in detail the ladies' fashions worn on the opening night of a fictitious theater (acc. to Chalfant).

In 1882, the Great Sierra Consolidated Silver Mining Company was organized to develop the Tioga Mine on a ridge just east of Tioga Pass. Routes to this mine were spectacular, accessible first only by the Bloody Canyon-Mono Pass trail. Later an even more precipitous trail was built over the mountains to Lundy, and 16,000 pounds of machinery—an engine, boiler, compressor, drills, pipe, and so on—impossible to pack in by mule, were hauled over this route on sleds in winter. A quote from the *Index* of March 1882 (this time probably not exaggerated) may arouse appreciation of the difficulties miners faced before the days of trucks and tractors:

The first ascent, from Mill Creek to the mouth of Lake Canyon, is 990 feet, almost perpendicular. From that point to the south end of Lake Oneida . . . is a rise of 845 feet. . . . The machinery will probably be hoisted straight up to the summit of Mount Warren ridge . . . an almost vertical rise of 2,160 feet. From the summit the descent will be made to Saddlebags Lake. . . . It is being transported on six heavy sleds admirably constructed of hardwood . . . a pair of bobsleds accompany the expedition, the latter being laden with bedding, provisions, cooking utensils, etc. The heaviest load is 4,200 pounds. Ten or twelve men, two mules, 4,500 feet of one-inch Manila rope, heavy double block and tackle, and all the available trees along the route are employed in 'snaking' the machinery up the mountain. . . .

After the company had spent $300,000 over a period of two years, financial disaster overtook it and work stopped abruptly.

Mining after 1890

Since Bodie's decline, gold and silver mining in Mono County has been small-scale only. Some thousands of dollars have been taken out by working tailings and by small mills. But the big bonanzas were elsewhere—Cripple Creek, the Klondike, Tombstone. Other metals have come into importance, in recent years tungsten, though most tungsten mines closed after 1956 when most government price support was removed. The Black Rock Mine southeast of Benton was in 1953 the second largest producer of tungsten in California, and the sixth largest in the United States. Prospecting continues, and usually there's someone looking for the Lost Cement Mine. But in recent years Mono County has produced little besides clay, pumice, sand and gravel, and stone. In 1972 total production was $528,000.

Farming and ranching

Mining had drawn thousands of men east of the Sierra and had stimulated the building of roads and the development of nearby farms, ranches, and sawmills. When the mines closed, most left. But two thousand stayed in Mono County, ranching and operating small sawmills. For the next thirty years, about one hundred farm families worked some 50,000 acres, diverting streams to flood some of the bottomlands. Most important was cattle ranching; the principal crops were hay, wheat, and barley. Good summer grazing for sheep was provided on the sagebrush slopes and in the high mountain meadows of the eastern Sierra. The severe droughts of 1863–1864, '71, and '77 had caused terrible losses of livestock. Animals died of thirst and starvation, for deep wells and irrigated pasture were then not common ranching practice. In '77 alone, southern California sheepmen lost an estimated 2,500,000 head. Spurred by these repeated droughts, ranchers began driving their animals into the High Sierra, where natural meadows offered dependable summer feed. John Muir's first acquaintance with the Sierra came as he herded sheep from the San Joaquin Valley to the high Tuolumne meadows.

Ranching declined drastically during the 1920s and '30s because of depressions and loss of markets, then increased as cattle raising became profitable once again. Shepherds still bring their sheep to the mountain meadows in summer, though the month-long drive from Bakersfield and Lancaster now takes only one day in a truck. In 1969 Mono County ranchers produced livestock and other farm products worth $861,000. Farms are fewer today, thirty-four, but larger; half are more than a thousand acres. In two of the county's fertile valleys—Long Valley and Mono Basin—ranching today consists largely of dry grazing on leases from the City of Los Angeles. Most of the water from these two valleys now flows into the Los Angeles Aqueduct.

Water for Los Angeles

During the early 1900s, the growing city of Los Angeles was short of water; the Owens River appeared to be a convenient source. The 25-year fight over water rights between Owens Valley citizens and the City's Department of Water and Power is well detailed in Nadeau's book *The Water Seekers*. The sad story need not be repeated here. One of the points causing bitter disagreement was the plan for a dam at the lower end of Long Valley. Finally in 1932, Los Angeles Mayor Fred Eaton's Long Valley ranch was purchased and construction of the dam begun. To control the streams, the City then began buying ranches and their water rights as far north as Lee Vining Creek. All waters tributary to Owens River flow naturally into Crowley Lake; streams north of Deadman Summit, which drained into Mono Lake, were diverted and joined to the Owens River by a tunnel driven through the Mono Craters. Within the Craters, much to their surprise, the tunnel builders encountered steam, hot water, volcanic gases, and ground cavings which doubled the cost of the tunnel, completed after great difficulties in 1940.

With ever more people asking for ever more water, the City in 1970 completed its Second Aqueduct, increasing total capacity by 48 per cent and increasing average delivery to 420 million gallons per day. To fill this "Second Barrel," the City increased its ground water pumping in Owens Valley and diverted the entire flow of the four major Mono Basin streams—Lee Vining, Walker, Parker, and Rush creeks.

The making of Inyo-Mono's vacation land

The eastern Sierra (Inyo-Mono) has natural attractions in abundance— great beauty, high mountains, hundreds of lakes, dozens of streams, fish, game, and a wide variety of scenery. Before 1920, a few people came to enjoy these attractions—but a very few. Had even more people known about the region's beauties, they *could* not have come. They worked fifty hours a week, six days a week; furthermore, it was a rugged two-day trip from Los Angeles. Automobiles were still a novelty, and anyone venturesome enough to drive up the east side had little more to follow than tracks through the sagebrush. Boiling radiators demanded quantities of water, and cars were expected to sink to their axles at least once or twice in the loose sand and pumice.

As California's people voted many millions for highways, a share was spent on El Camino Sierra, now known as U.S. Highway 395. At the same time, wages began going up, hours going down, automobiles going faster, and vacations getting longer. The growth of southern California during and after World War II provided an immense population center only seven hours away—millions of people with the time and money and desire to camp, hike, fish, hunt, and ski. The Inyo National Forest, now one of the ten most popular forests in the nation, counted close to five million visitor days in 1975.

In the late 1930s, a few local people, seeing skis on the horizon, built small portable ski tows and powered them with car engines. They set them up wherever the snow was suitable—as on the slope of McGee Mountain, Deadman Summit, or Conway Summit, usually close to Highway 395, for side roads were not kept open. A crowd of skiers in those days might be all of fifteen people.

After the war, skiing boomed in many parts of the country. Fifty or a hundred week-end skiers might come to Mammoth Mountain's rope tows, sometimes hiking several miles or riding a weasel if the road was snow blocked. The completion of an all-weather road to Mammoth Mountain's north slope in 1954 and the construction of a double chair lift in 1955 put Mammoth on the skier's map. A minimum six-month ski season, dependable snow, wonderfully variable terrain, and the proximity of two population centers have made Mammoth one of the country's outstanding winter resorts. More and more lifts and the opening of the June Mountain ski area in 1961 have changed recreation from a summer-only to an all-year industry. By 1972 tourists and recreation were bringing twenty-five million dollars a year to Mono County.

Mining was the key that unlocked the treasure chest of the eastern Sierra, one of the last regions of California to be settled. The Spanish-Mexicans and the men of the trading ships, so important to the state's early growth, left no mark east of the mountains. Vast deserts on three sides, and an immense mountain barrier on the other kept white men away until relatively late in California's development. Ranching succeeded mining. Now the magnificent mountain scenery, the long snow season, and the back country wilderness are the treasures that bring people flocking—to the Mammoth Lakes Sierra.

RECOMMENDED READING

Billeb, Emil W. *Mining Camp Days*. Berkeley: Howell-North Books, 1968. Life in Tonopah 1905, Bodie 1908–20, Mono Lake RR & Lumber Co., Lundy, Benton, etc.

Chalfant, Willie A. *Gold, Guns, and Ghost Towns*. Stanford: Stanford University Press, 1947. Nevada and eastern Sierra mining tales—humorous, exciting, authentic—by the man who edited the *Inyo Register* for fifty-five years. Highly recommended.

DeDecker, Mary. *Mines of the Eastern Sierra*. Glendale: La Siesta Press, 1966. Cloth and paper. True stories of the booms and busts.

Eaton, Evelyn. *Snowy Earth Comes Gliding*. Independence: Draco Foundation, 1974. Personal account of associations with the Paiutes and the Indian Way. Full-page photos of the exceptional carvings of Raymond Stone, Paiute sculptor and pipe-maker.

Farquhar, Francis P. *History of the Sierra Nevada*. Berkeley: University of California Press, 1965. Cloth and paper. A joy to read, a scholar's delight.

Johnson, Russ and Anne. *The Ghost Town of Bodie*. Bishop: Chalfant Press, 1967. Cloth and paper. Bodie as reported in the newspapers of its day. Many photos.

Nadeau, Remi A. *The Water Seekers*. Salt Lake City: Peregrine Smith, revised edition, 1974, cloth. Paper edition by Chalfant Press, Bishop. Back in print, the story of the Los Angeles Aqueduct—the long, bitter fight, not quite over, between Owens Valley people and the Department of Water and Power. Essential reading.

Reed, Adele. *Old Bottles and Ghost Towns*. Bishop: published by the author, 272 Shepard Lane, 1961. Wanderings to nearby ghost towns. Many illustrations.

Smith, Genny and Adele Reed. *Historic Mammoth Postcards*. 1975. Historic photos of Old Mammoth 1877–1937. Junior Women's Club, P.O. Box 1556, Mammoth Lakes.

Wedertz, Frank. *Bodie 1859–1900*. Bishop: Chalfant Press, 1969. Cloth and paper. Extensive coverage of Bodie. Many old photographs.

Wheat, Margaret. *Survival Arts of the Primitive Paiutes*. Reno: University of Nevada Press, 1967. The Old Ways—all but disappeared—of gathering food, making clothing, building shelters. Exceptional photographs depicting Paiute skills.

Notes

1. Some say a raft took passengers to a "dancing platform" built on the far side of Lake Mary; others say dancing was on a barge, pushed up and down the lake by long poles. The August 13, 1879, *Mammoth City Herald* tells of Jerry McCarthy's new dancing pavilion on the lake's west side where on Sundays there was "music, dancing, picnicking under the trees, flirting, real love making and we don't know what all."

2. A Calvert descendant states emphatically that Lake Mary was not named for her grandmother but that both Lakes Mary and Mamie were named for Bodie dancehall girls. She says that George carried mail from Bodie to Pine City on skis but she does not believe that her grandparents lived here. Another story has it that for a time the Mammoth Mine was operated by an English company and that Lakes Mary and George were named for the king and queen of England.

3. Casa Diablo's and Long Valley's steam may eventually be harnessed to turbines. Long Valley, a potential source of geothermal energy, has been one of the target areas of the U.S.G.S. Geothermal Research Program during the 1970s. A 9,000-foot exploratory well was authorized in 1976. This drilling is expected to provide critical evidence in confirming or denying significant geothermal potential.

4. Just opposite the turnoff to the Inyo Crater Lakes, a dirt road branches right from Highway 395 to an outstanding viewpoint called Lookout Mountain. The chief attraction is the superb panoramic view—especially of the Sierra Crest to the west and south. There are also excellent views of several barren, rough-surfaced obsidian domes to the west, the blocky, crown-shaped Mono Craters to the north, the White Mountains on the skyline to the east, and Long Valley and Crowley Lake to the southeast.

5. Sideroad to Bald Mountain. Just north of Deadman Summit there is a pumice road leading east to the top of Bald Mountain, a marvelous viewpoint from which to see almost all the country described in this guidebook. It is a particularly beautiful drive in the early evening. On the way there is a worthwhile side trip to the Indiana Summit Natural Area, a virgin Jeffrey pine woodland where no grazing or logging has been permitted. The contrast with the rest of the forest is striking—here the grass grows tall and the trees make a natural park with no stumps or slash. To heighten the contrast, you will also drive through forestland that was clear cut to supply lumber for early communities. Visitors are welcome to visit the fire lookout on the summit. The road is well signed and safe for passenger cars as long as you stay in the road tracks and stay out of the soft pumice.

6. The informative and artistic exhibits at the ranger station are well worth stopping for. They include displays on the plant communities of Mono Basin, the rocks, the old mining camps, and on the Paiute Indians.

7. Rock Creek has cut a strange, 500-foot gorge into the pink and tan rocks of the Bishop tuff, exposing their marvelously varied colors and textures in its vertical walls. A trail follows the creek through the gorge for about eight miles, from Paradise Camp on the old road to the junction of the old and new Sherwin Grade roads near Tom's Place. The most scenic hike (the gorge is deeper) and also the easiest (it's all downhill if you can arrange to be met) is from the first bridge across Rock Creek, five miles north of Paradise Camp on the old road, downstream to Paradise.

8. A local tale that refuses to die is that White Mountain Peak really is higher than Mount Whitney. Supposedly the first surveyors fudged—either on orders or to please someone, I never do get that straight—and three generations of engineers (highly trained geodists) have all conspired to change the height of this one peak. The truth is that the Coast and Geodetic Survey determined the elevation of White Mountain Peak by reciprocal vertical angle in 1950 as 14,246 feet, which supersedes a 1913 determination of 14,242 feet. Since modern instruments make it possible to measure more precisely, the most recent measurement of Mount Whitney, 14,494.164 feet—by first-order leveling in 1940—also varies a few feet from previous ones.

9. The cool seasons and, in summer, the cool evenings are choice times to wander the tan, arid world of the high desert east of Highway 395. Forests of pinyon and Jeffrey pine, groves of aspen, and in spring carpets of lavender lupine and magenta mimulus make it far less bleak than it seems at a distance. (See the 1972 Inyo Forest map.) Although many of the roads are in pumice, they are safe for passenger cars if you observe a few precautions—have a full gas tank, take water with you, and *stay in the road tracks*. Pumice is as treacherous as sand. Venturing cross-country or on little used side roads, even with 4-wheel drive, is asking for trouble.

10. Deer you see in the eastern Sierra south of Mono Lake may be either Inyo or Rocky Mountain mule deer. However, the validity of the Inyo mule deer as a distinct subspecies is questionable. North of Mono Lake only Rocky Mountain mule deer are present.

11. Valentine Eastern Sierra Reserve. In 1972 Carol Valentine and the Valentine Foundation donated these 136 acres, belonging to Edward Robinson Valentine (Robinsons Department Stores) and friends since 1915, to the University of California. It is managed by U.C. Santa Barbara. Though surrounded by developments, the reserve itself is wild and undisturbed, an ideal site for teaching and research.

Index

Agnew Lake, 67–68
Agnew Meadow, 11–13, 61–66
Agnew Pass, 64, 65
Alder, 102
Alger Lake, 68–69
Alkali Lakes, 6
Aqueduct, Los Angeles, 139–140
Arrowhead Lake, 48–49
Ashley Lake, 59
Aspen, 88, 90
Aurora, 33, 134

Badger Lakes, 63–64
Baldwin, Mount, 41
Barney Lake, 48–49
Barrett Lake, 50–51
Beaver, 113
Beaver Dam, 40
Beck Lakes, 58
Benton, 5–7, 27–28, 135, 136
Benton Crossing, 5–6, 80
Berry, service, 104
Big McGee Lake, 40–41
Blackbird, 126
Bloody Canyon. *See* Mono Pass
Bloody Mountain, 83
Bluebird, 126
Bodie, 28, 32–33, 136–137
Bodey, Bill, 134
Bottomless Pit, 47
Box Lake, 38
Brush: antelope, 104; bitter, 104; rabbit, 106; sage, 106
Buckeye Canyon, 72
Buckwheat, 93

Carson Peak, 65
Casa Diablo, 20–21
Cherry, bitter, 104
Chickadee, 124
Chickaree, 113
Chickenfoot Lake, 38
Chinquapin, 106
Chipmunk: least, 110; lodgepole, 112; Alpine, 114
Cinquefoil, 94
Clark Lakes, 64–65, 68
Coldwater Canyon, 48–50
Columbine, 96
Convict Canyon, Lake, 7–8, 41–43, 73
Conway Summit, 33
Cony. *See* Pika
Crater Creek, 55–56
Crater Meadows. *See* Red Cones

Craters, formation of, 23
Crestview, 22
Crocker Lake, 41
Crowley Lake, 3–4
Crystal Crag, Lake, 19, 51
Currant, 104

Daisy, 100
Davis Lake, 39–40
Deadman Creek, 21, 22, 82
Deer, 114
Deer Creek, 52–53, 54–55
Deer Lakes, 51–52
Delphinium, 100
Devil's Postpile National Monument, 11–14, 56–60
Devil's Punchbowl, 23
Dipper, 124–125
Dogtown Diggings, 133
Dorothy, Lake (Convict Canyon), 41–42
Dorothy Lake (Rock Creek), 37
Duck Lake, Pass, 48–49, 84

Earthquake Fault, 11
Eastern Brook Lakes, 38
Ediza, Lake, 61–62
El Camino Sierra, 1
Elephant heads, 100
Emerald Lake, 49–50

Fern Creek, Lake, 66
Finch: Cassin's purple, 126; Sierra rosy, 127
Fir: white, 90; red, 91
Fireweed, 98
Fish Creek, 55–56
Flag, western blue, 100
Forget-me-not, 102
Francis Lake, 36–37
Frémont, Captain John, 132

Garnet Lake, 64, 65, 66
Gem Lake (Rush Creek), 67–68
Gem Lakes (Rock Creek), 38
Genevieve, Lake, 42
Gentian, 102
George, Lake, 19, 20, 50–52
Gilia, 98
Golden Lake, 41
Grant Lake, 25
Grass Lake, 41
Green Lakes, 72
Groundsel, golden, 96
Ground squirrel: white-tailed antelope, 107; California, 108; Belding, 112; golden-mantled, 112

Grouse, 121
Gull, 121–122
Gull Lake, 24

Heart Lake (Mammoth), 48
Heart Lake (Rock Creek), 38
Heather: white, 94; red, 96
Hellebore, false, 93
Hemlock, 92
Hidden Lakes, 38
High Trail, 63–64
Hilton Creek, Lakes, 3, 4, 39–40
Holcomb Lake, 59
Horseshoe Lake, 20, 52–53
Hot Creek, 9
Hot Creek State Fish Hatchery, 9

Iceberg Lakes, 61–62
Indian. *See* Paiutes
Inyo, meaning of, 4–5
Inyo Craters, 21, 23, 24, 82
Iron Mountain, 58, 59
Island Crossing, 55–56

Jackrabbit: black-tailed, 108; white-tailed, 110
Jay, 122
John Muir Trail, 14, 34, 49, 53, 54, 55, 56, 62, 64
Johnson Lake, 59
Junco, 127
June Lake Basin, 24–25, 66–69
Juniper, 88

Kenneth Lake, 36–37
King Creek, 57

Lake Canyon, 71–72
Larkspur, 100
Laurel, bog, 96
Laurel Creek, Canyon, Lakes, 9–10, 43–44
Lee Vining, 29, 30. *See also* Vining, Leroy
Lily: corn, 93; Mariposa, 93; tiger, 94
Little Lakes Valley. *See* Rock Creek
Long Lake, 37–38
Lost Cement Mine, 22, 135–136
Lundy Canyon, Lake, 32, 71–72. *See also* May Lundy Mine
Lupine, 102

Mack Lake, 38
Mamie, Lake, 20
Mammoth City, Mines, 16–17, 45, 136
Mammoth Crest, 51–52, 83
Mammoth Lakes Basin: roads, 10, 11, 15–20; trails, 43–53
Mammoth Mountain: origin of, 19; skiing, 11, 12, 140–141; trail, 47–48

Mammoth Rock, 18, 83
Manzanita, 104
Maps, 34–35; geologic, 78–79
Marmot, 114–115
Marsh Lake, 38
Mary, Lake, 19, 20
May Lundy Mine, 32, 71–72, 138
McGee Creek, Canyon, 4, 40–41
McLeod Lake, 15, 52–53
Meadow Lake, 41
Middle Fork of the San Joaquin River, trails, 54–66
Mildred, Lake, 41–42
Mill Creek. *See* Lundy Canyon
Minaret Falls, Lake, 59–60
Minarets, 26
Minaret Summit, 11–12, 53–54
Mint, 100
Monkey flower, 96
Monkshood, 100
Mono, meaning of, 31
Mono Craters, 24, 27, 82, 140
Mono Lake, 30–31
Mono Mills, 27–28
Mono Pass (Bloody Canyon), 26, 70
Mono Pass (Rock Creek Canyon), 38–39
Monoville, 133–134
Morgan Lakes, Pass, 37–38
Morrison, Mount, 7, 8
Mountaineering, 35–36
Mullein, 96

Nutcracker, 122, 124

Obsidian, 23
Olaine, Lake, 60
Old Mammoth Road, 16–19
Oneida, Lake, 72
Onion, wild, 98
Orchis, rein, 93
Ouzel, 124–125
Owens River, 5, 6, 21

Paintbrush, 98
Paiutes, 10, 26, 28, 29, 31, 128–131
Panorama Dome, 45–46
Panum Crater, 23, 27, 82
Parker Lake, 69–70
Parsnip, 94
Pennyroyal, 100
Penstemon, 98
Phlox, 100
Pika, 115
Pine: pinyon, 88; Jeffrey, 90; lodgepole, 90–91; western white, 91–92; whitebark, 92
Poppy, 93

Porcupine, 111
Primrose, 96
Pumice, 23, 24, 27, 82
Purple Lake, 48–49
Pussypaws, 98

Quail, 121

Rabbitbrush, 106
Rainbow Falls, 15, 56–57
Rat, kangaroo, 108
Red Cones, 52–53, 54–55
Reds Meadow, 11–15, 53, 54–56
Ritter Range, 12, 26
River Trail, 63–64
Robin, 125–126
Rock Creek Canyon, Lake, 2, 36–39
Rocks: sedimentary, 80; volcanic, 81–82; igneous, 81–83; granitic, 83; metamorphic, 83–84
Rosalie Lake, 62
Rose, 102
Round Lake, 40

Saddlebag Lake, 70–71
Sagebrush, 106
Sage hen, 121
San Joaquin Mountain, 24, 65
San Joaquin River. *See* Middle Fork of the San Joaquin River
Sardine Lakes, 70
Seven Lakes Point, 47
Shadow Creek, Lake, 61–62, 84
Sherwin Creek, Lakes, 9, 10, 44–45
Sherwin Tollroad, 2, 136
Shooting star, 100
Silver Lake, 25, 64–65, 67–69
Skelton Lake, 48–49
Skunk, 108
Sky Meadow, 49–50
Snowbush, 104
Soda Springs, 59
Sotcher Lake, 55
Sparrow, white-crowned, 127
Squirrel. *See* Ground squirrel

Steelhead Lake (McGee Creek), 41
Steelhead Lake (Tioga), 71
Stick-seed, 102
Sulphur-flower, 94
Summit Lake (Bloody Canyon), 70
Summit Lake (Rock Creek Canyon), 38–39
Summit Meadow, 57–58
Superior Lake, 58

Tamarack Lakes, 36–37
Tanager, 126
Thousand Island Lake, 63–64, 68
Thrush, 125
Tioga Pass, Mine, 29, 70–71, 138
T. J. Lake, 50–51
Tom's Place, 2
Trail Lakes, 38–39
Trout: rainbow, 117, 118; golden, 117, 118; cutthroat, 118–119; Eastern brook, 119; brown, 119
Twin Lakes (Bridgeport), 72
Twin Lakes (Mammoth), 16, 45–48

Valentine Lake, 44
Valley View Point, 45–46
Vining, Leroy, 26, 29, 133
Virginia Lakes, 72
Vivian Lake, 62
Volcanic Ridge, 62

Walker, Joseph R., 132
Walker Lake, 70
Wall flower, 94
Waugh Lake, 67–68
Weber Lake, 67–68
Whiteheads, swamp, 94
White Mountains, 4, 5
Whitmore Hot Springs, 5, 6
Whitney Survey, 25–26
Willow, 102
Wilson Butte, 23
Wyetheia, 96

Yarrow, 94
Yosemite National Park, 29
Yost Lake, 66–67

See front cover for upper half of map.

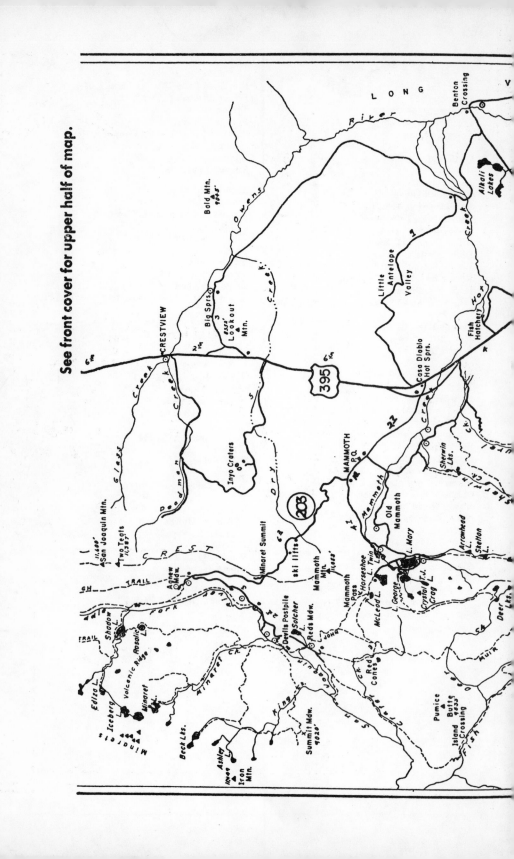